13

Wilhelmy

BISHOP BURTON COLLEGE

D1420370

T011596

Accession Number......24.5.16

Class Number........636·15

THOUGHTS ON HUNTING

PETER BECKFORD

From a painting in possession of the Hon. Miss Pitt of Steepleton

THOUGHTS ON
HUNTING

In a Series of
Familiar Letters to a Friend

by

PETER BECKFORD, ESQ.

WITH AN INTRODUCTION
AND NOTES BY
J. OTHO PAGET

FOREWORD BY
MICHAEL CLAYTON

J. A. ALLEN & CO. LTD.

First published in 1781,

new edition 1981.

this edition 1993

Foreword copyright © Michael Clayton.

J. A. ALLEN & CO. LTD.,
1, Lower Grosvenor Place,
London. SW1W 0EL.

British Library Cataloging in Publication Data
Beckford, Peter
Thoughts on Hunting
1. Foxhounds
2. Title
636.7'53   SF429.F6

ISBN 0 85131 367 1

Printed in Hong Kong by Dah Hua Printing Co. Ltd.

FOREWORD
by Michael Clayton

Every sport or pastime needs legend as well as fact to sustain its most passionate enthusiasts. Foxhunting has certainly been richer in legend, in mystery, than most other recreations. I am sure this is partly because it has always suited the Establishment of hunting that this should be so. One Master of Foxhounds was quite perturbed when I proposed publishing a series of articles in *Horse and Hound* about the life style of the fox.

"Steady on," he protested. "There's a lot of mystery about the fox, and it will not do anyone much good if we tear that mystery away."

There is still a residual feeling today that foxhound breeding is such a difficult, abstruse mystery that it should not be discussed too publicly. Certainly its ramifications are recorded in such a way that only a few brave souls will delve into them and dare to express an opinion.

Fortunately, the major influences in postwar hound breeding, the Duke of Beaufort, Sir Peter Farquhar, and Capt. Ronnie Wallace, have not pursued a secretive policy. They have talked and spoken readily about their policies and aims in breeding hounds which can pursue foxes in a countryside where vast changes have been wrought by urbanisation, and an increase in plough land.

Not only the eminent authorities on the sport, but lesser lights have felt able to expound their views on hound breeding, and the management of hunting, in recent years. Some amateur huntsmen have dared to endeavour to explain to the ignoramuses of the mounted field what the man blowing the horn in front is trying to do; and why he sometimes cannot do it!

One of the reasons why leading Masters have become so much readier to explain and discuss their sport with their followers is the recognition that hunting has recently attracted far more recruits who did not have an inherited "horsey" or hunting background.

I am not so sure that this was always quite the advantage which has been claimed. Children brought up in a devoted foxhunting household *may* imbibe the lifetime's passion for the Chase; they may equally be put off the sport for life, preferring indoor games to those cold, wet mornings at the covert side which their parents insisted were such fun.

Like the Roman Catholic religion, foxhunting finds some of its most passionate adherents are converts who have discovered its joys somewhat later than their schooldays.

Nevertheless, the degree of ignorance about the sport among postwar mounted fields is disturbing, and indeed a positive disadvantage at times. Hunts have done their best, aided by the Pony Club, to explain the need to avoid damaging farm crops and to shut gates when stock is grazing. There have even been attempts to improve standards of dress. How do you explain to a middle aged gentleman, newly drawn to the sound of hound and horn, that he looks an absolute mess on a horse?

New foxhunters *can* acquire basic advice and information with a little trouble. Indeed, sooner or later, someone will tell them – possibly in scathing terms – that it simply will not do to ride over hounds, or a field of seeds.

Yet who will tell them to read Beckford? Or Surtees? Or Whyte-Melville?

To go into the hunting field without the benefit of these sporting riches is an immense disadvantage. Surteesian characters can still be found; how much more amusing is time spent at the covert side if you can identify a modern Facey Romford, or a Soapy Sponge.

Whyte-Melville's advice on buying and keeping hunters is still immensely entertaining and worthwhile for the modern sportsman who optimistically involves himself with these fragile and expensive beasts.

Beckford is the keystone of the arch for the foxhunter's library. Not to have made his mere acquaintance is a disgrace; not to know his pages intimately, and to have imbibed at least an ounce of his wisdom, is a gross deprivation for anyone aspiring to be a foxhunter.

This new edition of his "Thoughts on Hunting" is therefore a marvellous opportunity for a whole generation of hunting folk to gain fresh access to the essential literary background of their sport.

Peter Beckford was born in 1740, and died in 1811; his experience of foxhunting therefore preceded the "golden age" of Leicestershire hunting in the early 19th century. He was far removed from the pretensions and aspirations of Nimrod, the hunting correspondent for whom the Chase represented riding over Leicestershire on a Thoroughbred, preferably in the company of an Earl.

Beckford lived in North Dorset, an area nowadays part of the Portman Hunt country. Most of my early hunting was in that delightful country, but it was some years before I realised that Stepleton House, near Blandford Forum, was Beckford's old home.

The Portman country is divided strictly between an upland area of hills and little valleys, easy to cross on a horse before the days of barbed wire, and the Vale below. The Portman has a stretch of vale below Shaftesbury; a different prospect entirely for the man riding to hounds: huge thorn hedges grow on low banks; there are frequent drops; and every hedge is guarded by a formidable ditch. It is a country which requires a bold horse and rider.

We can deduce from Beckford that he was not a vale man; indeed he was not a thruster in any sense. What then was his contribution to the sport? Why should we bother to read him today? The answer is simply that hounds, not horses, are the key to understanding the Chase, and Beckford produced the first realistic guide to their breeding, care and handling in the hunting field.

He treated his subject in a series of 24 letters to a friend, and the clarity and elegance of his style show that he was not just another Dorset squire with a view of life sharply circumscribed by the kennel and the latest harvest.

He was the son of a comparitively rich West Indian planter, and had received a better education than most of his class, attending Westminster School and New College, Oxford where he read Classics and History and acquired several foreign languages. Later he was to travel widely, spending much time in Italy, before settling down to rural life in Dorset.

Beckford acquired his early love of hunting with a pack of beagles in Cranbourne Chase, that great hunting ground in North East Dorset where the ownership of the Stepleton estate carried certain sporting rights.

From small beagles, which he doubtless followed on foot, Beckford graduated, by acquiring and breeding, to a type of hound known then as a fox-beagle, which could be hunted while mounted. Later he acquired his own pack of foxhounds, and hunted Cranbourne Chase and surrounding areas regularly.

Thoughts on Hunting was published in August, 1781, and represented the first serious attempt to lay down principles and methods in foxhunting. It must be remembered that in medieval England deer hunting was first in order of nobility and priority. It was the gradual clearance of the great forests, accelerating in the 18th century, which increased the popularity of foxhunting, raising the fox from mere vermin to a worthy beast of the chase.

Beckford's book answered a real need; by 1796 it had achieved considerable renown and had gone into four editions.

It is clear that in Beckford's day foxes were harder to find in many parts of Britain than they are today. This is particularly interesting, because modern Dorset is one of the best foxed counties I know. Even before the excesses of the 19th century, Beckford was already condemning such practices as the bag-fox. He does not aspire to lay down firm rules for every hunting country, but his advice on handling hounds in the field is still absolutely relevant, and of inestimable value to modern huntsmen and their followers.

He clearly had that invisible thread, that communication with hounds, which the exceptional huntsman should possess. His advice on hounds, at a time when animal welfare was not of much general interest, was enlightened and sympathetic . . . . . . "flogging hounds in the kennel (the frequent practice of most huntsmen) I hold in abhorrence; it is unreasonable, unjust and cruel . . . . . ."

And how is this for advice to a modern mounted field? "When your hounds are at fault, let not a word be said: let such as follow them ignorantly and unworthily, stand all aloof – Procul, O procul este profani! – for whilst such are chattering, not a hound will hunt."

His detailed descriptions of kennel management are of absorbing interest, although modern research *has* produced some improvements on his recommendation of a cure for distemper: "an ounce of Peruvian bark in a glass of port wine, taken twice a day."

The wit and wisdom of "Thoughts on Hunting" belies Beckford's assertion that "foxhunting, however lively and animating it may be in the field, is but a dull, dry subject to write upon . . . . . ."

Stepleton House still exists, and on the opposite side of the road is a row of cottages converted from the model kennel buildings which Beckford described and mapped in his book.

Some foxhunters used to touch their hats when jogging past Stepleton House. Indeed, I have done so myself when hunting in that country, and someone asked what I was doing. "Thoughts on Hunting" will make this small mystery, and a great many more important matters crystal clear to the modern foxhunter.

Perhaps after reading this book, the sportsman will one day make a pilgrimage to Stepleton Church, where a memorial tablet on a vault bears the following inscription which will be inaccurate as long as anyone cares about the greatest field sport of them all:

To
the memory of
PETER BECKFORD, ESQ.
who departed this life
A.D. 1811
aged 71 years.

We die and are forgotten; 'tis Heaven's decree;
Thus the fate of others will be the fate of me.

INTRODUCTION

MORE than a hundred years have elapsed since Beckford wrote *Thoughts on Hunting*, yet to this day the book remains a standard work on the subject. There had been no text-book on hunting previous to its appearance, and there has been nothing to rival it since. The ordinary reader fights shy of the yellow-toned page discoloured with the stain of years, and thinks—often rightly—that any literature of our great-grandfathers must be of a prosy nature. Nowadays a book, whether it be for instruction or amusement, must be distilled and compressed to its smallest compass. The bulky tome may fill a place in the bookshelf, but its virgin leaves will remain uncut for ever. In consideration for the age in which he lived, we could have forgiven Beckford if he had been slightly long-winded, but every word is to the point, and there is not a sentence we would wish left out. The book is purely technical, and yet those who know nothing of the subject read it with pleasure.

I have not been able to gather many reliable facts about the personal character of our author, but whoever reads his *Thoughts on Hunting* will, I think, agree with me that the man who wrote them was a sportsman and a gentleman. Can there be higher praise than this? Every line in the book bespeaks him a fox-hunter, and yet he was able to appreciate the mysteries of hare-hunting. Humane, kind-hearted and fond of animals, still, when he found a fox he was never satisfied until he had run him to ground or killed him. It would be hopeless to try and explain these things to those outside the craft, but we know that it is impossible for a good sportsman to be cruel. A fox-hunter may love the fox, but he loves the hound more, and he cannot spare the life of one without being cruel to the other.

Peter Beckford, born in 1740, was the son of Julines Beckford, whose brother William was the celebrated Lord Mayor and father of the author of *Vathek*. Five years after the birth of Peter his father purchased the house and manor of Stapleton, or Steepleton-Iwerne, in Dorsetshire, together with certain rights in Cranbourn Chase, from Thomas Fownes, who bought it from George Pitt in 1654. This Mr. Fownes appears to have been an excellent sportsman, and was one of the first masters who kept a pack exclusively for hunting the fox. He was also one of the pioneers in the scientific breeding of the fox-hound, and his pack was supposed to have been the most perfect in England, not only for looks, but for the style in which they hunted a fox. Like many other good men who have devoted a lifetime to sport, he took no thought of riches for himself, and in the end want of money forced him to sell his estate. Mr. Bowes, of Yorkshire, bought the pack for what at that date was considered an enormous price, but their subsequent history I have not been able to trace, though it is unlikely masters of that day would allow blood to be wasted which had proved itself to be good.

Julines Beckford does not appear to have kept a regular pack of hounds, but as his boyhood had been spent in Jamaica, it was perhaps a form of amusement that he did not understand. We, however, read that he appointed keepers to look after the deer in certain parts of Cranbourn Chase, so that it is evident he was interested in sport.

Young Peter must have been initiated early into the mysteries of sport, and we can imagine him as a boy with a few couple of the ancient breed of buck-hounds pursuing the deer in Cranbourn Chase. We are told these hounds were not particular what they hunted—deer, hares, foxes, and marten-cats were hunted impartially. It was the duty of the keepers of the Chase to keep down the vermin, and it was probably with these men that Peter first imbibed his love of hunting a fox. The population in and around the Chase was of a very sporting character, for they were all descendants of either poachers or keepers. These men would naturally be delighted to see the young squire of Stapleton developing sporting tastes, and would gladly impart their knowledge of woodcraft to him.

BECKFORD'S HOUSE, STEEPLETON-IWERNE

A slight stretch of imagination and we can see Peter, a lad of twelve or thereabouts, galloping off to the Chase on his pony in the fresh crispness of an autumn morning. By arrangement the keepers meet him at a certain spot with eight or ten couple of buck-hounds, but on this occasion it is not deer that are to be hunted.

A litter of cubs have been located in a patch of gorse in one of the open parts of the Chase, and as they have been making havoc amongst the rabbits it has been decided to reduce their numbers. A crowd of footpeople await the young squire's appearance, and under the direction of the head keeper they proceed to form a circle round the gorse where the cubs are supposed to be. There are several terriers, and nearly every man carries a spade, for they fully anticipate having to dig. The cubs have, however, moved elsewhere, but there is an old fox at home, and hounds are soon bustling him from one clump of gorse to another. Every time he attempts to escape he is met by a chorus of yells. Peter, in the middle of the gorse, is wild with excitement, dashing wildly from one side to the other, and occasionally viewing the fox. The old varmint begins to think there is more danger in stopping in the covert than in going away, and just when he is supposed to be on the further side, he breaks through the cordon and gets clear away. The noises that are made to stop the fox bring the hounds to the scene, and away they go in view to the disgust of all except Peter, who gallops after them in an ecstasy of delight. The open space is soon crossed and hounds disappear amongst the trees; but there is a riding handy, and our young sportsman hastens down the track with hounds running a little to the left. At last the limits of the Chase are reached, and hounds cross some rough heathy ground which brings them on to cultivated land. Peter's pony is showing symptoms of distress, for he is not in very good condition, the pace has been fast and the day hot; but scent is not so good now, and there is every appearance of the hunt coming to an end. Hounds also are not showing any desperate keenness to recover the scent, and are turning over in their minds the shortest way back to kennels. Then Peter sees some men in a cornfield half a mile away, frantically waving their hats. Digging his heels into the pony's fat sides, he holloas to the hounds and gallops with them to the distant cornfield. The men have been reaping wheat with the sickle, and seeing the tired fox lie down in the long stubble they promptly surrounded him. Peter rides into the stubble, which reaches nearly to his pony's girths, the fox jumps up in the middle of the pack, there is a shrill little holloa, and they run into him before he can get out of the field. The little heart had throbbed wildly throughout the exciting incidents of the hunt, and every moment would be engraved deep on his memory, leaving an impression that nothing in after-life could obliterate.

The next few years at Westminster School would not afford much opportunity for hunting, except during the holidays, and we may conclude that Peter had to devote most of his time to study until he was twenty-three. Julines Beckford, the father, was himself a man of very good ability, and was desirous that his son should lack nothing that education could impart.

Peter's innate love of sport found vent at first in keeping a pack of harriers, but these soon gave way to fox-hounds. Thomas Fownes had given the neighbouring squires and yeomen a taste of fox-hunting in its legitimate form, so that when Beckford announced his intention of reviving the glories of the Cranbourn Chase hunt he was welcomed on all sides. From what source or sources he procured the foundation of his pack it is now impossible to ascertain, but judging the man from his writing, one does not deem it likely that he would spare either trouble or expense in getting the best blood. We may also consider it an established fact that by dint of careful breeding he brought his pack to a very high state of perfection; but what was their ultimate fate I have not yet been able to trace. The Cranbourn Chase country was not, even in Beckford's day, an ideal spot for hunting, as he says himself; but being then less cultivated and fenced it was probably much better than as we know it now. They had, however, good sport and killed their foxes, so that it may be presumed they enjoyed themselves, which is after all the chief object for which we hunt. The country which Beckford hunted was probably that which now is known as the South Dorset. We know he hunted beyond the Stour, as we have it on his authority, the occasion (p. 190) being when he crossed it in a flood and lost several hounds. To the north is the Blackmore vale, which is nearly as good a country as any in the shires, being a wide expanse of grass, though it is greatly spoilt by the majority of fences being planted on banks. From the little one can gather of Beckford's doings as set down by himself, I imagine he was not a very hard rider, and the big banks of the vale may have had no great attraction for him.

Cranbourn Chase was a royal forest in the time of King John, and it then became the property of an Earl of Salisbury, by whom it was sold to the Earl of Pembroke. The next owner was a Lord Shaftesbury, who sold it to Mr. Freke, of Shroton, and it thus descended to Lord Rivers. The Rev. W. Chafin, in his *Anecdotes of Cranbourn Chase*, says there were many serious fights between poachers and keepers. About the year 1786 a severe battle was fought, the combatants being equally divided; the keepers were, however, armed with staves and short hangers, whilst the poachers only carried flails. The keepers, finding they were getting the worst of the encounter, retired amongst the trees, where it was impossible to use the flail, and at close quarters the hangers soon carried the day. The leader of the gang, a soldier from Blandford, had his hand cut off, another man was killed, and the remainder were all taken prisoners. History relates that prisoners and wounded were haled before his honour Peter Beckford, Esq., at that time Ranger of the Chase, who committed them for trial at the next assizes, after first procuring medical aid to bind up their wounds.

The family of Beckford was supposed to have originally

come from Gloucestershire, but there is no record to establish the claim between the family who lived there in the thirteenth century and the man who was the direct ancestor of the author of this book. This ancestor was also called Peter Beckford, and was one of the richest men in Jamaica, but where he came from or how he became possessed of his riches history does not relate. Jamaica was at one time a favourite resort for the buccaneers of the Spanish main, and many a highly respected pirate retired to that island to spend the remainder of his days in peace after a stormy life on the ocean. Occasionally, when His Majesty of England had not other work for his ships to do, one of these sea-robbers would be captured and hung from the yard-arm, but as a rule, if he confined his attentions to the unhappy stranger and respected the union jack, the hard-working pirate had not much to fear. It is quite certain that many families in Jamaica are descended from successful bucca-neers, and it is not unlikely that Peter Beckford, Commander-in-chief and Governor of the island, may have been a pirate chief or the son of one. Whatever his origin, this Peter must have been a very able and energetic man, or he would not, on the death of the Governor, have been elected to fill that post. We are told that he was the owner of several plantations and of slaves by the hundred. Peter Beckford, his son, was Speaker of the House of Assembly, and was the father of thirteen children. Two sons, William and Julines, came to England, and were at the time of their arrival possessed of considerable wealth. William had inherited his grandfather's energy and strength of character, so that we find, instead of allowing his capital and time to be idle, he entered very successfully into business as a merchant in the city of London. Twice was he made Lord Mayor, and on one celebrated occasion he demanded audience of the king and protested stoutly against the infringements of certain rights. His son William, the author of *Vathek*, was a man who could probably have made his mark in the world had he not been hampered with too much riches, but he lacked the fixity of purpose which was one of the strong points in his father's character. His collection of art treasures at Fonthill Abbey was perhaps larger than any single individual has ever owned.

Julines Beckford was more of a student than his brother, and enjoyed the quiet retirement of a country life, but we find that he was at one time the member for Salisbury. He married Elizabeth, daughter of Solomon Ashly, Ashly St. Ledgers, Northamptonshire. The result of that marriage was Peter, the author of this book and the subject of this short history, who in 1773 married Louisa, daughter of Lord Rivers. Peter's son became the third Lord Rivers by a special Act of Parliament, and his great-granddaughter married the ninth Duke of Leeds, so that the present master of the Bedale is the direct descendant of the man whose name all fox-hunters honour.

Beckford sat for Morpeth in 1768, and in 1789 he travelled in Italy, when he wrote an account of his travels. Sir Egerton Brydges, in *Retrospective Review*, says: "Never had fox or hare the honour of being chased to death by so accomplished a hunter; never was a huntsman's dinner graced with such urbanity and wit. He would bag a fox in Greek, find a hare in Latin, inspect his kennels in Italian, and direct the economy of his stables in excellent French." Of course we understand by this that Beckford was a brilliant conversationalist and an excellent linguist, but I think it would have annoyed him, in spite of the intended compliment to read of his bagging a fox and of his giving orders to his stud-groom in French.

The first edition of *Thoughts on Hunting* was published in 1781, when Beckford was forty-one years of age, and the proof of the excellence of the book is in the way it has stood the test of time. You turn to its pages for information, and you find pleasure in gleaning the fruits from the experience of a master in the art. If you flatter yourself you are beginning to know something of the subject, you find yourself agreeing with the author in every particular, and in any way you may differ, you are almost persuaded by his gentle reasoning. If you are an utter novice at the game, a close study of the book will start you on that path of knowledge which experience alone can complete. I have loved and venerated the author for a great many years, so that to me the task of editing his book is an honour which I greatly appreciate.

Through the kindness and courtesy of the Misses Pitt,[1] the present owners of Steepleton, I was able to see the house where Beckford lived and the interesting pictures which are reproduced in this volume. The house is practically as it was in Beckford's time and of course the greater part of the structure dates to a much earlier period, the basement and cellars being in existence when Elizabeth was queen. Though I have read and admired this work for years, I had no idea that the author's home was standing in its original condition and contained personal relics of the man. My most sanguine hope was to find an engraving of the old house and to look on some new building that covered the site. Therefore my joy and surprise was great to see the house itself, the intellectual features of Peter Beckford in a life-size portrait, and the excellent paintings of his hounds.

My visit to Steepleton was unfortunately very short, but I enjoyed every moment of the hour I spent there. The grey stone walls whispered to me the tale of a country gentleman's life more than a hundred years ago, and the wood-crowned hill seemed to echo with the notes of Peter's horn. The house is just what your imagination would conceive Beckford's home to be—beautiful yet unpretentious, with the picturesque surroundings that are only to be found in England's most ancient homes. I would gladly have lingered on in the sunshine and the scent of flowers, looking at the scene as it is to-day and filling in the details of the past as my imagination painted them. The rumble of a not far-distant train recalled to me the need for hurrying and the time I was due back at Blandford. Following my guide into the garden amongst flower-beds and shrubs, we dived under a yew arch, and to my surprise there was the church—a pretty little building covered with ivy and

[1] Great-granddaughters of Beckford.

creepers, seemingly shut off from the clamour of the outside world, and with a look of restful repose that ought to be conducive to devotions. Within the church one feels the presence of the dead; outside in the sunshine and beneath the trees Peter lives; but here in the peaceful shadows beneath our feet lie his bones, and instinctively we tread lightly, lest we should disturb his rest.

On the marble slab of the vault is this simple inscription:

P. B.
SIBI
ET
SUIS
MDCCCIX.

Then on a memorial tablet is the name in full and the date of death, with this rather curious epitaph:

"We die and are forgotten—'tis Heaven's decree;
Thus the fate of others will be the fate of me."

Out again into the bright sunlight, and I was asked would I like to see the kennels, which of course was exactly what I did want to see. Therefore, on we went down the gravel path, by the edge of a large ornamental lake, where tall yews threw dark shadows on the water, and through kitchen-gardens surrounded by high walls of age-toned brick. Here we called the head gardener to our assistance, and coming out into the road I was confronted with a low tile-roofed building, covered with roses and creepers, which is still known as "the kennels." Now they are used as dwelling-houses for workmen on the estate, and the little flower gardens in front are planted where was once the kennel yard. It took me some little time to reconstruct the place as it was, but by opening doorways that had been walled up and blocking up others, the kennels grew gradually upon me. Here was the huntsman's house at this end, there the boiling house, and the original arches are still in the walls showing the feeding place or hounds' main lodging-rooms. Some of the flagstones, which must have often listened to the old story of legs and feet, are now used as a pathway to one of the cottages. Not

fifty yards distant is the running stream which Beckford
insists on should always be in the grass-yard; but here nature
and man have contrived to make serious alterations. The
trees under which the Cranbourn Chase hounds used to
gambol are cut down and others have grown up in their
place, whilst the actual scene of the grass-yard is now an
osier-bed. This, I think, shows that the ornamental lake was
not in Peter's reign, as the damming up of the water must
have caused the hounds' playground to become a swamp.

Back to the house we went by way of the stables, which
have evidently been shorn of much of their ancient glory;
but the main building has not suffered any alteration.
and only the wings have been pulled down. Close to the
house are some outbuildings, which have certainly been
kennels at some period, and they may have been used
for shooting-dogs, but according to my fancy it was there
that young Peter kept his pack of beagles.

In the drawing-room Peter welcomes me from his portrait
with a pleasant smile, and I can almost imagine him pressing
me to see the pictures of his hounds in the next room.
There I see three excellent oil-paintings of hounds by
Sartorius, a well-known animal painter of that period,
which are here reproduced. After looking at these pictures
it is easy to believe that Beckford's pack had a great
reputation in those days. On the staircase is a large picture
without either name or date, containing one large hound,
which I believe to be a harrier, and some smaller ones
which are undoubtedly portraits of his beagles. This
picture is not nearly so well painted as the others, but
it gives one a very fair idea of the type of hound. The
painting of the pack with the two hunt servants is particularly interesting as showing the costumes of that
period. It will be noticed that the men carry short swords
or hangers by their sides, and I believe they wore them
by virtue of their master's office as Ranger of the Chase.
This picture, however, met with an accident and had to
be restored, so that the outlines of the hounds are not
so good as in the two others.

At the moment Beckford commenced to breed a pack of fox-hounds, others were doing the same thing in different parts of England, and the middle of the eighteenth century may be considered the period when the movement became general. For those who took the trouble to travel to different kennels there was ample material to choose from, and the few years it took to build up a first-rate pack proves the goodness of that material. The hour had arrived when the excellence of our English hound was to be recognised, and his many different qualities improved by judicious breeding. The one or two names of men that have been handed down were not the only breeders, and the fox-hound of to-day owes many of his good qualities to quiet country gentlemen, who were little known in their own time and are never heard of now.

Whilst Mr. Meynell was forming his celebrated pack in the Midlands, Beckford and others were doing similar good work in different counties. Because the names of their hounds do not appear in the pedigrees of our packs, it does not follow their blood does not flow now in the veins of the lions of the field and the winners on the flags at Peterboro'. I have not the slightest doubt that Beckford's choicest strains have helped to form some of the best packs that are in existence to-day; but breeders then were as selfish as they are now. Whatever the animal we may wish to breed, we are always ready to forget the claims of the man from whom we obtain the strain, if by so doing we get more credit to ourselves when the animal eventually produced becomes a success.

If the few facts which I have here set down concerning the individuality of our author prove half as interesting to those who read them as they have been to me in collecting, I shall feel more than satisfied. The many readers and admirers of Beckford would view with horror the slightest alteration in the original text, and I am not sure whether they will not consider my few notes a sacrilege. I have much pleasure in stating that the text is exactly the same as in the original edition. My hope is, with the illustrations and notes, to make the book more widely known amongst those to whom heretofore Beckford has been only a name. No man or woman ought to be allowed in the hunting-field until they have read and thoroughly digested *Thoughts on Hunting*—I mean the original phase, not my additions.

J. OTHO PAGET

P.S.—My notes may be distinguished from the author's by being in brackets.

PREFACE

As the Author of the following Letters has been charged with inhumanity, and yet conjectured to be a Clergyman, it is now become necessary to publish his name: and, though it may not be usual to answer an anonymous writer,[1] yet, as it is not impossible that some readers may have adopted his sentiments, this consideration, and this alone, induces the Author to answer the objections which the critic hath so wantonly made. Whatever may be the imperfection of these Letters, the Author is desirous that it should fall as it ought, upon himself only. The objections, which he thinks were unnecessarily made, he has endeavoured to remove. All intentional cruelty he entirely disclaims. His appeal from that accusation lies to those whom he addresses as his judges; not (as the critic may think) because they are equally barbarous with himself, but because Sportsmen *only* are competent to decide.

THE AUTHOR

[1] In the *Monthly Review*.

PREFACE

IT is rather singular to observe but worthy of remark by the Sporting World that, till Mr. Beckford's book appeared, no work on the subject of HUNTING had been published, except an anonymous publication, in 1733, entitled *An Essay on Hunting*.[1] This latter work displays much good sense and practical knowledge: it has been reprinted with great success.

The biography of the Author of *Letters on Hunting* might be said to be *multum in parvo*. But, short as it may be, it is entitled to our notice. Peter Beckford, Esq., of Stapleton, in Dorsetshire, died at the age of seventy years. As a gentleman hunter, not a stancher one was to be found in his whole county. His judgment in the choice of hounds, and the skill he displayed in the management of his establishment, claimed the praise of all those persons who witnessed it. In his selection of horses, and all other animals, his judgment was considered equally conspicuous. In the character of an Author, his *Letters on Hunting*, which have gone through several editions, have not only been pronounced excellent by the Sporting World, but completely show that Mr. Beckford was master of the subject on which he wrote. His elegant and hospitable residence in Dorsetshire was one of the most delightfully picturesque situations in that part of the country. In a word, a truer sportsman never crossed a horse, followed a pack of hounds, or leaped a gate, than Peter Beckford, Esq.

THE EDITOR

October 2nd, 1820

[1 A very interesting little work; but the author is evidently only a hare-hunter. The chapter on the various sorts of hounds and their different peculiarities is worth reading.]

CONTENTS

LETTER I

LETTER XIV

LETTER XV

LETTER XVI

LETTER XVII

LETTER XVIII

LIBRARY
BISHOP BURTON COLLEGE
BEVERLEY HU17 8QG

LETTER XXIII

LETTER XXIV

ILLUSTRATIONS

LETTER I

Bristol Hot-Wells, March 20, 1779

YOU could not, my friend, have chosen a better season than the present, to remind me of sending you my Thoughts on Hunting; for the accident that brought me hither is likely to detain me some time: besides I have no longer a plea for not obeying your commands. Hitherto, indeed, I had excused myself, in hopes that some publication on the subject might have rendered these Letters needless; but since nothing of the kind, although so much wanted, has appeared; as I am now sufficiently unoccupied to undertake the task, I shall not think it a trifling subject, if you think it a necessary one: and I wish that my own experience of the diversion may enable me to answer the many questions which you are pleased to propose concerning it.

Knowing your partiality to rhyme, I could wish to send you my thoughts in verse; but as this would take up more time, without answering your purpose better, I must beg you to accept them in humble prose, which, in my opinion, is better suited to the subject. Didactic essays should be as little clogged as possible: they should proceed regularly and clearly: should be easily written, and as easily understood; having less to do with words than things. The game of *crambo* is out of fashion, to the no small prejudice of the rhyming tribe; and before I could find a rhyme to *porringer*, I should hope to finish a great part of these Letters. I shall, therefore, without further delay, proceed upon them:—this, however, I must desire to be first understood between us—that when, to save trouble to us both, I say a thing *is*, without tacking a salvo to the tail of it, such as, *in my opinion — to the best of my judgment*, &c. &c.—you shall not call my humility in question, as the assertion is not meant to be mathematically certain. When I have any better authority than my own, such as

Somerville, for instance (who, by the bye, is the only one that has written intelligibly on this subject), I shall take the liberty of giving it you in his own words, to save you the trouble of turning to him.

You may remember, perhaps, that when we were hunting together at Turin, the hounds having lost the stag, and the *piqueurs* (still more at fault than they) being ignorant which way to try, the king bid them ask *Milord Anglois*: nor is it to be wondered at, if an Englishman should be thought to understand the art of hunting, as the hounds which this country produces are universally allowed to be the best in the world. Whence, I think, this inference may be drawn—that although every man who follows this diversion may not understand it, yet it is extraordinary, of the many who do, that one only, of any note, should have written on the subject. It is rather unfortunate for me, that this ingenious sportsman should have preferred writing an elegant poem to an useful lesson; since, if it had pleased him, he might easily have saved me the trouble of writing these Letters. Is it not strange, in a country where the press is one continued labour with opinions of almost every kind, from the most serious and instructive to the most ridiculous and trifling; a country, besides, so famous for the best hounds, and the best horses to follow them; whose authors sometimes hunt, and whose sportsmen sometimes write—that only the practical part of hunting should be known? There is, however, no doubt, that the practical part of it would be improved, were it to be accompanied by theory.

France, Germany, and Italy, are also silent, I believe, on the subject; though each of these countries has had its sportsman. Foxes, it is true, they never hunt, and hares but seldom, yet the stag, and wild boar, both in France and in Germany, are still pursued with the utmost splendour and magnificence. In Italy, there has been no hunting since the death of the Duke of Parma: he was very fond of it; and, I apprehend, all hunting in that country ceased with him. The only sportsmen now remaining are gentlemen in green coats, who, taking their *couteaux de chasse* along with them, walk into the fields to catch small birds, which they call *andar a la caccia*, or, in plain English, *going a-hunting*: yet it has not been so with horsemanship: *that* has been treated scientifically by all—in Italy, by Pignatelli; in Germany, by Isenbourg; and in France, by La Guerinière. Nor are the useful lessons of the Duke of Newcastle confined to this country only; they are both read and practised everywhere: nor is *he* the *only* noble lord who has written on the subject— while, upon hunting, all are silent: and were it not for the muse of Somerville, who has so judiciously and so sweetly sung, the dog, that useful, that honest, that faithful, that disinterested, that entertaining animal, would be suffered to pass unnoticed and undistinguished.

A northern court, indeed, did honour this animal with a particular mark of approbation and respect; but the fidelity of the dog has since given place to the sagacity of the elephant.[1] Naturalists, it is true, have included dogs in the specific descriptions that they have given us of animals. Authors may have written on hunting, and booksellers may know many who to sportsmen are unknown; but I again repeat, that I know not any writer, ancient or modern, from the time of Nimrod to the present day (one only excepted), who has given any useful information to a sportsman.[2]

It may be objected, that the hunting of a pack of hounds depends upon the huntsman; and that the huntsman, generally speaking, is an illiterate fellow, who seldom can either read or write—this cannot well be denied—I must therefore observe, that it is impossible for the business of a kennel to go on as it ought, unless the master himself knows something of it. There must be an understanding somewhere; and without it, no gentleman can enjoy in perfection this noble diversion.

[1] Vide Mr. Pope's Letter to Mr. Cromwell.

[2] Many French authors have given rules for hunting the hare and stag: to make this passage less exceptionable, therefore, it may be better perhaps, instead of *sportsman*, to read *fox-hunter*.

It was the opinion of a great sportsman, that it is not less difficult to find a perfect huntsman than a good prime minister. Without taking upon me to determine what requisites may be necessary to form a good prime minister, I will describe some of those which are essentially necessary towards forming a perfect huntsman; qualities which, I will venture to say, would not disgrace more brilliant situations; such as a clear head, nice observation, quick apprehension, undaunted courage, strength of constitution, activity of body, a good ear, and a good voice.

There is not any one branch of knowledge, commonly dignified with the title of art, which has not such rudiments or principles as may lead to a competent degree of skill, if not to perfection, in it; while hunting, the sole business of some, and the amusement of most of the youth in this kingdom, seems left entirely to chance. Its pursuit puts us both to greater expense, and also to greater inconvenience, than any other; yet, notwithstanding this, we trust our diversion in it to the sole guidance of a huntsman: we follow just as he shall choose to conduct us; and we suffer the success, or disappointment, of the chase, to depend solely on the judgment of a fellow who is frequently a greater brute than the creature on which he rides. I would not be understood to mean by this, that a huntsman should be a scholar, or that every gentleman should hunt his own hounds. It is not necessary a huntsman should be a man of letters: but give me leave to observe, that, had he the best understanding, he would frequently find opportunities of exercising it and intricacies which might put it to the test. You will say, perhaps, there is something too laborious in the occupation of a huntsman, for a gentleman to take it upon himself; you may also think it is beneath him: I agree with you in both; yet I hope that he may have leave to understand it.—If he follow the diversion, it is a sign of his liking it; and if he like it, surely it is some disgrace to him to be ignorant of the means most conducive to it.

I find there will be no necessity to say much to you in commendation of a diversion which you professedly admire: [1] it would be needless, therefore, to enumerate the heroes of antiquity who were taught the art of hunting, or the many great men (among whom was the famous Galen) who have united in recommending it. I shall, however, remind you, that your beloved hero, Henry the Fourth of France, made it his chief amusement (his very love-letters, strange as it may appear, being filled with little else); and that one of the greatest ministers which our own country ever produced, was so fond of this diversion, that the first letter he opened, as I have been told, was generally that of his huntsman. [2] In most countries, from the earliest times, hunting has been a principal occupation of the people, either for use or amusement; and many princes have made it their chief delight; a circumstance which occasioned the following *bon mot*: Louis the Fifteenth was so passionately fond of this diversion, that it occupied him entirely. The King of Prussia, who never hunts, gives up a great deal of his time to music, and himself plays on the flute. A German, last war, meeting a Frenchman, asked him very impertinently, "*Si son maître chassoit toujours?*" "*Oui, oui,*" replied the other—"*il ne joue jamais de la flute.*" The reply was excellent; but it would have been as well for mankind, perhaps, if that great man had never been otherwise employed. Hunting is the soul of a country life: it gives health to the body, and contentment to the mind; and is one of the few pleasures that we can enjoy in society, without prejudice either to ourselves or our friends.

[1] Since the above was written, hunting has undergone a severe censure (vide *Monthly Review* for September, 1781); nor will anything satisfy the critic, less than its total abolition. He recommends feats of agility to be practised and exhibited instead of it. Whether the amendment proposed by the learned gentleman be desirable or not, I shall forbear to determine; taking the liberty, however, to remind him, that as hunting hath stood its ground from the earliest times, been encouraged and approved by the best authorities, and practised by the greatest men, it cannot now be supposed either to dread criticism or to need support. Hunting originates in Nature itself; and it is in perfect correspondence with this law of Nature, that the several animals are provided with necessary means of attack and defence.

[[2] Probably Sir Robert Walpole.]

The *Spectator* has drawn with infinite humour the character of a man who passes his whole life in pursuit of trifles; and it is probable that other Will Wimbles might still be found. I hope, however, that he did not think they were solely confined to the country. Triflers there are of every denomination. Are we not all triflers? and are we not told that all is vanity? The *Spectator* without doubt, felt great compassion for Mr. Wimble; yet Mr. Wimble might not have been a proper object of it; since it is more than probable that he was a happy man, if the employment of his time in obliging others, and pleasing himself, can be thought to have made him so. Whether vanity mislead us or not in the choice of our pursuits, the pleasures or advantages which result from them will best determine. I fear that the occupation of few gentlemen will admit of nice scrutiny: occupations therefore that amuse, and are at the same time innocent; that promote exercise, and conduce to health; though they may appear trifles in the eyes of others, certainly are not so to those who enjoy them. Of this number, I think I may reckon hunting; and I am particularly glad that the same author furnishes a quotation in support of it: "For my own part," says this elegant writer, "I intend to hunt twice a week, during my stay with Sir Roger; and shall prescribe the moderate use of this exercise to all my country friends, as the best physic for mending a bad constitution, and preserving a good one." The inimitable Cervantes also honourably mentions this diversion: he makes Sancho say—"Mercy on me, what pleasure can you find, any of ye all, in killing a poor beast that never meant any harm!" that the Duke may reply—"You are mistaken, Sancho: hunting wild beasts is the most proper exercise for knights and princes; for in the chase of a stout noble beast, may be represented the whole art of war, stratagems, policy, and ambuscades, with all other devices usually practised to overcome an enemy with safety. Here we are exposed to the extremities of heat and cold: ease and laziness can have no room in this diversion. By this we are inured to toil and hardship; our limbs are strengthened, our joints made supple, and our whole body hale and active: in short, it is an exercise that may be beneficial to many, and can be prejudicial to none." Small indeed, is the number of those who, in the course of five thousand years, have employed themselves in the advancement of useful knowledge. Mankind have been blest with but one Titus, that we know of; and it is to be feared, he has had but few imitators. Days and years fly away; nor is any account taken of them; and how many may reasonably be supposed to pass, without affording even amusement to others, or satisfaction to ourselves? Much more, I think, might be said in favour of the Wimbles; but it must be confessed, that the man who spends his whole time in trifles, passes it contemptibly, compared with those who are employed in researches after knowledge useful to mankind, or in professions useful to the state.

I am glad to find that you approve of the plan I propose to observe in the course of these Letters; wherein it shall be my endeavour not to omit anything which it may be necessary for you to know; at least, as far as my own observation and experience will give me leave. The experience that I have had may be of use to you at present: others, perhaps, hereafter, may write more judiciously and more fully on the subject: you know it is my interest to wish that they would. The few who have written on hunting, refer you to their predecessors, for great part of the information you might expect from them; and who their predecessors were, I have yet to learn. Even Somerville is less copious than I could wish, and has purposely omitted what is not to be found elsewhere; I mean receipts for the cure of such diseases as hounds are subject to: he holds such information cheap, and beneath his lofty muse. Prose has no excuse; and you may depend on every information that I can give. The familiar manner in which my thoughts will be conveyed to you in these Letters, may sufficiently evince the intention of the author: they are written with no other design than to be of use to sportsmen. Were my aim to amuse, I would not endeavour to instruct: a song might suit the purpose better than an essay. To improve health, by promoting exercise; to excite gentlemen who are fond of hunting to obtain the knowledge necessary to enjoy it in perfection; and to lessen the punishments which are too often inflicted on an animal so friendly to man—are the chief ends intended by the following Letters.

I shall not pretend to lay down rules which are to be equally good in every country; I shall think myself sufficiently justified in recommending such as have been tried with success in the countries where I have generally hunted. As almost every country has a different dialect, you will also excuse, I hope, any terms that may not be current with *you*: I will take the best care I can that the number shall be small. It is needless, I think, to advise you not to adopt too easily the opinions of other men. You will hear a tall man say, It is folly to ride any but large horses; and every little man in company will immediately sell his little horses, buy such as he can hardly mount, and ride them in hilly countries, for which they are totally unfit. Pride induces some men to dictate; indolence makes others like to be dictated to; so both parties find their account in it. You will not let this mislead you: you will dare to think for yourself. Nor will you believe every man, who pretends to know what you like better than you do yourself. There is a degree of coxcombry, I believe, in everything. You have heard, I make no doubt, that greyhounds are either black, or white, or black and white; and if you have any faith in those who say they know best, they will tell you that there are no others.[1] Prejudice, however, is by far too blind a guide to be depended on.

I have read somewhere, that there is no book so bad, but a judicious reader may derive some advantage from the reading of it: I hope these Letters will not prove the only exception. Should they fall into the hands of such as are not sportsmen, I need not, I think, make any excuses to

---

[1] There is a fashion in greyhounds: some coursers even pretend, that *all* not being of the fashionable colour, are curs, and not greyhounds. Greyhound seems to be a corruption from some other word; most probably from gaze-hound.

them for the contents, since the title sufficiently shows for whom they were designed. Nor are they meant for such sportsmen as need not instruction, but for those that do; to whom, I presume, in some parts at least, they may be found of use. Since a great book has been long looked upon as a great evil, I shall take care not to sin that way at least; and shall endeavour to make these Letters as short as the extent of my subject will admit.

You will rally me, perhaps, on the choice of my frontispiece; but why should not hunting admit the patronage of a lady? The ancients, you know, invoked Diana at setting out on the chase, and sacrificed to her at their return: is not this enough to show the propriety of my choice? At all events, I assure myself that you will approve her attendants, *Health*, and *Contentment*.

I shall now take my leave of you for the present. In my next Letter I shall proceed according to your desire, till I have answered all your questions. Remember, you are not to expect entertainment: I wish that you may find some instruction: the dryness of the subject may excuse *your* want of the one, and I cannot doubt of your indulgence whilst I am obeying your commands, though *I* should fail in the other.

LETTER II

SINCE you intend to make hunting your chief amusement in the country, you are certainly in the right to give it some consideration before you begin; and not, like Master Stephen in the play, first buy a hawk, and then hunt after a book to keep it by. I am glad to find that you intend to build a new kennel; and, I flatter myself, the experience that I have had may be of some use to you in building it: it is not only the first thing that you should do, but it is also the most important. As often as your mind may alter, so often may you easily change from one kind of hound to another; but your kennel will still remain the same; will still keep its original imperfections, unless altered at a great expense; and be less perfect at last than it might have been made at first, had you pursued a proper plan. It is true, hounds may be kept in barns and stables: but those who keep them in such places can best inform you, whether their hounds are capable of answering the purposes for which they were designed. The sense of smelling, the *odora canum vis*, as Virgil calls it, is so exquisite in a hound, that I cannot but suppose every stench is hurtful to it. It is that faculty on which all our hopes depend; it is *that* which must lead us over greasy fallows, where the feet of the game we pursue, being clogged, leave little scent behind; as well as over stony roads, through watery meads, and where sheep have stained the ground.

Cleanliness is not only absolutely necessary to the nose of the hound, but also to the preservation of his health. Dogs are naturally cleanly animals; they seldom, when they can help it, dung where they lie: air, and fresh straw, are necessary to keep them healthy. They are subject to the mange; a disorder to which poverty and nastiness will very much contribute. *This*, though easily stopped at its first appearance, if suffered to continue long, may lessen the powers of the animal; and the remedies which are

THE KENNELS AT STEEPLETON, NOW CONVERTED INTO COTTAGES

then to be used, being in themselves violent, must injure his constitution. It had better be prevented: let the kennel therefore, be an object of your particular care.

> Upon some little eminence erect,
> And fronting to the ruddy dawn; its courts
> On either hand wide opening to receive
> The sun's all-cheering beams, when mild he shines,
> And gilds the mountain tops.

Let such as Somerville directs be the situation: its size must be suited to the number of its inhabitants: the architecture of it may be conformable to your own taste. Useless expense I should not recommend; yet, as I suppose you will often make it a visit, at least in the hunting season, I could wish it might have neatness without, as well as cleanliness within, the more to allure you to it. I should, for the same reason, wish it to be as near to your house as you will give it leave. I know there are many objections to its being very near: I foresee still more to it being at a distance. There is a vulgar saying, that it is the master's eye that makes the horse fat: I can assure you, that it is even more necessary in the kennel, where cleanliness is not less essential than food.

There are, I make no doubt, many better kennels than mine; some of which you should see before you begin to build. You can but make use of my plan, in case that you like no other better. If, in the meantime, I am to give you my opinion what a kennel ought to be, I must send you a description of my own, for I have not seen many others.

I would advise you to make it large enough at first, as any addition afterwards must spoil the appearance of it. I have been obliged to add to mine, which was built from a plan of my own, and intended, at first, for a pack of beagles. My feeding-yard being too small, I will endeavour to remedy that defect in the plan I send you, which plan may be still enlarged, or lessened, as you think fit, or as your occasions may require. The feeding-troughs should be wide at the bottom, and must have wooden covers.

I think two kennels absolutely necessary to the well-being of the hounds: when there is but one, it is seldom sweet; and, when cleaned out, the hounds, particularly in winter, suffer both whilst it is cleaning, and as long as it remains wet afterwards. To be more clearly understood by you, I shall call one of these the *hunting-kennel*, by which I mean that kennel into which the hounds intended to hunt the next day, are drafted. Used always to the same kennel, they will be drafted with little trouble; they will answer to their names more readily, and you may count your hounds into the kennel with as much ease as a shepherd counts his sheep out of the fold.

When the feeder first comes to the kennel in a morning, he should let out the hounds into the outer court; and in bad weather he should open the door of the hunting-kennel, lest want of rest should incline them to go into it. The lodging-room should then be cleaned out, the doors and windows of it opened, the litter shaken up, and the kennel made sweet and clean, before the hounds return to it again. The great court and the other kennels, are not less to be attended to, nor should you pass over in silence any omission that is hurtful to your hounds.

The floor of each lodging-room should be bricked, and sloped on both sides to run to the centre, with a gutter left to carry off the water, that when they are washed, they may be soon dry. If water should remain, through any fault in the floor, it should be carefully mopped up; for as warmth is in the greatest degree necessary to hounds after work, so damps are equally prejudicial. You will think me, perhaps, too particular in these directions; yet there can be no harm in your knowing what your servants ought to do; as it is not impossible but it may be sometimes necessary for you to see that it is done. In your military profession, you are perfectly acquainted with the duty of a common soldier; and though you have no farther business with the minutiæ of it, without doubt you still find the knowledge of them useful to you. Believe me, they may be useful *here*; and you will pardon me, I hope, if I wish to see you a

Martinet in the kennel, as well as in the field. Orders given without skill are seldom well obeyed; and where the master is either ignorant or inattentive, the servant will be idle.

I also wish, that, contrary to the usual practice in building kennels, you would have three doors; two in the front, and one in the back; the last to have a lattice-window in it, with a wooden shutter, which is constantly to be kept closed when the hounds are in, except in summer, when it should be left open all the day. This door answers two very necessary purposes: it gives an opportunity of carrying out the straw when the lodging-room is cleaned, and, as it is opposite to the window, will be a means to let in a thorough air, which will greatly contribute to keep it sweet and wholesome. The other doors will be of use in drying the room when the hounds are out; and as one is to be kept shut, and the other hooked back (allowing just room for a dog to pass), they are not liable to any objection. The great window in the centre should have a folding shutter; half, or the whole, of which, may be shut at nights, according to the weather: and your kennels, by that means, may be kept warm or cool, just as you please to have them. The two great lodging-rooms are exactly alike, and, as each has a court belonging to it, are distinct kennels, situated at the opposite ends of the building; in the centre of which is the boiling-house and feeding-yard; and on each side a lesser kennel, either for hounds that are drafted off, hounds that are sick, or lame; or for any other purposes, as occasion may require: at the back of which, as they are but half the depth of the two great kennels, are places for coals, &c. for the use of the kennel: there is also a small building in the rear, for hot bitches: the plan will show you the size of the whole. The floors of the inner courts, like those of the lodging-rooms, are bricked, and sloped towards the centre; and a channel of water, brought in by a leaden pipe, runs through the middle of them. In the centre of each court, is a well, large enough to dip a bucket, to clean the kennels: this must be faced with stone, or it will be often out of repair:—in the feeding-yard it should have a wooden cover.

The benches, which must be open, to let the urine through, should have hinges and hooks in the wall, that they may fold up, for the greater conveniency in washing out the kennel: they should also be made as low as possible, that a hound, when he is tired, may have no difficulty in jumping up, and at no time may be able to creep under.[1] Let me add, that the boiler should be of cast-iron.

The rest of the kennel consists of a large court in front, which is also bricked, having a grass-court adjoining, and a little brook running through the middle of it. The earth that was taken out of it, is thrown up into a mount, where the hounds, in summer, delight to sit. This court is planted round with trees, and has, besides, a lime-tree, and some horse-chestnut trees, near the middle of it, for the sake of shade. A high pale incloses the whole; part of which, to the height of about four feet, is close; the other open; the interstices are about two inches wide. The grass-court is pitched near the pale, to prevent the hounds from scratching out. Grass is the dog's best emetic; and in this he is his own physician. If you cannot guess the intention of the posts which you see in the courts, there is scarcely an inn window on any road, where the following line will not let you into the secret:

> "So dogs will p— where dogs have p—'d before."

This is done to save the trees, to which the urinary salts are prejudicial. If they be at first backward in coming to them, bind some straw round the bottom, and rub it with galbanum. The brook in the grass-court may serve as a stew: your fish will be very safe.[2]

At the back of the kennel is a house, thatched and furzed up on the sides, big enough to contain at least a load of

[1] Benches cannot be too low. If, owing to the smallness of the hound, it should be difficult to render them low enough, a projecting ledge will answer the same purpose; and the benches may be boarded at bottom, to prevent the hound from creeping under.

[2] It may also be used as a cold bath, for such hounds as stand in need of it: for lameness in the stifle, and for strains, it will be found of service.

straw. Here should be a pit ready to receive the dung, and a gallows for the flesh. The gallows should have a thatched roof, and a circular board at the posts of it, to prevent vermin from climbing up. If you can inclose a piece of ground adjoining to your kennel, for such dog-horses as may be brought to you alive, it will be of great use; as it might be dangerous to turn them out where other horses go; for you may not always be able to discover their disorders. *Hither* you may also bring your hounds, after they have been fed, to empty themselves; *here* you will have more opportunities of seeing them than in the kennel; and will be enabled, therefore, to make your draft for the next day with greater accuracy.

A stove, I believe, is made use of in some kennels; but, where the feeder is a good one, a mop, properly used, will render it unnecessary. I have a little hay-rick in the grass-yard, which I think is of use, to keep the hounds clean, and fine in their coats: you will find them frequently rubbing themselves against it: the shade of it also is useful to them in summer. If ticks at any time be troublesome in your kennel, let the walls of it be well washed: if that should not destroy them, the walls must then be white-washed.

In the summer, when you do not hunt, one kennel will be sufficient: the other may then be set apart for the young hounds, who should also have the grass-court adjoining to it. It is best, at that time of the year, to keep them separate; and it prevents many accidents which otherwise might happen; nor should they be put together till the hunting season begins.[1] If your hounds be very quarrelsome, the feeder may sleep in a cot in the kennel adjoining; and, if they be well chastised at the first quarrel, his voice will be sufficient to settle all their differences afterwards.[2] Close to the door of the kennel, let there be

[1] The dogs and the bitches may also be kept separate from each other during the summer months, where there are conveniences for it.

[2] In a kennel in Oxfordshire, the feeder pulls a bell, which the hounds understand the meaning of: it silences them immediately, and saves him the trouble of getting out of his bed.

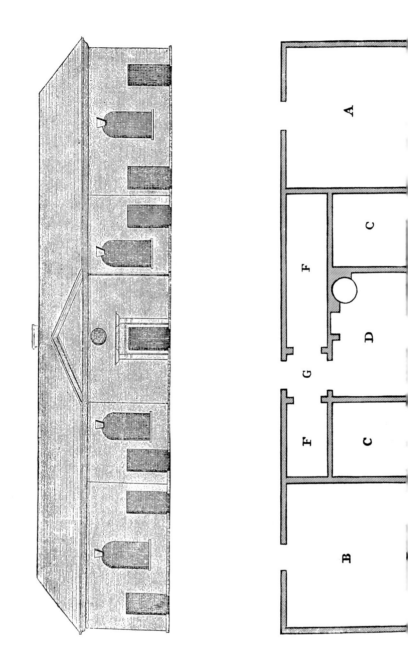

H

	ft. in.		ft. in.	ft. in. height
A. Lodging Rooms	18 " 4.	by	16 "	18 height
a. Court	20.	by	18 " 4.	
B. Lodging Room to the Hunting Kennel	18 " 4.	by	16 "	18
b. Court	20.	by	18 " 4.	
C. Smaller Lodging Rooms	10 " 1.	by	9 " 4½.	18
c. Courts	20.	by	9 " 4½.	18
D. Boiling House	15 " 4½.	by	10.	18
E. Feeding Court	20.	by	15 " 4½.	
F. Places for Coals &c	19 " 4.	by	5 " 1.	
F.	9 " 4.	by	5 " 1.	
G. Passage	5 " 6.	by	5 " 1.	
H. Great Court				
I. Grass Court				

always a quantity of little switches; which three narrow boards, nailed to one of the posts, will easily contain.[1]

My kennel is close to the road-side, but it was unavoidable. This is the reason why my front pale is close, and only the side ones open: it is a great fault: avoid it if you can, and your hounds will be the quieter.

Upon looking over my Letter, I find that I begin by recommending, with Mr. Somerville, a high situation for the kennel, and afterwards talk of a brook running through the middle of it: I am afraid that you will not be able to unite these two advantages; in which case, without doubt, water should be preferred. The mount that I have mentioned will answer all the purposes of an eminence: besides, there should be moveable stages on wheels, for the hounds to lie upon; at any rate, however, let your soil be a dry one.[2]

You will, perhaps, think my lodging-rooms higher than is necessary. I know that they are considerably higher than is usual; the intention of which is, to give more air to the hounds; and I have not the least doubt that they are the better for it. I will no longer persecute you with this unentertaining subject, but send you a plan from my own kennel, and take my leave of you.

P.S.—I send only the ground-plan and elevation, as the size of the outer court, and grass-court, are perfectly immaterial; the one should not be small, and the other should be as large as you can conveniently make it.

[1] When hounds are perfectly obedient, whips are no longer necessary; switches in my opinion, are preferable. The whips I use are coach-whips, three feet long, the thong half the length of the crop: they are more handy than horse-whips, correct the hounds as well, and hurt them less.

[[2] The hill is to be preferred to the running water, and the soil should be a stiff clay. Kennels should never be built on gravel. Clay certainly holds moisture, but at the same time it prevents any moisture rising from below. There is always water beneath gravel, and the heat of the hounds' bodies will draw it up from any depth. This is the cause of that terrible scourge kennel-lameness, which is nothing else but rheumatism. If kennels are already built on gravel, the floor should be taken up, the ground excavated, and three feet of clay puddled in. Of course spouting should be attended to, and if there is any high ground above the kennel floor, drains should be made to carry off surface water.]

LETTER III

I BEGIN this Letter with assuring you that I have done with the *kennel*: without doubt, you will think I had need. If I have made even the name frightful to you, comfort yourself with the thoughts that it will not appear again.

Your criticism on my switches I think unjust. You tell me, that self-defence would of course make you take that precaution. Do you always walk with a whip in your hand? —or do you think that a walking-stick, which may be a good thing to knock a dog on the head with, would be equally proper to correct him, should he be too familiar? You forget, however, to put a better substitute in the room of them.

You desire to know what kind of hound I would recommend. As you mention not for any particular chase, or country, I understand you generally; and shall answer, that I most approve of hounds of the middle size. I believe all animals of that description are strongest, and best able to endure fatigue. In the height, as well as the colour of hounds, most sportsmen have their prejudices; but in their shape, at least, I think they must all agree. I know sportsmen who boldly affirm, that a small hound will oftentimes beat a large one; that he will climb hills better, and go through cover quicker;—whilst others are not less ready to assert, that a large hound will make his way in any country; will get better through the dirt than a small one; and that no fence, however high, can stop him. You have now three opinions; and I advise you to adopt that which suits your country best. There is, however, a certain size, best adapted for business; which I take to be that between the two extremes; and I will venture to say, that such hounds will not suffer themselves to be disgraced in any country. Somerville, I find, is of the same opinion.

But here a mean
Observe, nor the large hound prefer, of size

Gigantic; he in the thick-woven covert
Painfully tugs, or in the thorny brake,
Torn and embarrass'd, bleeds: but if too small,
The pigmy brood in every furrow swims;
Moil'd in the clogging clay, panting they lag
Behind, inglorious; or else shivering creep,
Benumb'd and faint, beneath the shelt'ring thorn;
For hounds of middle size, active and strong,
Will better answer all thy various ends,
And crown thy pleasing labours with success.

I perfectly agree with you, that, to look well, they should be all nearly of a size; and I even think that they should all look of the same family.

Facies non omnibus una,
Nec diversa tamen, qualem decet esse sororum.

If handsome withal, they are then perfect. With regard to their being sizeable, what Somerville says is so much in your way, that I shall send it to you.

As some brave captain, curious and exact,
By his fix'd standard forms in equal ranks
His gay battalion, as one man they move
Step after step, their size the same, their arms
Far gleaming, dart the same united blaze:
Reviewing generals his merit own.
How regular! how just!—and all his cares
Are well repaid, if mighty GEORGE approve.
So model thou thy pack, if honour touch
Thy gen'rous soul, and the world's just applause.

There are necessary points in the shape of a hound, which ought always to be attended to by a sportsman; for, if he be not of a perfect symmetry, he will neither run fast, nor bear much work: he has much to undergo, and should have strength proportioned to it. Let his legs be straight as arrows; his feet round, and not too large; his shoulders back; his breast rather wide than narrow; his chest deep; his back broad; his head small, his neck thin; his tail thick and brushy: if he carry it well, so much the better. This last point, however trifling it may appear to you, gave rise to a very odd question. A gentleman (not much acquainted with hounds), as we were hunting together the other day, said: "I observe, Sir, that some of your dogs' tails stand up, and some hang down; pray, which do you reckon *the best hounds?*" Such young hounds as are out at the elbows, and such as are weak from the knee to the foot, should never be taken into the pack.

I find that I have mentioned a small head, as one of the necessary requisites of a hound; but you will understand it as relative to *beauty only*; for, as to *goodness*, I believe large-headed hounds are in no wise inferior. Somerville, in his description of a perfect hound, makes no mention of the head, leaving the size of it to Phidias to determine; he, therefore, must have thought it of little consequence. I send you his words.

> See there, with countenance blythe
> And with a courtly grin, the fawning hound
> Salutes thee cow'ring; his wide-op'ning nose
> Upwards he curls, and his large sloe-black eyes
> Melt in soft blandishments, and humble joy:
> His glossy skin, or yellow-pied, or blue,
> In lights or shades, by Nature's pencil drawn,
> Reflects the various tints: his ears and legs,
> Fleckt here and there in gay enamel'd pride,
> Rival the speckled pard: his rush-gown tail
> O'er his broad back bends in an ample arch.
> On shoulders clean, upright and firm he stands:
> His round cat-foot, straight hams, and wide-spread thighs,
> And his low-dropping chest, confess his speed:
> His strength, his wind, or on the steepy hill,
> Or far-extended plain; in every part
> So well proportion'd, that the nicer skill
> Of Phidias himself can't blame thy choice.
> Of such compose thy pack.

The colour I think of little moment; and am of opinion with our friend Foote, respecting his negro friend that a good dog, like a good candidate, cannot be of a bad colour.

Men are too apt to be prejudiced by the sort of hound which they themselves have been most accustomed to. Those who have been used to the sharp-nosed fox-hound, will hardly allow a large-headed hound to *be* a fox-hound; yet they both equally are: speed and beauty are the chief excellences of the one; while stoutness, and tenderness of nose, in hunting,[1] are characteristic of the other. I could tell you, that I have seen very good sport with very unhandsome packs, consisting of hounds of various sizes, differing from one another as much in shape and look as in their colour; nor could there be traced the least sign of consanguinity amongst them. Considered separately, the hounds were good; as a pack of hounds, they were not to be commended; nor would you be satisfied with anything that looked so very incomplete. You will find nothing so essential to your sport, as that your hounds should run well together; nor can this end be better attained, than by confining yourself, as near as you can, to those of the same sort, size, and shape.

A great excellence in a pack of hounds, is the head they carry; and that pack may be said to go the fastest, that can run ten miles the soonest; notwithstanding the hounds, separately, may not run so fast as many others.[2] A pack of hounds, considered in a collective body, go fast, in proportion to the excellence of their noses, and the head they carry; as that traveller generally gets soonest to his journey's end who stops least upon the road. Some hounds that I have hunted with, would creep all through the same hole, though they might have leapt the hedge, and would follow one another in a string, as true as a team of cart-horses. I had rather see them, like the horses of the sun, *all a-breast*.

A friend of mine killed thirty-seven brace of foxes in one season: twenty-nine of the foxes were killed without any intermission. I must tell you, at the same time, that they were killed with hounds bred from a pack of harriers;

---

[1] Il parait que la finesse de l'odorat, dans les chiens, dépend de la grosseur plus que de la longueur du museau.—BUFFON.

[2] [The most essential thing in a pack of hounds is the head they carry.]

"they spread like a sky-rocket"

nor had they, I believe, a single skirter belonging to them. There is a pack now in my neighbourhood, of all sorts and sizes, which seldom miss a fox; when they run, there is a long string of them, and every fault is hit off by an old southern hound. However, out of the last eighteen foxes that they hunted, they killed seventeen; and I have no doubt, that, as they become more complete, more foxes will escape from them. Packs which are composed of hounds of various kinds, seldom run well together; nor do their tongues harmonize; yet they generally, I think, kill most foxes: but unless I like their style of killing them, whatever may be their success, I cannot be completely satisfied. I once asked the famous Will Crane, how his hounds behaved. *"Very well, Sir,"* he replied: *"they never come to a fault but they spread like a sky-rocket."* Thus it should always be.

A famous sportsman asked a gentleman what he thought of his hounds. "Your pack is composed, Sir," said he, "of dogs which any other man would *hang:* they are all *skirters.*" This was taken as a compliment. However, think not that I recommend it to you as such; for, though I am a great advocate for style in the killing of a fox, I never forgive a professed skirter: where game is in plenty, they are always changing, and are the loss of more foxes than they kill.

You ask me, how many hounds you ought to keep? It is a question not easy to answer: from twenty to thirty couple are as many, I think, as you should ever take into the field.[1] The propriety of any number must depend upon the strength of your pack, and the country in which you are to hunt: the quantity of hounds necessary to furnish that number for a whole season, must also depend on the country *where* you hunt; as some countries lame hounds more than others. The taking out too many hounds, Mr. Somerville very properly calls *an useless incumbrance.* It is not so material what the number is, as it is that all your hounds should be steady, and as nearly as possible of equal speed.

[1 From fifteen to twenty couple are quite enough, and more than that number do harm rather than good.]

When packs are very large, the hounds are seldom sufficiently hunted to be good. Few people choose to hunt every day; and, if they did, it is not likely that the weather in winter would give them leave. You would always be obliged, therefore, either to take out a very large pack, or a great number of hounds must be left behind: in the first case, too many hounds in the field would probably spoil your sport; in the second, hounds that remain long without work, always get out of wind, and oftentimes become riotous. About forty couple, I think, will best answer your purpose. Forty couple of hunting hounds will enable you to hunt three, or even four, times in a week; and, I will venture to say, will kill more foxes than a greater number. Hounds, to be good, must be kept constantly hunted; and if I should hereafter say, a fox-hound should be above his work, it will not be a young fox-hound that I shall mean; for he should seldom be left at home, as long as he is able to hunt: the old and lame, and such as are low in flesh, you should leave; and such as you are sure idleness cannot spoil.

It is a great fault to keep too many old hounds. If you choose that your hounds should run well together, you should not continue *any*, longer than five or six seasons; though there is no saying, with certainty, what number of seasons a hound will last. Like us, some of them have better constitutions than others, and consequently will bear more work; and the duration of all bodies depends as much on the usage that they meet with, as on the materials of which they are made.

You ask, whether you had not better buy a complete pack at once, than be at the trouble of breeding one? Certainly you had, if such an opportunity should offer. It sometimes happens, that hounds are to be bought for less money than you could breed them. The gentleman to whom my house formerly belonged, had a most famous pack of fox-hounds. His goods, &c., were appraised and sold; which, when the appraiser had done, he was put in mind of the hounds. "Well, gentlemen," said he, "what shall I appraise *them at*? *A shilling a-piece?*" "Oh, it is too little!" "Is it so?" said the appraiser—"why, it is more than *I would give for them, I assure you.*"

Hounds are not bought so cheap *at Tattersall's.*

LETTER IV

I A M glad that you do not disapprove the advantage I have made of my friend Somerville. I was doubtful whether you would not have censured me for it, and have compared me to some of those would-be fine gentlemen, who, to cut a figure, tack an embroidered edging on their coarse cloth. I shall be cautious, however, of abusing your indulgence, and shall not quote my poet oftener than is necessary; but where we think the same thing, you had better take it in his words than mine. I shall now proceed to the feeding of hounds, and management of them in the kennel.

A good feeder is an essential part of your establishment. Let him be young and active, and have the reputation at least of not disliking work: he should be good-tempered, for the sake of the animals entrusted to his care; and who, however they may be treated by him, cannot complain. He should be one who will strictly obey any orders that you may give, as well with regard to the management as to the breeding of the hounds; and should not be solely under the direction of your huntsman. It is true, I have seen it otherwise: I have known a pack of hounds belong, as it were, entirely to the huntsman; a stable of horses belong to the groom; while the master had little more power in the direction of either, than a perfect stranger. This you will not allow. I know that you choose to keep the supreme command in your own hands; and, though you permit your servants to remonstrate, you do not suffer them to disobey. He who allows a huntsman to manage his hounds without control, literally keeps them for the huntsman's amusement. You desire to know what is required of a feeder: I will tell you as well as I can.

As our sport depends entirely on that exquisite sense of smelling so peculiar to the hound, care must be taken to preserve it; and cleanliness is the surest means. The keeping your kennel *sweet* and *clean*, cannot therefore be too much recommended to the feeder; nor should you on any account, admit the least deviation from it. If he sees *you* exact, he will be so himself. This is a very essential part of his business. The boiling for the hounds, mixing of the meat, and getting it ready for them at proper hours, your huntsman will of course take care of; nor is it ever likely to be forgotten. I must caution you not to let your dogs eat their meat too hot; I have known it attended with bad consequences; you should also order it to be mixed up as thick as possible. When the feeder has cleaned his kennel in the morning, and prepared his meat, it is usual for him, on hunting days (in an establishment like yours), to exercise the horses of the huntsman and whipper-in; and, in many stables, it is also the feeder who looks after the huntsman's horse, when he comes in from hunting; whilst the huntsman feeds the hounds. When the hounds are not out, the huntsman and whipper-in, of course, will exercise their own horses; and, that day, the feeder has little else to mind but the cleaning of his kennel. Every possible contrivance has been attended to in the plan that I sent you, to make that part of his work easy; all the courts, except the grass court, being bricked and sloped on purpose. There is also plenty of water, without any trouble of fetching it; and a thorough air throughout the kennels, to assist in drying them again. Should you choose to increase your number of servants in the stable, the business of the feeder may be confined entirely to the kennel. There should be always two to feed the hounds properly; the feeder and the huntsman.

Somerville strongly recommends cleanliness in the following lines:

> O'er all let cleanliness preside; no scraps
> Bestrew the pavement, and no half-pick'd bones,
> To kindle fierce debate, or to disgust
> That nicer sense, on which the sportsman's hope,
> And all his future triumphs, must depend.
> Soon as the growling pack with eager joy
> Have lapp'd their smoking viands, morn or eve,

From the full cistern lead the ductile streams,
To wash thy court well pav'd; nor spare thy pains,
For much to health will cleanliness avail.
Seek'st thou for hounds to climb the rocky steep,
And brush th' entangled covert, whose nice scent
O'er greasy fallows, and frequented roads,
Can pick the dubious way?—banish far off
Each noisome stench; let no offensive smell
Invade thy wide inclosure, but admit
The nitrous air and purifying breeze.

So perfectly right is the poet in this, that if you can make your kennel a visit every day, your hounds will be the better for it. When I have been long absent from mine, I have always perceived a difference in their looks. I shall now take notice of that part of the management of hounds in the kennel which concerns the huntsman, as well as the feeder. Your huntsman must always attend the feeding of the hounds, which should be drafted, according to the condition they are in. In all packs, some hounds will feed better than others: some there are that will do with less meat; and it requires a nice eye, and great attention, to keep them all in equal flesh: it is what distinguishes a good kennel-huntsman, and has its merit. It is seldom that huntsmen give this particular all the attention which it deserves: they feed their hounds in too great a hurry; and not often, I believe, take the trouble of casting their eye over them before they begin; and yet to distinguish with any nicety the order that a pack of hounds are in, and the different degrees of it, is surely no easy task; and, to be done well, requires no small degree of circumspection. You had better not expect your huntsman to be very exact: where precision is required, he will most probably fail.

When I am present myself, I make several drafts. When my huntsman feeds them, he calls them all over by their names, letting in each hound as he is called: it has its use; it uses them to their names, and teaches them to be obedient. Were it not for this, I should disapprove of it entirely; since it certainly requires more coolness and deliberation to distinguish with precision which are best entitled to precedence, than this method of feeding will admit of; and unless flesh be in great plenty, those that are called in last may not have a taste of it. To prevent this inconvenience, such as are low in flesh had better be all drafted off into a separate kennel;[1] by this means, the hounds that require *flesh* will all have a share of it. If any be much poorer than the rest, they should be fed again: such hounds cannot be fed too often. If any in the pack be too fat, *they* should be drafted off, and not suffered to fill themselves. The others should eat what they will of the meat. The days my hounds have greens, or sulphur, they generally are let in all together; and such as require *flesh*, have it given to them afterwards. Having a good kennel-huntsman, it is not often that I take this trouble; yet I seldom go into my kennel, but I indulge myself in the pleasure of seeing food given to such hounds as appear to me to be in want of it. I have been told, that in one kennel, in particular, the hounds are under such excellent management, that they constantly are fed with the door of the feeding-yard open; and the rough nature of the fox-hound is changed into so much politeness, that he waits at the door till he is invited in; and, what perhaps is not less extraordinary, he comes out again, whether he has satisfied his hunger or not, the moment he is desired—the effect of discipline. However, as this is not absolutely necessary, and hounds may be good without it; and as I well know that your other amusements will not permit you to attend to so much manœuvring—I would by no means wish you to give such power to your huntsman. The business would be injudiciously done, and most probably would not answer your expectations. The hound would be tormented *mal-à-propos*; an animal so little deserving of it from our hands, that I should be sorry to disturb his hours of repose by unnecessary severity. You will perceive that it is a nice affair; and, I assure you,

---

[1] By thus separating from the rest such as are poor, you will proceed to the feeding of your hounds with more accuracy and less trouble; and though they be at first drafted off in the manner above described, it is still meant that they should be let in to feed, one by one, as they answer to their names; or else, as it will frequently happen, they may be better fed than taught.

I know no huntsman who is equal to it. The gentleman who has carried this matter to its utmost perfection, has attended to it regularly himself; has constantly acted on fixed principles, from which he has never deviated; and, I believe, has succeeded to the very utmost of his wishes. All hounds (and more especially young ones) should be called over often in the kennel;[1] and most huntsmen practise this lesson as they feed their hounds: they flog them while they feed them; and if they have not always a belly-full one way, they seldom fail to have it the other.[2] It is not, however, my intention to oppose so general a practice, in which there may be some utility; I shall only observe, that it should be used with discretion; lest the whip should fall heavily, in the kennel, on such as never deserve it in the field.

My hounds are generally fed about eleven o'clock;[3] and, when I am present myself, I take the same opportunity to make my draft for the next day's hunting. I seldom, when I can help it, leave this to my huntsman; though it is necessary that he should be present when the draft is made, that he may know what hounds he has out.

[1] There is no better method of teaching a hound obedience; when you call him he should approach you; and when you touch him with your stick, he should follow you anywhere.

[2] "Thus we find, eat or not eat, work or play, whipping is always in season." (Vide *Monthly Review*). The critic treats this passage with great severity. He would have spared it, without doubt, had he understood that it was introduced on purpose to correct the abuse of kennel-discipline. Unacquainted as the reviewer seems to be with the subject, it is no wonder that he should mistake a meaning, perhaps rather unfairly stated by the author, in favour of that humanity which he is supposed so much to want. Hounds are called in to feed, one by one, and such only are corrected as come uncalled for: nor is correction unjust, so long as it shall fall on the disobedient only. Obedience is an useful lesson, and though it cannot be *practised* too often, it should be *taught* them at a more idle time.

[3] Having found it necessary to alter my method of feeding hounds, it may not be improper to take notice of it here. They are now fed at eight o'clock, instead of eleven. Their first feed is of barley and oatmeal mixed, an equal quantity of each. Flesh is afterwards mixed up with the remainder, for such hounds as are poor, who are then drafted off into another kennel, and let in to feed altogether. When the flesh is all eaten, the pack are again let in, and are by this means cheated into a second appetite. At three o'clock, those that are to hunt the next day are drafted into the hunting-kennel; they are then let into the feeding-yard, where a small quantity of oatmeal (about three buckets) is prepared for them, mixed up thick. Such as are tender, or bad feeders, have a handful of boiled flesh given to them afterwards. When they are not to hunt the next day, they are fed once only, at eleven o'clock.

It is a bad custom to use hounds to the boiling-house: it is apt to make them nice, and may prevent them from ever eating the kennel meat. What they have should always be given them in the feeding-yard; and for the same reason, though it be flesh, it should have some meal mixed with it.

If your hounds be low in flesh, and have far to go to cover, they may all have a little thin lap again in the evening; but this should never be done if you hunt early.[1] Hounds, I think, should be sharp set before hunting: they run the better for it.[2]

If many of your hounds, after long rest, should be too fat,[3] feeding them for a day or two on thinner meat than you give the others, will be found, I believe, to answer better than the usual method of giving them the same meat, and stinting them in the quantity of it.

If your hounds be not walked out, they should be turned into the grass-court to empty themselves, after they have been fed: it will contribute not a little to the cleanliness of the kennel.

I have heard, that it is a custom in some kennels to shut up the hounds for a couple of hours after they come in from hunting, before they are fed; and that other hounds are shut up with them, to lick them clean.[4] My usual way is to send in a whipper-in before them, that the meat may be got ready against they come, and they are fed *immediately*: having filled their bellies, they are naturally inclined to rest. If they have had a severe day, they are fed again some hours after.[5] As to the method above mentioned, it may be

---

[1] Hounds that are tender feeders cannot be fed too late, or with meat too good.

[2] Vide note, page 29.

[3] Hounds that rest should not be suffered to become fat. It would be accounting very badly for the fatness of a hound, to say, "He is fat because he has not worked lately;" since he ought to have been kept lower on that account.

[4] If hounds be shut up as soon as they come in from hunting, they will not readily leave the benches afterwards; for if they be much fatigued, they will prefer rest to food.

[5] My hounds are generally fed twice on the days they hunt. Some will feed better the second time than the first; besides, the turning them out of the lodging-house refreshes them: they stretch their limbs, empty their bodies; and, as during this time their kennel is cleaned out, and litter shaken up, they settle themselves better on the benches afterwards.

more convenient, perhaps, to have the hounds all together; but I cannot think it necessary, for the reason that is given; and I should apprehend, a parcel of idle hounds shut up amongst such as are tired and inclined to rest, would disturb them more than all their licking would make amends for. When you feed them twice, keep them separate till after the second feeding: it would be still better, were they not put together till the next morning.

Every day, when hounds come in from hunting, they ought carefully to be looked over, and invalids should immediately be taken care of.[1] Such as have sore feet, should have them well washed out with brine, or pot-liquor. If you permit those hounds that are unable to work, to run about your house, it will be of great service to them. Such as are ill, or lame, ought to be turned out into another kennel; it will be more easy to give them *there* the attention they may require, both as to medicine and food.

Every Thursday during the hunting-season, my hounds have one pound of sulphur given them in their meat; and every Sunday throughout the year they have plenty of greens boiled up with it: I find it better to fix the days, as it is then less liable to be forgotten. I used to give them the wash from the kitchen, but I found it made them thirsty; and it is now omitted in the hunting-season. A horse fresh killed is an excellent meal for hounds, after a very hard day; but they should not hunt till the third day after it. The bones broken are good food for poor hounds, as there is great proof in them. Sheep-trotters are very sweet food, and will be of service when horse-flesh is not to be had. Bullock's bellies may be also of some use, if you can get nothing else. Oatmeal, I believe, makes the best meat for hounds: barley is certainly the cheapest; and in many kennels they give barley on that account; but it is heating, does not mix up so well, nor is there so much proof in it as in oatmeal. If mixed (an equal quantity of each), it will then do very

[1] Hounds that come home lame should not be taken out the next hunting day, since they may appear sound without being so. At the beginning of the season, the eyes of hounds are frequently injured: such hounds should not be hunted, and, if their eyes continue weak, they should lose a little blood.

well; but barley alone will not. Much also depends on the goodness of the meal itself, which is not often attended to. If you do not use your own, you should buy a large quantity of it any time before harvest, and keep it by you: there is no other certainty, I believe, of having it *old*; which is more material, perhaps, than you are aware of. I have heard, that a famous Cheshire huntsman feeds his hounds with wheat, which he has found to be the best food: he gives it them with the bran. It would cause no little disturbance in many neighbourhoods, if other sportsmen were to do the same.

I am not fond of *bleeding* hounds, unless they want it; though it has long been a custom in my kennel to *physic* them twice a year; after they leave off hunting, and before they begin: it is given in hot weather, and at an idle time: it cools their bodies, and, without doubt, is of service to them. If a hound be in want of physic, I prefer giving it in balls.[1] It is more easy to give in this manner the quantity that he may want, and you are more certain that he takes it. In many kennels they also bleed them twice a year; and some people think that it prevents madness. The anointing of hounds, or *dressing* them, as huntsmen call it, makes them fine in their coats: it may be done twice a year, or oftener, if you find it necessary. As I shall hereafter have occasion to write on the diseases of hounds, and their cures, I will send you at the same time a receipt for this purpose. During the summer months, when my hounds do not hunt, they have seldom any flesh allowed them, and are kept low, contrary, I believe, to the usual practice of most kennels where mangey hounds, in summer, are but too often seen. Huntsmen sometimes content themselves with checking this disorder, when with less trouble, perhaps, they might prevent it. A regular course of whey and vegetables, during the hot months, must certainly be wholesome, and is, without doubt, the cause that a mangey hound is an unusual sight in my kennel. Every Monday and Friday my hounds

---

[1] One pound of antimony, four ounces of sulphur, and syrup of buckthorn q. s. to give it the consistency of a ball. Each ball weighs about seven drachms.

go for whey, till the hunting season begins; are kept out several hours; and are often made to swim through rivers, during the hot weather.[1] After the last physic, and before they begin to hunt, they are exercised on the turnpike road, to harden their feet, which are washed with strong brine as soon as they come in. Little straw is necessary during the summer; but when they hunt they cannot have too much, or have it changed too often. In many kennels they do not boil for the hounds in summer, but give them meal only: in mine it is always boiled; but with this difference, that it is mixed up thin, instead of thick. Many give spurge-laurel in summer, boiled up in their meat: as I never use it, I cannot recommend it. The physic that I give, is two pounds of sulphur, one pound of antimony, and a pint and a half of syrup of buckthorn, for about forty couple of hounds.[2] In the winter season, let your hounds be shut up warm at night. If, after hunting, any hounds be missing, the straw-house door should be left open; and, if they have had a hard day, it may be as well to leave some meat there for them.

I have inquired of my feeder (who is a good one, and has had more experience in these matters than any one that you perhaps may get) how he mixes up his meat. He tells me, that, in his opinion, oatmeal and barley mixed (an equal quantity of each) make the best meat for hounds. The oatmeal he boils for half an hour, and then puts out the fire, puts the barley into the copper, and mixes both together. I asked him, why he boiled one, and not the other? He told me, that boiling, which made oatmeal thick, made barley thin; and that when you feed with barley only, it should not be put into the copper, but be scalded with the

---

[1] Hounds should be walked out every day in the summer. Success in the future season will largely depend on the trouble that has been taken in getting the pack fit beforehand. In the six weeks previous to the commencement of the season, hounds should have at least two hours' exercise on the roads daily, and twice a week they should have six hours', if the sun is not too hot. On these occasions the men may take them out three hours before breakfast with one lot of horses and three hours afterwards with fresh mounts. If a saving of horses is a consideration, and the men can ride bicycles, these useful machines may be substituted.]

[2] Vide page 23.

liquor, and mixed up in a bucket. I find there is in my kennel a large tub on purpose, which contains about half a hogshead.

You little think, perhaps, how difficult it is to be a good kennel-huntsman; nor can you, as yet, know the nicety that is required to feed hounds properly. You are not aware, that some hounds will hunt best when fed late; others when fed early; that some should have but little; that others cannot have too much:—however, if your huntsman observe the rules that I have here laid down, his hounds will not do much amiss. But should you at any time wish to *renchérir* upon the matter, and feed each particular hound so as to make the most of him, you must learn it of a gentleman in Leicestershire, to whom the noble science of fox-hunting is more beholden than to any other. I shall myself say nothing further on the subject; for as your huntsman will not have the sense of the gentleman I allude to, nor *you*, perhaps, his patience, an easier method I know will suit you best. I shall only advise you, while you endeavour to keep your hounds in good order, not to let them become *too fat*: it will be impossible for them to run, if they be so. A fat alderman would cut a mighty ridiculous figure, were he inclined to run a race.

LETTER V

THERE is an active vanity in the minds of men which is favourable to improvement; and in every pursuit, while something remains to be attained, so long will it afford amusement: you will therefore find pleasure in the breeding of hounds, in which expectation is never completely satisfied; and it is on the sagacious management of this business that all your success will depend. Is it not extraordinary, that no other country should equal us in this particular, and that the very hounds procured from hence should degenerate in another climate?

> In thee alone, fair land of liberty!
> Is bred the perfect hound, in scent and speed
> As yet unrivall'd, while in other climes
> Their virtue fails, a weak degen'rate race.—SOMERVILLE.

Happy climate for sportsmen! where Nature seems, as it were, to give them an exclusive privilege of enjoying this diversion. To preserve this advantage, however, care should be taken in the breed: I shall, therefore, according to your desire, send you such rules as I observe myself. Consider the size, shape, colour, constitution, and natural disposition, of the dog you breed from, as well as the fineness of his nose, his stoutness, and method of hunting. On no account breed from one that is not *stout*, that is not *tender-nosed*, or that is either a *babbler*[1] or a *skirter*.

> Observe with care his shape, sort, colour, size:
> Nor will sagacious huntsmen less regard
> His inward habits; the vain babbler shun,
> Ever loquacious, ever in the wrong:
> His foolish offspring shall offend thy ears
> With false alarms, and loud impertinence:
> Nor less the shifting cur avoid, that breaks

[1] Babbling is one of the worst faults that a hound can be guilty of; it is constantly increasing, and is also catching. This fault, like many others, will sometimes run in the blood.

Illusive from the pack: to the next hedge
Devious he strays; there ev'ry muse he tries:
If haply then he cross the streaming scent,
Away he flies vain-glorious; and exults
As of the pack supreme, and in his speed
And strength unrivall'd. Lo! cast far behind,
His vex'd associates pant, and lab'ring strain
To climb the steep ascent. Soon as they reach
Th' insulting boaster, his false courage fails:
Behind he lags, doom'd to the fatal noose,
His master's hate, and scorn of all the field.
What can from such be hop'd, but a base brood
Of coward curs, a frantic, vagrant race?—SOMERVILLE.

It is the judicious cross that makes the pack complete.[1] The faults and imperfections in one breed may be rectified from another; and, if this be properly attended to, I see no reason why the breeding of hounds may not improve till improvement can go no further. If you find a cross hit, pursue it.[2] Never put an old dog to an old bitch. Be careful that they be healthy which you breed from, or you are not likely to have a healthy offspring. Should a favourite dog skirt a little, put him to a thorough line-hunting bitch, and such a cross may succeed. My objection to the breeding from such a hound is, that, as skirting is what most fox-hounds acquire from practice, it had better not be made natural to them. A very famous sportsman has told me, that he frequently breeds from brothers and sisters. As I should be very unwilling to urge any thing in opposition to such authority, you had better try it; and if it succeed in hounds, it is more, I believe, than it usually does in other animals. A famous cocker assured a friend of mine, that the third generation, which he called a nick, he had found to succeed very well, but

---

[1] I have seen fox-hounds that were bred out of a Newfoundland bitch and a fox-hound dog. They are monstrously ugly, are said to give their tongues sparingly, and to tire soon. The experiment has not succeeded: the cross most likely to be of service to a fox-hound, is the beagle. I am well convinced, that a handsome bony, tender-nosed, stout beagle would, occasionally, be no improper cross for a high-bred pack of fox-hounds.

[2] After the first season, I breed from all my young dog-hounds who have beauty and goodness to recommend them, to see what whelps they get.

BECKFORD'S HOUNDS AND HUNT SERVANTS

From a painting at Steepleton by Sartorius

no nearer. As I have tried neither one nor the other, I cannot speak with any certainty about them.

Give particular orders to your feeder to watch over the bitches with a cautious eye, and separate such as are going to be proud, before it be too late. The advances they make, frequently portend mischief as well as love, and, if not prevented in time, will not fail to set the whole kennel together by the ears, and may occasion the death of your best dogs: care only can prevent it.[1]

> Mark well the wanton females of thy pack,
> That curl their taper tails, and frisking court
> Their pyebald mates enamour'd: their red eyes
> Flash fires impure; nor rest nor food they take,
> Goaded by furious love. In sep'rate cells
> Confine them now, lest bloody civil wars
> Annoy thy peaceful state.—SOMERVILLE.

I have known huntsmen perfectly ignorant of the breed of their hounds, from inattention in this particular; and I have also known many good dogs fall a sacrifice to it.

The earlier in the year you breed, the better; January, February, and March, are the best months. Late puppies seldom thrive; if you have any such, put them to the best walks.[2] When the bitches begin to get big, let them not hunt any more: it proves frequently fatal to the puppies, sometimes to the bitch herself; nor is it safe for them to remain much longer in the kennel. If one bitch have many puppies, more than she can well rear, you may put some of them to another bitch; or, if you destroy any of them, you may keep the best coloured. They sometimes will have an extraordinary number: I have known an instance of one having fifteen; and a friend of mine, whose veracity I cannot doubt, has assured me that a hound in his pack brought forth sixteen, all alive. When you breed from a very favourite sort, and can have another bitch warded at the same time, it will have this advantage, it will enable

---

[1] When the bitches are off their heat, they should be suffered to run about the house a day or two, before they are taken out to hunt.

[2] Of the early whelps I keep five or six, of the late ones only two or three.

you to save all the puppies. Give particular orders that
the bitches be well fed with flesh; they should also have
plenty of milk; nor should the puppies be taken from them
till they are able to take care of themselves:[1] they will soon
learn to lap milk, which will relieve the mother. The
bitches, when their puppies are taken away from them,
should be physicked; they should have three purging-balls
given them, one every other morning, and plenty of whey
the intermediate day. If a bitch bring only one or two puppies, and you have another bitch that will take them; by
putting the puppies to her, the former will be soon fit to
hunt again: she should, however, be physicked first; and
if her dugs be annointed with brandy and water, it will
also be of service. The distemper makes dreadful havoc
with whelps at their walks, greatly owing, I believe, to the
to the little care that is taken of them there. I am in doubt
whether it might not be better to breed them up yourself,
and have a kennel on purpose.[2] You have a large orchard
paled in, which would suit them exactly; and what else

[1 It is most important to keep the pups healthy until they are ready to go to
their walks, and it is as well to employ a boy to spend his entire time in looking
after them. At a month old they will begin drinking milk if the boy takes a little
trouble in tempting them, and the bitch will thus have her task made easier. When
the pups are ten days or a fortnight old they should be put in movable kennels
and taken on clean ground, the bitch being allowed to roam where she lists, but the
pups may be kept in with a wire run. As soon as the pups will lap readily they
should be fed three times a day, and soaked bread or biscuit added when they will
eat it. A lad fond of animals will do this work better than a man, with the occasional
supervision of the huntsman. The dew claws may be removed at about a month
old, a sharp pair of scissors being used for the purpose. Each litter should be
marked in the ear with a different letter or number in Indian ink, so that there will
be no confusion when they come back from walk. The best plan is to use a letter
and number together, and thus by changing the combination several litters can
be marked with one or two letters. This, when done properly, makes branding
unnecessary. When the pups are about eight or nine weeks old they should be
sent out to walk; but before going they should be dressed with a mixture of yellow
sulphur and lard in equal parts, adding about four teaspoonsfuls of turpentine
to a pound of sulphur. Unless the pups look well when they go out you cannot
expect them to be in good order on their return.]

[2 This has been proved impossible. Hounds to be reared successfully must go
out to walk; the risks of accidents and distemper will have to be chanced. The
best plan is to give a handsome luncheon to the puppy walkers and prizes for the
best hounds; this will encourage the farmers to look after their charges and make
them take an interest in the pack. The hounds that survive the dangers of walks
always appear to have more sense than those that are kept at home.]

is wanted might easily be obtained. There is, however, an objection that perhaps may strike you: if the distemper once get amongst them, they must all have it; yet, notwithstanding *that*, as they will be constantly well fed, and will lie warm, I am confident it would be the saving of many lives. If you should adopt this method, you must remember to use them early to go in couples; and, when they become of a proper age, they must be walked out often; for, should they remain confined, they would neither have the shape, health, or understanding, which they ought to have. When I kept harriers, I bred up some of the puppies at a distant kennel; but, having no servants there to exercise them properly, I found them much inferior to such of their brethren as had the luck to survive the many difficulties and dangers which they had undergone at their walks: these were afterwards equal to any thing, and afraid of nothing; while those that had been nursed with so much care, were weakly and timid, and had every disadvantage attending private education.

I have often heard, as an excuse for hounds not hunting a cold scent, that they were *too high bred*. I confess, I know not what that means; but this I know, that hounds are frequently *too ill-bred* to be of any service. It is judgment in the breeder, and patience afterwards in the huntsman, that make them hunt.[1]

Young hounds are commonly named when first put out, and sometimes, indeed, ridiculously enough; nor is it easy, when you breed many, to find suitable or harmonious names for all; particularly as it is usual to name all the whelps of one litter with the same letter, which (to be systematically done) should also be the initial letter of the dog that got them, or the bitch that bred them. A baronet of my acquaintance, a literal observer of the above rule, sent three young hounds of one litter to a friend, all their names beginning, as *he said*, with the letter G: *Gowler, Govial, and Galloper.*

---

[1] Hounds which I had thought *stiff-nosed* for many years, I have seen hunt the coldest scent, when once the impatience of youth had left them.

LIBRARY
BISHOP BURTON COLLEGE
BEVERLEY HU17 8QG

It is, indeed, of little consequence what huntsmen call
their hounds; yet, if you dislike an unmeaning name, would
it not be as well to leave the naming of them till they are
brought home? They soon learn their names, and a shorter
list would do. Damons and Delias would not then be
necessary; nor need the sacred names of Titus and Trajan
be thus degraded. It is true, there are many odd names which
custom authorises; yet I cannot think, because some drunken
fellow or other has christened his dog Tipler, or Tapster,
that there is the least reason to follow the example. Pipers
and Fiddlers, for the sake of their music, we will not object
to; but Tiplers and Tapsters your kennel will be much
better without.

However extraordinary you may think it, I can assure you
that I have myself seen a *white* Gipsey, a *grey* Ruby, a *dark*
Snowball, and a Blueman, of any colour but *blue*. The
huntsman of a friend of mine being asked the name of
a young hound, said "it was *Lyman.*" "Lyman!" said his
master, "why, James, what does Lyman mean?" "Lord,
Sir!" replied James, "what does *any thing mean?*" A farmer,
who bred up two couple of hounds for me, whose names
were Merryman and Merrylass, Ferryman and Furious,
upon my inquiring after them, gave this account: "Merryman and Merrylass are both dead; but Ferryman, Sir, is a
fine dog, and so is *Ferrylass.*" Madam, a usual name among
hounds, is often, I believe, very disrespectfully treated:
I had an instance of it the other day in my own huntsman,
who, after having rated Madam a great deal to no purpose
(who, to confess the truth, was much given to do otherwise
than she should), flew into a violent passion, and hallooed
out as loud as he could, *Madam, you d—d bitch!*

As you desire a list of names, I will send you one. I have
endeavoured to class them according to their different
genders; but you will perceive that some names may be
used indiscriminately for either. It is not usual, I believe,
to call a pointer Ringwood, or a greyhound Harmony;
and such names as are expressive of speed, strength, courage,
or other natural qualities in a hound, I think most applicable

to them. Damons and Delias I have left out; the bold Thunder, and the brisk Lightning, if you please may supply their places; unless you prefer the method of the gentleman I told you of, who intends naming his hounds from the p—ge; and, I suppose, he at the came time will not be unmindful of the p—y c—rs.

If you mark the whelps in the side (which is called branding them) when they are first put out (or perhaps it may be better done after they have been out some time), it may prevent their being stolen.

When young hounds are first taken in, they should be kept separate from the pack; and, as it will happen at a time of the year when there is little or no hunting, you may easily give them up one of the kennels and grass-court adjoining. Their play ends frequently in a battle; it therefore is less dangerous, where all are equally matched. What Somerville says on this subject is exceedingly beautiful.

> But here, with watchful and observant eye,
> Attend their frolicks, which too often end
> In bloody broils and death. High o'er thy head
> Wave thy resounding whip, and with a voice
> Fierce-menacing o'er-rule the stern debate,
> And quench their kindling rage; for oft, in sport
> Begun, combat ensues; growling they snarl,
> Then on their haunches rear'd, rampant they seize
> Each other's throats; with teeth and claws, in gore
> Besmear'd, they wound, they tear, till on the ground,
> Panting, half dead the conquer'd champion lies:
> Then sudden all the base ignoble crowd
> Loud-clam'ring seize the helpless worried wretch,
> And, thirsting for his blood, drag diff'rent ways
> His mangled carcass on th' ensanguin'd plain.
> O, breasts of pity void! t' oppress the weak,
> To point your vengeance at the friendless head,
> And with one mutual cry insult the fall'n!
> Emblem too just of man's degen'rate race.

If you find that they take a dislike to any particular hound, the safest way will be to remove him, or it is probable they will kill him at last. When a feeder hears the hounds quarrel in the kennel, he halloos to them to stop them. He then goes in among them, and flogs every hound he can come near. How much more reasonable, as well as more efficacious, would it be, were he to see which were the combatants, before he speaks to them? Punishment would then fall, as it ought, on the guilty only. In all packs there are some hounds more quarrelsome than the rest; and it is to them we owe all the mischief that is done. If you find that chastisement cannot quiet them, it may be prudent to break their holders; for since they are not necessary to them for the meat they have to eat, they are not likely to serve them in any good purpose.

Young hounds ought to be fed twice a day, as they seldom take kindly at first to the kennel meat, and the distemper is most apt to seize them at this time. It is better not to round them till they are thoroughly settled; nor should it be put off till the hot weather, for then they would bleed too much.[1] If any of the dogs be thin over the back, or any more quarrelsome than the rest, it will be of use to cut them: I also spay such bitches as I think I shall not want to breed from; they are more useful, are stouter, and are always in better order; besides, it is absolutely necessary, if you hunt late in the spring, or your pack will be very short for want of it. It may be right to tell you, that the latter operation does not always succeed; it will be necessary, therefore, to employ a skilful person, and one on whom you can depend; for, if it be ill done, though they cannot have puppies, they will go to heat notwithstanding, of which I have known many instances; and that, I apprehend, would not answer your purpose, at any rate. They should be kept low for several days before the operation is performed, and must be fed on thin meat for some time after.

[1] It may be better, perhaps, to round them at their quarters, when about six months old; should it be done sooner, it would make their ears tuck-up.[1] The tailing of them is usually done before they are put out; it might be better perhaps, to leave it till they are taken in. Dogs must not be rounded at the time they have the distemper upon them; the loss of blood would weaken them too much.

[1 The operation of rounding the ears is not now practised in some kennels, but if skilfully done it does not cause much pain, and saves them being torn in thick coverts.]

You ask me, what number of young hounds you should breed, to keep up your stock? It is a question, I believe, that no man can answer. It depends altogether on contingencies. The deficiencies of one year must be supplied the next. I should apprehend, from thirty to thirty-five couple of old hounds, and from eight to twelve couple of young ones, would, one year with another, best suit an establishment which you do not intend should much exceed forty couple. This rule you should at the same time observe— never to part with a useful old hound, or enter an unhandsome young one.

I would advise you, in breeding, to be as little prejudiced as possible in favour of your own sort; but send your best bitches to the best dogs, be they where they may. Those who breed only a few hounds, may by chance have a good pack; while those who breed a great many (if, at the same time, they understand the business) reduce it to a certainty. You say, you wish to see your pack as complete as Mr. Meynell's: believe me, my good friend, unless you were to breed as many hounds, it is totally impossible. Those who breed the greatest number of hounds have a right to expect the best pack; at least, it must be their own fault if they have it not.

NAMES OF HOUNDS

A

DOGS

Able
Actor
Adamant
Adjutant
Agent
Aider
Aimwell
Amorous
Antic
Anxious
Arbiter
Archer
Ardent
Ardor
Arrogant
Arsenic
Artful
Artist
Atlas
Atom
Auditor
Augur
Awful

BITCHES

Accurate
Active
Actress
Affable
Agile
Airy
Amity
Angry
Animate
Artifice
Audible

B

DOGS

Bachelor
Baffler
Banger
Barbarous
Bellman
Bender
Blaster
Bluecap
Blueman
Bluster
Boaster
Boisterous
Bonnyface
Bouncer
Bowler
Bragger
Bravo
Brawler
Brazen
Brilliant
Brusher
Brutal
Burster
Bustler

BITCHES

Baneful
Bashful
Bauble
Beauteous
Beauty
Beldam
Bellmaid
Blameless
Blithsome
Blowzy
Bluebell
Bluemaid
Bonny
Bonnybell
Bonnylass
Boundless
Bravery
Brevity
Brimstone
Busy
Buxom

C

DOGS

Caitiff
Caliban
Capital
Captain
Captor
Carol
Carver
Caster
Castwell
Catcher
Catchpole
Caviller
Cerberus
Challenger
Champion
Charon
Chaser
Chaunter
Chieftain
Chimer
Chirper
Choleric
Claimant
Clamorous
Clangour
Clasher
Climbank
Clinker
Combat
Combatant
Comforter
Comrade
Comus
Conflict
Conqueror
Conquest
Constant
Contest
Coroner
Cottager
Counsellor
Countryman
Courteous
Coxcomb
Craftsman
Crasher
Critic
Critical
Crowner
Cruiser

44

Crusty
Cryer
Curfew
Currier

BITCHES

Capable
Captious
Careless
Careful
Carnage
Caution
Cautious
Charmer
Chauntress
Cheerful
Cherriper
Chorus
Circe
Clarinet
Clio
Comely
Comfort
Comical
Concord
Courtesy
Crafty
Crazy
Credible
Credulous
Croney
Cruel
Curious

D

DOGS

Damper
Danger

Dangerous
Dapper
Dapster
Darter
Dasher
Dashwood
Daunter
Dexterous
Disputant
Downright
Dragon
Dreadnought
Driver
Duster

BITCHES

Dainty
Daphne
Darling
Dashaway
Dauntless
Delicate
Desperate
Destiny
Dian
Diligent
Docile
Document
Doubtful
Doubtless
Dreadful
Dreadless
Dulcet

E

DOGS

Eager
Earnest

Effort
Elegant
Eminent
Envious
Envoy
Errant
Excellent

BITCHES

Easy
Echo
Ecstasy
Endless
Energy
Enmity
Essay

F

DOGS

Factious
Factor
Fatal
Fearnought
Ferryman
Fervent
Finder
Firebrand
Flagrant
Flasher
Fleece'm
Fleecer
Flinger
Flippant
Flourisher
Flyer
Foamer
Foiler
Foreman

Foremost
Foresight
Forester
Forward
Fulminant
Furrier

BITCHES

Fairmaid
Fairplay
Faithful
Famous
Fanciful
Fashion
Favourite
Fearless
Festive
Fickle
Fidget
Fiery
Fireaway
Firetail
Flighty
Fourish
Flurry
Forcible
Fretful
Friendly
Frisky
Frolic
Frolicsome
Funnylass
Furious
Fury

G

DOGS

Gainer
Gallant

Galliard
Galloper
Gamboy
Gamester
Garrulous
Gazer
General
Genius
Gimcrack
Giant
Glancer
Glider
Glorious
Goblin
Governor
Grapler
Grasper
Griper
Growler
Grumbler
Guardian
Guider
Guiler

BITCHES

Gaiety
Gaily
Gainful
Galley
Gambol
Gamesome
Gamestress
Gaylass
Ghastly
Giddy
Gladness
Gladsome
Governess
Graceful
Graceless

Gracious
Grateful
Gravity
Guilesome
Guilty
Guiltless

H

DOGS

Hannibal
Harbinger
Hardiman
Hardy
Harlequin
Harasser
Havoc
Hazard
Headstrong
Hearty
Hector
Heedful
Hercules
Hero
Highflyer
Hopeful
Hotspur
Humbler
Hurtful

BITCHES

Handsome
Harlot
Harmony
Hasty
Hazardous
Heedless
Hellen
Heroine

Hideous
Honesty
Hostile

I & J

DOGS

Jerker
Jingler
Impetus
Jockey
Jolly
Jollyboy
Jostler
Jovial
Jubal
Judgment
Jumper

BITCHES

Jealousy
Industry
Jollity
Joyful
Joyous

L

DOGS

Labourer
Larum
Lasher
Laster
Launcher
Leader
Leveller
Liberal
Libertine

Lictor
Lifter
Lightfoot
Linguist
Listener
Lounger
Lucifer
Lunatic
Lunger
Lurker
Lusty

BITCHES

Lacerate
Laudable
Lavish
Lawless
Lenity
Levity
Liberty
Lightning
Lightsome
Likely
Lissome
Litigate
Lively
Lofty
Lovely
Luckylass
Lunacy

M

DOGS

Manager
Manful
Marschal
Marksman
Marplot
Martial

Marvellous
Matchem
Maxim
Maximus
Meanwell
Medler
Menacer
Mendall
Mender
Mentor
Mercury
Merlin
Merryboy
Merryman
Messmate
Methodist
Mighty
Militant
Minikin
Miscreant
Mittimus
Monarch
Monitor
Motley
Mounter
Mover
Mungo
Musical
Mutinous
Mutterer
Myrmidon

BITCHES

Madcap
Madrigal
Magic
Maggoty
Matchless
Melody
Merrylass

Merriment
Mindful
Minion
Miriam
Mischief
Modish
Monody
Music

N

DOGS

Nervous
Nestor
Nettler
Newsman
Nimrod
Noble
Nonsuch
Novel
Noxious

BITCHES

Narrative
Neatness
Needful
Negative
Nicety
Nimble
Noisy
Notable
Notice
Notion
Novelty
Novice

P

DOGS

Pæan
Pageant

Paragon
Paramount
Partner
Partyman
Pealer
Penetrant
Perfect
Perilous
Pertinent
Petulant
Phœbus
Piercer
Pilgrim
Pillager
Pilot
Pincher
Piper
Playful
Plodder
Plunder
Politic
Potent
Prater
Prattler
Premier
President
Presto
Prevalent
Primate
Principal
Prodigal
Prompter
Prophet
Prosper
Prosperous
Prowler
Pryer

BITCHES

Passion
Pastime

Patience
Phœnix
Phrenetic
Phrensy
Placid
Playful
Playsome
Pleasant
Pliant
Positive
Precious
Prettylass
Previous
Priestess
Probity
Prudence

R

DOGS

Racer
Rager
Rallywood
Rambler
Ramper
Rampant
Rancour
Random
Ranger
Ransack
Rantaway
Ranter
Rapper
Rattler
Ravager
Ravenous
Ravisher
Reacher
Reasoner
Rector

Regent
Render
Resonant
Restive
Reveller
Rifler
Rigid
Rigour
Ringwood
Rioter
Risker
Rockwood
Romper
Rouser
Router
Rover
Rudesby
Ruffian
Ruffler
Rumbler
Rümmager
Rumour
Runner
Rural
Rusher
Rustic

BITCHES

Racket
Rally
Rampish
Rantipole
Rapid
Rapine
Rapture
Rarity
Rashness
Rattle
Ravish
Reptile

Resolute
Restless
Rhapsody
Riddance
Riot
Rival
Roguish
Ruin
Rummage
Ruthless

S

DOGS

Salient
Sampler
Sampson
Sanction
Sapient
Saucebox
Saunter
Scalper
Scamper
Schemer
Scourer
Scrambler
Screamer
Screecher
Scuffler
Searcher
Settler
Sharper
Shifter
Signal
Singer
Singwell
Skirmish
Smoker
Social
Solomon

Solon
Songster
Sonorous
Soundwell
Spanker
Special
Specimen
Speedwell
Spinner
Splendour
Splenetic
Spoiler
Spokesman
Sportsman
Squabbler
Squeaker
Statesman
Steady
Stickler
Stinger
Stormer
Stranger
Stripling
Striver
Strivewell
Stroker
Stroller
Struggler
Sturdy
Subtile
Succour
Suppler
Surly
Swaggerer
Sylvan

BITCHES

Sanguine
Sappho
Science

Scrupulous
Shrewdness
Skilful
Songstress
Specious
Speedy
Spiteful
Spitfire
Sportful
Sportive
Sportly
Sprightly
Stately
Stoutness
Strenuous
Strumpet
Surety
Sybil
Symphony

T

DOGS

Tackler
Talisman
Tamer
Tangent
Tartar
Tattler
Taunter
Teaser
Terror
Thrasher
Threatner
Thumper
Thunderer
Thwacker
Thwarter
Tickler
Tomboy

Topmost
Topper
Torment
Torrent
Torturer
Tosser
Touchstone
Tracer
Tragic
Trampler
Transit
Transport
Traveller
Trial
Trier
Trimbush
Trimmer
Triumph
Trojan
Trouncer
Truant
Trueboy
Trueman
Trudger
Trusty
Trywell
Tuner
Turbulent
Twanger
Twig'em
Tyrant

BITCHES

Tattle
Telltale
Tempest
Tentative
Termagant

Terminate
Terrible
Testy
Thankful
Thoughtful
Tidings
Toilsome
Tractable
Tragedy
Trespass
Trifle
Trivial
Trollop
Troublesome
Truelass
Truemaid
Tunable
Tuneful

V

DOGS

Vagabond
Vagrant
Valiant
Valid
Valorous
Valour
Vaulter
Vaunter
Venture
Venturer
Venturous
Vermin
Vexer
Victor
Vigilant
Vigorous

Vigour
Villager
Viper
Volant
Voucher

BITCHES

Vanquish
Vehemence
Vehement
Vengeance
Vengeful
Venomous
Venturesome
Venus
Verify
Verity
Vicious
Victory
Victrix
Vigilance
Violent
Viperous
Virulent
Vitiate
Vivid
Vixen
Vocal
Volatile
Voluble

W

DOGS

Wanderer
Warbler
Warning

Warrior
Warhoop
Wayward
Wellbred
Whipster
Whynot
Wildair
Wildman
Wilful
Wisdom
Woodman
Worker
Workman
Worthy
Wrangler
Wrestler

BITCHES

Waggery
Waggish
Wagtail
Wanton
Warfare
Warlike
Waspish
Wasteful
Watchful
Welcome
Welldone
Whimsey
Whirligig
Wildfire
Willing
Wishful
Wonderful
Worry
Wrathful
Wreakful

LETTER VI

AFTER the young hounds have been rounded and are well reconciled to the kennel, know the huntsman, and begin to know their names, they should be put into couples, and walked out amongst sheep.

If any be particularly snappish and troublesome, you should leave the couples loose about their necks in the kennel, till you find they are more reconciled to them. If any be more stubborn than the rest, you should couple them to old hounds rather than to young ones; and you should not couple *two dogs* together, when you can avoid it. Young hounds are awkward at first; I should therefore advise you to send out a few only at a time, with your people on foot; they will soon afterwards become handy enough to follow a horse; and care should be taken that the couples be not too loose, lest they should slip their necks out of the collar, and give trouble in catching them again.

When they have been walked often in this manner amongst the sheep, you may then uncouple a few at a time, and begin to chastise such as offer to run after them; but you will soon find that the cry of *ware sheep*, will stop them sufficiently without the whip; and the less this is used the better. With proper care and attention, you will soon make them ashamed of it; but if once suffered to taste blood, you may find it difficult to reclaim them. Various are the methods used to break such dogs from sheep: some will couple them to a ram, but that is breaking them with a vengeance: you had better hang them. A late lord of my acquaintance, who had heard of this method, and whose whole pack had been often guilty of killing sheep, determined to punish them, and to that intent put the largest ram he could find into his kennel. The men with their whips and voices, and the ram with his horns, soon put the whole kennel into confusion and dismay; and the hounds and the ram were then left together. Meeting a friend soon after, "Come," says he, "come with me to the kennel, and see what rare sport the ram makes among the hounds: the old fellow lays about him stoutly, I assure you. Egad he trims them: there is not a dog dares look him in the face." His friend, who is a compassionate man, pitied the hounds exceedingly, and asked, if he was not afraid that some of them might be spoiled? "No; d—n them," said he, "they deserve it, and let them suffer." On they went: all was quiet: they opened the kennel door, but saw neither ram nor hound. The ram by this time was entirely eaten up, and the hounds, having filled their bellies, were retired to rest.

Without doubt it is best, when you air your hounds, to take them out separately; the old ones one day, another day the young:[1] but as I find your hounds are to have their whey at a distant dairy, on those days both old and young may be taken out together, observing only to take the young hounds in couples when the old ones are along with them. Young hounds are always ready for any kind of mischief, and idleness might make even old ones too apt to join them in it. Besides, should they break off from the huntsman, the whipper-in is generally too ill-mounted at this season of the year, easily to head and bring them back. Run no such risk. My hounds were near being spoiled by the mere accident of a horse's falling: the whipper-in was thrown from his horse; the horse ran away, and the whole pack followed: a flock of sheep, which were at a little distance, took fright, began to run, and the hounds pursued them: the most vicious set on the rest, and several sheep were soon pulled down and killed. I mention this, to show you what caution is necessary while hounds are idle; for though the fall of the horse was not to be attributed to any fault of the man, yet had the old hounds been taken out by themselves, or had all the young ones been in couples, it is probable that so common an accident would not have produced so extraordinary an effect.

[1] It would be better still, to take out your hounds every day, the old and young separately, when it can be done without inconvenience; when it cannot, a large grass-court will partly answer the same purpose.

It is now time to stoop them to a scent. You had better enter them at their own game; it will save you much trouble afterwards. Many dogs, I believe, like that scent best which they were first blooded to; but be that as it may, it is certainly most reasonable to use them to that which it is intended they should hunt. It may not be amiss, when they first begin to hunt, to put light collars on them. Young hounds may easily get out of their knowledge; and shy ones, after they have been much beaten, may not choose to return home: collars in that case, may prevent their being lost.

You say, you should like to see your young hounds run a trail-scent. I have no doubt that you would be glad to see them run over an open down, where you could so easily observe their action and their speed. I cannot think the doing of it once or twice could hurt your hounds; and yet, as a sportsman, I dare not recommend it to you. All that I shall say of it is, that it would be less bad than entering them *at hare*. A cat is as good a trail as any; but on no account should any trail be used after your hounds are stooped to a scent.

I know an old sportsman who enters his young hounds first at a cat, which he drags along the ground for a mile or two, at the end of which he turns out a badger, first taking care to break his teeth: he takes out about two couple of old hounds along with the young ones, to hold them on. He never enters his young hounds but at vermin; for he says, *"train up a child in the way he should go, and when he is old he will not depart from it."*

Summer hunting, though useful to young hounds, is prejudicial to old ones; I think, therefore, you will do well to reserve some of the best of your draft-hounds to enter your young hounds with, selecting such as are most likely to set them a good example. It is needless to tell you they should not be skirters, but, on the contrary, should be fair-hunting hounds; such as love a scent, and that hunt closest on the line of it: it will be necessary that some of them should be good finders, and all must be steady. Thus you procure for your young hounds the best instructors, and at the same time prevent two evils which would necessarily ensue, were they taught by the whole pack— one, that of corrupting, and getting into scrapes, such as are not much wiser than themselves; and the other, that of occasioning much flogging and rating, which always shies and interrupts the hunting of an old hound. An old hound is a sagacious animal, and is not fond of trusting himself in the way of an enraged whipper-in, who, as experience has taught him, can flog severely, and can flog unjustly. By attending to this advice, you will improve one part of your pack, without prejudice to the other; while such as never separate their young hounds from the old, are not likely to have any of them steady.

You ask, at what time you should begin to enter your young hounds? that question is easily answered; for you certainly should begin with them *as soon as you can.* The time must vary in different countries: in corn countries, it may not be possible to hunt till after the corn is cut; in grass countries, you may begin sooner; and, in woodlands, you may hunt as soon as you please. If you have plenty of foxes, and can afford to make a sacrifice of some of them, for the sake of making your young hounds steady, take them first where you have least riot, putting some of the steadiest of your old hounds amongst them. If in such a place you are fortunate enough to find a litter of foxes, you may assure yourself you will have but little trouble with your young hounds afterwards.[1]

Such young hounds as are most riotous at first, generally speaking, I think, are best in the end. A gentleman in my neighbourhood was so thoroughly convinced of this, that he complained bitterly of a young pointer to the person who gave it him, because he had done *no mischief.* However, meeting the same person some time after, he told him the dog, he believed, would prove a good one at last. "How

[1 The first time you take out the entry at the commencement of the cub-hunting season, go, if possible, to a small covert or spinney where you are *certain* there is a litter of cubs, and use every means in your power to catch one. Don't make the young hounds sick by drawing unlikely places first.]

so?" demanded his friend; "it was but the other day that you said he was good for nothing." *"True; but he has killed me nineteen turkeys since that."*

If, owing to a scarcity of foxes, you should stoop your hounds at hare, let them by no means have the blood of her; nor, for the sake of consistency, give them any encouragement. Hare-hunting has one advantage: hounds are chiefly in open ground, where you can easily command them; but, notwithstanding that, if foxes be in tolerable plenty, keep them to their own game, and forget not the advice of the old sportsman.

Frequent *hallooing* is of use with young hounds: it keeps them forward, prevents their being lost, and hinders them from hunting after the rest. The oftener, therefore, a fox is seen and hallooed, the better: it serves to let them in, makes them eager, makes them exert themselves, and teaches them to be handy. I must tell you, at the same time I say this, that I by no means approve of much hallooing to old hounds; and though I frequently am guilty of it myself, it is owing to my spirits, which lead me into an error which my judgment condemns. It is true, there is a time when hallooing is of use, a time when it does hurt, and a time when it is perfectly indifferent; but it is long practice, and great attention to hunting, that must teach you the application.[1]

Hounds, at their first entering, cannot be encouraged too much. When they are become handy, love a scent, and begin to know what is *right*, it will be soon enough to chastise them for doing *wrong*; in which case, one severe beating will save a deal of trouble. You should recommend to your whipper-in, when he flogs a hound, to make use of his voice as well as his whip; and let him remember, that the smack of the whip is often of as much use as the lash,

[1 There is only one person whose voice should be heard cheering hounds, and that is the huntsman. Different people holloaing confuse both young and old hounds. A whipper-in with a good voice may do a great deal of harm, and he should be told never to speak except a rate or in putting the pack on to their huntsman. The Duke of Beaufort and Lord Lonsdale supply their huntservants with whistles to use instead of holloaing away from a covert, and I am surprised this excellent plan has not become more general.]

to one that has felt it.[1] If any be very unsteady, it will not be amiss to send them out by themselves, when the men go out to exercise their horses. If you have hares in plenty, let some be found sitting, and turned out before them; and you will soon find the most riotous will not run after them. If you intend them to be made steady from deer, they should often see deer, and they will not regard them; and if, after a probation of this kind, you turn out a cub before them, with some old hounds to lead them on, you may assure yourself they will not be unsteady long; for, as Somerville rightly observes,

> Easy the lesson of the youthful train,
> When instinct prompts, and when example guides.

Flogging hounds in the kennel (the frequent practice of most huntsmen) I hold in abhorrence: it is unreasonable, unjust, and cruel; and, carried to the excess we sometimes see it, is a disgrace to humanity. Hounds that are old offenders, that are very riotous, and at the same time very cunning, it may be difficult to catch; such hounds may be excepted; they deserve punishment wherever taken, and you should not fail to give it them *when you can*. This, you will allow, is a particular case, and necessity may excuse it; but let not the peace and quiet of your kennel be often thus disturbed. When your hounds offend, punish them; when caught in the fact, then let them suffer; and, if you be severe, at least be just.

When your young hounds stoop to a scent, are become handy, know a rate, and stop easily, you may then begin to put them into the pack, a few only at a time: nor do I think it advisable to begin this, till the pack have been out a few times by themselves, and are gotten well in blood. I should also advise you to take them the first day where they are most sure to find; as long rest makes all hounds riotous, and they may do that *en gaieté de cœur*, which they would not

---

[1] Hounds, like children, should never be unjustly punished, and should never be punished if a rating will serve the purpose. The education and correction of a pack should be done in private, not before a large field.]

think of at another time. Let your hounds be low in flesh when you begin to hunt: the ground is generally hard at that season, and they are liable to be shaken.

If your covers be large, you will find the straight horn of use; and I am sorry to hear that you do not approve of it. You ask me why I like it?—not as a *musician*, I can assure you. It signifies little, in our way, what the noise is, as long as it is understood.

LETTER VII

U N L E S S I had kept a regular journal of all that has been done in the kennel, from the time when my young hounds were first taken in, to the end of the last season, it would be impossible, I think, to answer all the questions which, in your last Letter, you ask concerning them. I wish that a memory, which is far from a good one, would enable me to give the information that you desire. If I am to be more circumstantial than in my former Letter, I must recollect as well as I can the regular system of my own kennel; and, if I am to write from memory, you will, without doubt, excuse the want of the *lucidus ordo*. It shall be my endeavour, that the information which these Letters contain shall not mislead you.

You wish me to explain what I mean by hounds being *handy*. It respects their readiness to do whatever is required of them; and particularly, when cast, to turn easily which way the huntsman pleases.[1]

I was told the other day by a sportsman, that he considers the management of hounds as a regular system of education, from the time when they are first taken into the kennel: I perfectly agree with this gentleman; and am well convinced that if you expect sagacity in your hound when he is old, you must be mindful what instruction he receives from you in his youth; for as he is, of all animals, the most docile, he is also most liable to bad habits. A diversity of character, constitution, and disposition, are to be observed amongst them; which, to be made the most of, must be carefully attended to, and differently treated. I do not pretend to have succeeded in it myself; yet you will perceive, perhaps, that I have given it some attention.

---

[1] My hounds are frequently walked about the courts of the kennel, the whipper-in following them, and rating them after the huntsman: this and the sending them out (after they have been fed) with the people on foot, contribute greatly to make them handy.

I begin to hunt with my young hounds in August. The employment of my huntsman the preceding months is to keep his old hounds healthy and quiet, by giving them proper exercise; and to get his young hounds forward.[1] They are called over often in the kennel: it uses them to their names, to the huntsman, and to the whipper-in. They are walked out often among sheep, hares, and deer: it uses them to a rate. Sometimes he turns down a cat before them, which they hunt up to, and kill; and, when the time of hunting approaches, he turns out badgers, or young foxes, taking out some of the steadiest of his old hounds to lead them on: this teaches them to hunt. He draws small covers and furze brakes with them, to use them to a halloo, and to teach them obedience. If they find improper game, and hunt it, they are stopped and brought back; and as long as they will stop at a rate, they are not chastised. Obedience is all that is required of them, till they have been sufficiently taught the game that they are to pursue: an obstinate deviation from it afterwards is *never pardoned*. It is an observation of the Marchese Beccaria, that "La certezza di un castigo, benche moderato, fara sempre una maggiore impressione, che non il timore di un altro piu terribile, unito colla speranza, della 'impunita."

When my young hounds are taken out to air, my huntsman takes them into that country in which they are designed to hunt. It is attended with this advantage: they acquire a knowledge of the country, and, when left behind at any time, cannot fail to find their way home more easily.

When they begin to hunt, they are first taken into a large cover of my own, which has many ridings cut in it, and where young foxes are turned out every year on purpose for them. *Here* they are taught the scent that they are to follow, are encouraged to pursue it, and are stopped from every other. *Here* they are blooded to fox. I must also tell

[1] Nothing will answer this purpose so well as taking them out often. Let your huntsman lounge about with them: nothing will make them so handy. Let him get off his horse frequently, and encourage them to come to him: nothing will familiarise them so much: too great restraint will oftentimes incline hounds to be riotous.

you, that, as foxes are plentiful in this cover, the principal earth is not stopped; and the foxes are checked back, or some of them let in, as may best suit the purpose of blooding. After they have been hunted a few days in this manner, they are then sent to more distant covers, and more old hounds are added to them: there they continue to hunt, till they are taken into the pack, which is seldom later than the beginning of September; for by that time they will have learned what is required of them, and they seldom give much trouble afterwards.[1] In September I begin to hunt in earnest; and after the old hounds have killed a few foxes, the young hounds are put into the pack, two or three couple at a time, till all have hunted. They are then divided; and as I seldom have occasion to take in more than nine or ten couple, one half are taken out one day, the other half the next, till all are steady.

Two other methods of entering young hounds I have practised occasionally, as the number of hounds have required; for instance, if that number be considerable (fifteen or sixteen couple), I make a large draft of my steadiest hounds, which are kept with the young hounds in a separate kennel, and are hunted with them all the first part of the season. This, when the old hounds begin to hunt, makes two distinct packs, and is always attended with great trouble and inconvenience. Nothing hurts a pack so much, as to enter many young hounds; since it must be considerably weakened, by being robbed of those which are the most steady; and yet young hounds can do nothing without their assistance. Such, therefore, as constantly enter their young hounds in this manner, will, sometimes at least, have two indifferent packs, instead of one good one.

In the other method, the young hounds are well awed from sheep, but never stooped to a scent till they are taken out with the pack: they are then taken out, a few only at a time; and, if your pack be perfectly steady, and well manned,

---

[1] Sport in fox-hunting, cannot be said to begin before October; but, in the two preceding months, a pack is either made or marred.

may not give you much trouble. The method I first mentioned, is that which I most commonly practise, being most suitable to the number of young hounds that I usually enter—nine or ten couple: if you have fewer, the last will be most convenient. The one which requires two distinct packs, is too extensive a plan to suit your establishment, requiring more horses and hounds than you intend to keep.[1]

Though I have mentioned, in a former Letter, from eight to twelve couple of young hounds, as a sufficient number to keep up your pack to its present establishment; yet it is always best to have a reserve of a few couple more than you want, in case of accidents; since, from the time you make your draft to the time of hunting, is a long period, and their existence, at that age and season, very precarious; besides, when they are safe from the disorder, they are not always safe from each other; and a summer seldom passes without some losses of that kind. At the same time I must tell you, that I should decline *entering* more than are necessary to keep up the pack; since a great number would only create useless trouble and vexation.

You wish to know what number of old hounds you should hunt with the young ones: that must depend on the strength of your pack, and the number which you choose to spare; if good and steady, ten or twelve couple will be sufficient.

My young hounds, and such old ones as are intended to hunt along with them,[2] are kept in a kennel by themselves

---

[1] To render fox-hunting perfect, no young hounds should be taken into the pack the first season; a requisite too expensive for most sportsmen. The pack should consist of about forty couple of hounds, that have hunted one, two, three, four, or five seasons. The young pack should consist of about twenty couple of young hounds, and about an equal number of old ones. They should have a separate establishment; nor should the two kennels be near enough to interfere with each other. The season over, the best of the young hounds should be taken into the pack, and the draft of old ones exchanged for them. To enable you every season to take in twenty couple of young hounds, many must be bred; and, of course, the greater your choice, the handsomer your pack will become. It will always be easy to keep up the number of old hounds; for, when your own draft is not sufficient, drafts from other packs may easily be obtained, and at a small expense. When young hounds are hunted together the first season, and have not a sufficient number of old hounds along with them, it does them more harm than good.

[2] Some also take out their unsteady hounds when they enter the young ones: I doubt the propriety of it.

till the young hounds are hunted with the pack. I need not, I am sure, enumerate the many reasons that make *this regulation* necessary.

I never trust my young hounds in the forest till they have been well blooded to fox, and seldom put more than a couple into the pack at a time:[1] the others are walked out amongst the deer when the men exercise their horses, and are severely chastised if they take any notice of them: they also draw covers with them; selecting those where they can best see their hounds, and most easily command them, and where there is the least chance to find a fox. On these occasions, I had rather they should have to rate their hounds than encourage them. It requires less judgment, and, if improperly done, is less dangerous in its consequences. One halloo of encouragement to a wrong scent, more than undoes all that you have been doing.

When young hounds begin to love a scent, it may be of use to turn out a badger before them: you will then be able to discover what improvement they have made. I mention a badger, on a supposition that young foxes cannot so well be spared; besides, the badger, being a slower animal, he may easily be followed, and driven the way you choose he should run.

The day you intend to turn out a fox, or badger, you will do well to send them amongst hares, or deer. A little rating and flogging, before they are encouraged to vermin, is of the greatest use; as it teaches them as well what they should not, as what they should, do. I have known a badger run several miles, if judiciously managed; for which purpose, he should be turned out in a very open country, and followed by a person who has more sense than to ride on the line of him. If he do not meet with a cover, or hedge, in his way, he will keep on for several miles; if he do, you will not be able to get him any farther. You should

---

[1] I sometimes send all my young hounds together into the forest, with four or five couple of old hounds only; such as I know they cannot spoil. As often as any of them break off to deer, they are taken up and flogged. When they lose one fox they try for another, and are kept out till they are all made tolerably steady.

give him a great deal of law, and you will do well to break his teeth.[1]

If you run any cubs to ground in an indifferent country, and do not want blood, bring them home, and they will be of use to your young hounds. Turn out bag-foxes to your young hounds, but never to your old ones. I object to them on many accounts: but of bag-foxes I shall have occasion to speak hereafter.

The day after your hounds have had blood, is also a proper time to send them where there is riot, and to chastise them, if they deserve it: it is always best to correct them when they cannot help knowing what they are corrected for. When you send out your hounds for this purpose, the later they go out the better; as the worse the scent is, the less inclinable will they be to run it, and, of course, will give less trouble in stopping them. It is a common practice with huntsmen, to flog their hounds most unmercifully in the kennel. I have already mentioned my disapprobation of it; but, if many of your hounds be obstinately riotous,[2] you may with less impropriety put a live hare into the kennel to them, flogging them as often as they approach her: they will then have some notion, at least, for what they are beaten; but let me entreat you, before this *charivari*[3] begins, to draft off your steady hounds: an animal to whom we owe so much good diversion, should not be ill-used unnecessarily. When a hare is put into the kennel, the huntsman and both the whippers-in

---

[1] The critic says, "there is neither justice nor equity in breaking his teeth." (Vide *Monthly Review*). I confess there is not; and I never know that it is done, but I feel all the force of the observation. It is a custom, as Shakespeare says on another occasion,

"More honour'd in the breach than the observance."

[2] This passage has also been thought deserving of censure, though its motive is humane. By these means the disobedient are taught obedience, and a more general punishment prevented, which the effect of bad example might otherwise make necessary.

[3] A confusion arising from a variety of noises. It is a custom in France and in Switzerland, if a woman marry sooner than is usual after the death of her husband, or a woman get the better of her husband when attempting to chastise her, and return the beating with interest—the neighbours give them a *charivari;* a kind of concert, composed of tongs, fire-shovels, kettles, brass pans, &c., &c.

"obliged to stop them often from hare

should be present; and the whippers-in should flog every hound, calling him by his name, and rating him as often as he is near the hare; and upon this occasion they cannot cut them too hard, or rate them too much. When they think they have chastised them enough, the hare should then be taken away, the huntsman should halloo off his hounds, and the whippers-in should rate them to him. If any one love hare more than the rest, you may tie a dead one round his neck, flogging him and rating him at the same time. This possibly may make him ashamed of it. I never bought a lot of hounds, some of which were not obliged to undergo this discipline. Either hares are less plentiful in other countries, or other sportsmen are less nice in making their hounds steady from them.

I would advise you to hunt your large covers with your young hounds: it will tire them out;[1] a necessary step towards making them steady;—will open the cover against the time you begin in earnest; and, by disturbing the large covers early in the year, foxes will be shy of them in the season, and show you better chases; besides, as they are not likely to break from thence, you can do no hurt to the corn, and may begin before it is cut.

If your hounds be very riotous, and you are obliged to stop them often from hare, it will be advisable to try on (however late it may be) till you find a fox; as the giving them encouragement should, at such a time, prevail over every other consideration.

Though all young hounds are given to riot, yet the better they are bred, the less trouble will they be likely to give. Pointers, well bred, stand naturally; and high-bred fox-hounds love their own game best. Such, however, as are very riotous, should have little rest: you should hunt them one day in large covers where foxes are in plenty;

---

[1] Provided that you have old hounds enough out to carry on the scent; if you have not a body of old hounds to keep up a cry on the right scent, the young ones, as soon as the ground becomes foiled, will be scattered about the cover, hunting old scents, and will not get on fast enough to tire themselves. Young hounds should never be taken into large covers where there is much riot, unless whippers-in can easily get at them.

the next day they should be walked out amongst hares and deer, and stopped from riot; the day following be hunted again, as before. Old hounds, which I have had from other packs (particularly such as have been entered at hare), I have sometimes found incorrigible; but I never yet knew a young hound so riotous, but, by this management, he soon became steady.

When hounds are rated and do not answer the rate, they should be coupled up immediately, and be made to know the whipper-in: in all probability this method will save any further trouble. These fellows sometimes flog hounds unmercifully, and some of them seem to take pleasure in their cruelty: I am sure, however, I need not desire you to prevent any excess in correction.

I have heard, that no fox-hounds will break off to deer, after once a fox is found. I cannot say that the experience I have had of this diversion will in anywise justify the remark: let me advise you, therefore, to seek a surer dependence. Before you hunt your young hounds where hares are in plenty, let them be awed and stopped from hare: before you hunt amongst deer, let them not only see deer, but let them draw covers where deer are; for you must not be surprised, if, after they are so far steady as not to run them in view, they should challenge on the scent of them. Unless you take this method with your young hounds before you put them into the pack, you will run a risk of corrupting the old ones, and may suffer continual vexation, by hunting with unsteady hounds. I have already told you, that, after my young hounds *are* taken into the pack, I still take out but very few at a time when I hunt among deer: I also change them when I take out others; for the steadiness they may have acquired could be but little depended on, were they to meet with any encouragement to be riotous.

I confess, that I think first impressions of more consequence than they are in general thought to be: I not only enter my young hounds to vermin on that account, but I even use them, as early as I can, to the strongest covers and thickest brakes; and I seldom find that they are shy of them afterwards. A friend of mine has assured me, that he once entered a spaniel to snipes, and the dog ever after was partial to them, preferring them to every other bird.

If you have martin-cats within your reach, as all hounds are fond of their scent, you will do well to enter your young hounds in the covers they frequent. The martin-cat, being a small animal, by running the thickest brakes it can find, teaches hounds to run cover, and is therefore of the greatest use. I do not much approve of hunting them with the old hounds: they show but little sport; are continually climbing trees; and as the cover they run seldom fails to scratch and tear hounds considerably, I think you might be sorry to see your whole pack disfigured by it. The agility of this little animal is really wonderful; and though it frequently falls from a tree in the midst of a whole pack of hounds, all intent on catching it, there are but few instances, I believe, of a martin's being caught by them in that situation.

In summer, hounds might hunt in an evening. I know a pack that, after having killed one fox in the morning with the young hounds, killed another in the evening with the old ones. Scent generally lies well at the close of the day; yet there is a great objection to hunting at that time; animals are then more easily disturbed, and you have a greater variety of scents than at an earlier hour.

Having given you all the information that I can possibly recollect, with regard to my own management of young hounds, I shall now take notice of that part of your last letter, where, I am sorry to find, our opinions differ. Obedience, you say, is everything necessary in a hound. and it is of little consequence by what means it is obtained. I cannot altogether concur in that opinion; for I think it very necessary that the hound should at the same time understand you: obedience, under proper management, will be a necessary consequence of it. Obedience, surely, is not all that is required of them: they should be taught to distinguish of themselves right from wrong, or I know not how they are to be managed when, as it frequently happens, we cannot see what they are at, and must take their words for it. A hound that hears a voice which has often rated him, and that hears the whip which he has often felt, I know will stop. I also know that he will commit the same fault again, if he has been accustomed to be guilty of it.

Obedience, you very rightly observe, is a necessary quality in a hound, for he is useless without it. It is, therefore, an excellent principle for a huntsman to set out upon; yet, good as it is, I think it may be carried too far. I would not have him insist on too much, or torment his hounds *mal-à-propos*, by forcibly exacting from them what is not absolutely necessary to your diversion. He intends, you say, to enter your young hounds at hare: is it to teach them obedience? Does he mean to encourage vice in them, for the sake of correcting it afterwards? I have heard, indeed, that the way to make hounds steady from hare, is to enter them at hare;[1] that is, to encourage them to hunt her. The belief of so strange a paradox requires more faith than I can pretend to.

It concerns me to be under the necessity of differing from you in opinion; but, since it cannot now be helped, we will pursue the subject, and examine it throughout. Permit me then to ask you, what it is that you propose from entering your hounds at hare? Two advantages, I shall presume, you expect from it: the teaching of your hounds to hunt, and teaching them to be obedient. However necessary you may think these requisites in a hound, I cannot but flatter myself that they are to be acquired by less exceptionable means. The method I have already mentioned to make hounds obedient, as it is practised in my own kennel— that of calling them over often in the kennel, to use them to their names,[2] and walking them out often among sheep, hares, and deer, from which they are stopped, to use them to a rate, in my opinion, would answer your purpose better.

[1] In proper hands, either method may do. The method here proposed seems best suited to fox-hounds in general, as well as to those who have the direction of them. The talents of some men are superior to all rules; nor is their success any positive proof of the goodness of their method. See page 54.

[2] See note, page 29.

The teaching your hounds to hunt, is by no means so necessary as you seem to imagine: *Nature* will teach it them; nor need you give yourself so much concern about it. *Art* will only be necessary to prevent them from hunting what they ought *not to hunt*; and do you think your method a proper one to accomplish it?

The first, and most essential, thing towards making hounds obedient, I suppose, is to make them understand you; nor do I apprehend that you will find any difficulty on their parts, but such as may be occasioned on yours.[1] The language that we use to them to convey our meaning should never vary; still less should we alter the very meaning of the terms we use. Would it not be absurd to encourage when we mean to rate? and, if we did, could we expect to be obeyed? You will not deny this; and yet you are guilty of no less an inconsistency, when you encourage your hounds to run a scent to-day, which you know, at the same time, you must be obliged to break them from to-morrow. Is it not running counter to justice and to reason?

I confess, that there is some use in hunting young hounds where you can easily command them; but even this you may pay too dearly for. Enter your hounds in small covers, or in such large ones as have ridings cut in them: whippers-in can then get at them; can always see what they are at; and I have no doubt that you may have a pack of fox-hounds steady to fox by this means, without adopting so preposterous a method as that of first making hare-hunters of them. You will find that hounds, thus taught what game they are to hunt, and what they are not, will stop at a word; because they will understand you; and, after they have been treated in this manner, a smack only of the whip will spare you the inhumanity of cutting your hounds in pieces (not very justly), for faults which you yourself have encouraged them to commit.

[1] Were huntsmen to scream continually to their hounds, using the same halloo whether they were drawing, casting, or running, the hounds could not understand them, and probably would show on every occasion as little attention to them as they would deserve.

In your last letter you seem very anxious. to get your young hounds well blooded to fox, at the same time that you talk of entering them at hare. How am I to reconcile such contradictions? If the blood of fox be of so much use, surely you cannot think the blood of hare a matter of indifference, unless you should be of opinion that a fox is better eating. You may think, perhaps, it was not intended they should hunt sheep; yet we very well know, that when once they have killed sheep, they have no dislike to mutton afterwards.

You have conceived an idea, perhaps, that a fox-hound is designed by Nature to hunt a fox: yet, surely, if that were your opinion, you would not think of entering him at any other game. I cannot, however, suppose Nature designed the dog which we call a fox-hound to hunt a fox only, since we very well know that he will also hunt other animals. That a well-bred fox-hound may give a preference to vermin, *cæteris paribus*, I will not dispute: it is very possible he may; but of this I am certain, that every fox-hound will leave a bad scent of fox for a good one of either hare or deer, unless he has been made steady from them; and in this I shall not fear to be contradicted. But, as I do not wish to enter into abstruse reasoning with you, or think it in anywise material to our present purpose, whether the dogs we call fox-hounds were originally designed by Nature to hunt fox, or not, we will drop the subject. I must, at the same time, beg leave to observe, that dogs are not the only animals in which an extraordinary diversity of species has happened since the days of Adam. Yet a great naturalist tells us, that man is nearer, by eight degrees, to Adam, than is the dog to the first dog of his race; since the age of man is fourscore years, and that of a dog but ten. It therefore follows, that if both should equally degenerate, the alteration would be eight times more remarkable in the dog than in man.

The two most necessary questions which result from the foregoing premises, are, Whether hounds entered at hare are perfectly steady afterwards to fox? and, Whether steadiness be not attainable by more reasonable terms? Having never hunted with gentlemen who follow this practice, I must leave the first question for others to determine; but, having always had my hounds steady, I can myself answer the second.

The objections that I have now made to the treatment of young hounds by some huntsmen, though addressed, my friend, to you, are general objections, and should not personally offend you. I know no man more just or more humane than yourself. For the disapprobation which you so strongly marked in your last letter, of the severity used in some kennels, the noble animal that we both admire is much beholden to you: your intention of being present yourself the first time a hound is flogged, to see how your new whipper-in behaves himself, is a proof of benevolence, which the Italian author of the most humane book[1] could not fail to commend you for. Huntsmen and whippers-in are seldom so unlucky as to have your feelings; yet custom, which authorizes them to flog hounds unmercifully, does not do away the barbarity of it. A gentleman seeing a girl skinning eels alive, asked her "if it was not very cruel?" "Oh, not at all, Sir," replied the girl; *"they be used to it!"*

[1] Dei delitti e delle pene.

LETTER VIII

Y O U desire to know if there be any remedy for the distemper among dogs: I shall therefore mention all the disorders that my hounds have experienced, and point out the remedies which have been of service to them. The distemper that you inquire about, is, I believe, the most fatal (the plague only excepted) that any animal is subject to: though not long known in this country, it is almost inconceivable what numbers have been destroyed by it in so short a period; several hundreds I can myself place to this mortifying account. It seems happily to be now on the decline; at least, is less frequent, and more mild; and probably, in time, may be entirely removed. The effects of it are too generally known, to need any description of them here—I wish the remedies were known as well![1]

A brother sportsman communicated to me a remedy, from which, he said, his hounds had found great benefit, viz. *an ounce of Peruvian bark in a glass of Port wine, taken twice a day*. It is not infallible, but in some stages of this disorder, is certainly of use. The hound most infected that ever I knew to recover, was a large staghound: he lay five days, without being able to get off the bench, receiving little nourishment during the whole time of the disorder, except this medicine, with which he drank three bottles of Port wine. You may think, perhaps, that the feeder drank

[1 All remedies to be of use in distemper must be given in the earlier stages of the disease. Directly a hound shows symptoms he should be isolated, and dosed with Gillard's compound or quinine until the fever abates, being kept meanwhile in a warm dry place, free from draughts. Eyes and nose should be sponged clean twice a day with tepid water, in which there is a little disinfectant. When the fever has gone, Pacita will he found a very useful tonic to restore the hound to health again. Like influenza in man, it is the ailments that are left behind that generally prove fatal in distemper. Each sick hound should have a small kennel to itself, with plenty of clean dry straw on the bench, and creosoted sawdust on the floor, which should not be swilled down. The droppings should be shovelled up and either burnt or covered with quicklime. They are the frequent cause of infection from one season to the other, the germs probably lying dormant and breeding in the ground.]

his share; and, probably, he might, had it not been sent
ready mixed up with the bark. I once tried the *poudre
unique*, thinking it a proper medicine for a disorder which
is said to be putrid; but I cannot say anything in its favour,
with regard to dogs at least. Norris's drops I have also
given, and with success. I gave a large tablespoonful of
them in an equal quantity of Port wine, three times a day:
as the dog grew better, I lessened the quantity. When dogs
run much at the nose, nothing will contribute more to the
cure of them than keeping that part clean: when that cannot
conveniently be done, emetics will be necessary: the best
that I know is, a large spoonful of common salt, dissolved
in three spoonfuls of warm water.[1] The first symptom of
this disorder, generally, is a cough. As soon as it is perceived among my young hounds, great attention is paid
to them. They have plenty of clean straw, and are fed
oftener and better than at other times: so long as they
continue to eat the kennel meat, they are kept together; as
soon as any of them refuse to feed, they are removed into
another kennel; the door of the lodging-room is left open
in the day, and they are only shut up at night: being out in
the air, is of great service to them. To such as are very bad,
I give Norris's drops; to others, emetics; while some only
require to be better fed than ordinary, and need no other
remedy.[2] They should be fed from the kitchen, when they
refuse the kennel meat. Sometimes they will lose the use of
their hinder parts: bleeding them, by cutting off the last
joint of the tail, may perhaps be of service to them. I cannot
speak of it with any certainty; yet I have reason to think
that I once saved a favourite dog by this operation. In
short, by one method or another, I think they may sometimes be recovered.

The likeliest preservative for those that are well, is
keeping them warm at night, and feeding them high. This

---

[1] The quantity of salt must be proportioned to the size of the dog, and to the
difficulty there may be to make him vomit.

[2] Hounds that have the distemper upon them have but little appetite. By feeding
two or three together, they eat more greedily.

disorder being probably infectious, it is better to provide an hospital for such as are seized with it, which should be in the back part of the kennel. There is no doubt that some kennels are healthier than others, and consequently less liable to it. I apprehend mine to be one of those; for, in a dozen years, I do not believe that I have lost half that number of old hounds, although I lose so great a number of whelps at their walks. Neighbouring kennels have not been equally fortunate: I have observed in some of them a disorder unknown in mine; I mean a swelling in the side, which sometimes breaks, but soon after forms again, and generally proves fatal at last. I once heard a friend of mine say, whose kennel is subject to this complaint, that he never knew but one instance of a dog that recovered from it. I have, however, since known another, in a dog that I had from him, which I cured by frequently rubbing with a digestive ointment: the tumour broke and formed again several times, till at last it entirely disappeared. The disorder that we have now been treating of has this, I think, in common with the putrid sore throat, that it usually attacks the weakest. Women are more apt to catch the sore throat than men; children than women; and young hounds more readily catch this disorder than old. When it seizes whelps at their walks, or young hounds when first taken from them, it is then most dangerous. I also think that madness, *their* inflammatory fever, is less frequent than it was before this disorder was known.

There are few disorders to which dogs are so subject as the mange. Air and exercise, wholesome food, and cleanliness, are the best preservatives against it. Your feeder should be particularly attentive to it; and when he perceives any spot upon them, let him rub it with the following mixture:

> A pint of train oil,
> Three quarters of a pint of turpentine,
> Three quarters of a pound of sulphur,
> Two ounces of sulphur vivus,
> Mixed well together, and kept in a bottle.

If the disorder should be bad enough to resist *that*, three mild purging balls (one every other day) should be given, and the dog laid up for a little while afterwards. For the red mange, you may use the following:[1]

> Four ounces of quicksilver,
> Two ounces of Venice turpentine,
> One pound of hog's-lard.

The quicksilver and turpentine are to be rubbed together till the globules all disappear. When you apply it, you must rub an ounce (once a day) upon the part affected, for three days successively. This is to be used when the hair comes off, or any redness appears.

How wonderful is the fatigue which a fox-hound undergoes! Could you count the miles that he runs, the number would appear almost incredible. This he undergoes cheerfully, and perhaps three times a week through a long season: his health, therefore, well deserves your care; nor should you suffer the least taint to injure it. Huntsmen are frequently too negligent in this point. I know one in particular, a famous one too, whose kennel was never free from the mange; and the smell of brimstone was oftentimes stronger, I believe, in the noses of his hounds than the scent of the fox. If you choose to try a curious prescription for the cure of the mange, in the *Phil. Trans.* No. 25, p. 451, you will find the following:

"Mr. Cox procured an old mongrel cur, all over mangy, of a middle size; and having some hours before fed him plentifully with cheese-parings and milk, he prepared his jugular vein; then he made a strong ligature on his neck, that the venal blood might be emitted with the greater impetus; after this, he took a young land spaniel, about the same bigness, and prepared his jugular vein likewise, that the descendant part might receive the mangy dog's blood, and the ascendant discharge his own into a dish: he trans-

[1 We are told that there are three distinct types of mange, but there are probably several variations of each. This mixture, when well rubbed into the skin, will be found a cure for nearly every variety: 1 lb. black sulphur, 1 pint train oil, ¼ pint turpentine, ½ lb. Stockholm tar, 2 ozs. glycerine.]

fused about fourteen or sixteen ounces of the blood of the *infected* into the veins of the *sound* dog. By this experiment there appeared no alteration in the sound one; but the mangy dog was, in about ten days or a fortnight's time, perfectly cured; and possibly this is the quickest and surest remedy for that disease, either in man or beast."

Hounds sometimes are bitten by vipers. Sweet-oil has been long deemed a certain antidote: some should be applied to the part, and some taken inwardly; though a friend of mine informs me, that the common cheese-rennet, externally applied, is a more efficacious remedy than oil, for the bite of a viper. They are also liable to wounds and cuts: Friar's balsam is very good, if applied immediately; yet, as it is apt to shut up a bad wound too soon, the following tincture, in such cases, may perhaps be preferable, at least after the first dressing or two:

> Of Barbadoes aloes, two ounces;
> Of myrrh, pounded, three ounces;
> Mixed up with a quart of brandy.

The bottle should be well corked, and put into a bark-bed, or dunghill, for about ten days or a fortnight. The tongue of the dog, in most cases, is his best surgeon; where he can apply *that*, he will seldom need any other remedy. A green, or seton, in the neck, is of great relief in most disorders of the eyes; and I have frequently known dogs, almost blind, recovered by it: it is also of service when dogs are shaken in the shoulders, and has made many sound. In the latter case, there should be two, one applied on each side, and as near to the shoulder as it is possible. The following ointment may be used to disperse swellings:

> Of fresh mutton-suet, *tried*, two pounds;
> Of gum-elemi, one pound;
> Of common turpentine, ten ounces.

[1] Turning a hound out of the kennel will sometimes cure a lameness in the shoulders. An attentive huntsman will perceive, from the manner of a hound's galloping, when this lameness takes place; and the hound should be turned out immediately. Care should be taken, that a hound turned out do not become fat.

[Hounds supposed to be shaken in the shoulders are generally suffering from a kennel lameness. The only remedy is to turn out of kennel and let them run loose.]

The gum is to be melted with the suet, and, when taken from the fire, the turpentine is to be mixed with it, straining the mixture while it is hot. Dogs frequently are stubbed in the foot. The tincture before mentioned, and this, or any digestive ointment, will soon recover them.[1] For strains, I use two-thirds of spirits of wine, and one of turpentine, mixed up together: the British oil is also good. Hounds, from blows, or other accidents, are often lame in the stifle: either of these, frequently applied, and long rest, are the likeliest means that I know of to recover them. The following excellent remedy for a strain, with which I have cured myself and many others, I have also found of benefit to dogs, when strained in the leg or foot:

Dissolve two ounces of camphor in half a pint of spirits of wine, and put to it a bullock's gall. The part affected must be rubbed before the fire three or four times a day.

Sore feet are soon cured with brine, pot-liquor, or salt and vinegar; a handful of salt to a pint of vinegar: if neither of these will do, mercurial-ointment may then be necessary. A plaster of black pitch is the best cure for a thorn, in either man, horse, or dog; and I have known it succeed after everything else had failed. If the part be much inflamed, a common poultice bound over the plaster will assist in the cure. Hounds frequently are lame in the knee, sometimes from bruises, sometimes from the stab of a thorn: digestive ointment rubbed in upon the part, will generally be of service.[2] I have also known good effects from a poultice of Goulard, changed two or three times a day: it must be sewed on, the dog kept by himself, and muzzled.

If hounds be much troubled with worms, the following is the best cure that I am acquainted with:

Of pewter pulverised, 1 drachm 10 grains;
Of Æthiop's mineral, 16 grains.

---

[1] An obstinate lameness is sometimes increased by humours: physic, in that case, may be necessary to remove it.

[2] If the knee continue foul, blisters, and long rest afterwards, are the most likely means to recover it.

This is to be taken three times: every other day, once: the dog should be kept warm, and from cold water. Whey, or pot-liquor, may be given him two or three hours after, and should be continued, instead of meat, during the time that he is taking the medicine. The best way of giving it, is to mix it up with butter, and then to make it into balls with a little flour.

When a dog is rough in his coat, and scratches much, two or three purging balls, and a little rest afterwards, seldom fail to get him into order again. To make dogs fine in their coats you should use the following dressing:

> One pound of native sulphur,
> One quart of train-oil,
> One pint of oil of turpentine,
> Two pound of soap.

My hounds are dressed with it two or three times only in a year: in some kennels, I am told, they dress them once in two months. The more frequently it is done, the cleaner, I suppose, your hounds will look. Should you choose to dress your puppies before they are put out to their walks, the following receipt, which I received from a friend of mine in Staffordshire (the person already mentioned in this Letter, an excellent sportsman, to whom I have many obligations), will answer the purpose best; and on their change of diet, from milk to meat, may be sometimes necessary:

> Three-quarters of an ounce of quicksilver,
> Half a pint of spirits of turpentine,
> Four ounces of hog's-lard,
> One pound of soft soap,
> Three ounces of common turpentine, in which
> the quicksilver must be killed.

Instinct directs dogs, when the stomach is out of order, to be their own physician; and it is to their example that we owe our knowledge how to relieve it. It may appear foreign to our present purpose; yet as it is much (if true) to the honour of animals in general, I must beg leave to add what a French author tells us—that also by the hippopotamus we are instructed how to bleed, and by the crane how to give a clyster. I have already declared my disapprobation of bleeding hounds, unless they absolutely want it: when they refuse their food, from having been over-worked; or when they have taken a chill, to which they are very subject; then the loss of a little blood may be of use to recover them. Sick hounds will recover sooner if suffered to run about the house, than if they be confined in the kennel.

Madness, thou dreadful malady, what shall I say to thee; or what preservative shall I find against thy envenomed fang! Somerville, who declines writing of lesser ills, is not silent on the subject of this.

> Of lesser ills the muse declines to sing,
> Nor stoops so low; of these each groom can tell
> The proper remedy.

I wish this worthy gentleman, to whom we have already been so much obliged, had been less sparing of his instructions; since it is possible that grooms may not have all the knowledge he supposes them to have, and their masters may stand in need of it. No man, I believe, will complain of being too well informed; nor is any knowledge unnecessary which is likely to be put in practice. The executive part is fully sufficient to trust in a groom's hands. Somerville's advice on the subject of madness is worth your notice:

> When Sirius reigns, and the sun's parching beams
> Bake the dry gaping surface, visit thou
> Each ev'n and morn, with quick observant eye,
> Thy panting pack. If in dark sullen mood
> The glouting hound refuse his wonted meal,
> Retiring to some close, obscure retreat,
> Gloomy, disconsolate; with speed remove
> The poor infectious wretch, and in strong chains
> Bind him suspected. Thus that dire disease,
> Which art can't cure, wise caution may prevent.

Plenty of water, whey, greens, physic, air, and exercise, such as I have before mentioned, have hitherto preserved my kennel from its baneful influence; and, without doubt, you will also find their good effects. If, notwithstanding, you should at any time have reason to suspect the approach of this evil, let your hounds be well observed at the time when they feed: there will be no danger while they can eat. Should a whole pack be in the same predicament, they must be chained up separately: and I should be very cautious what experiment I tried to cure them; for I have been told by those who have had madness in their kennels, and who have drenched their hounds to cure it, that it was the occasion of its breaking out a long time afterwards, and that it continued to do so as long as they gave them anything to put it off. If a few dogs only have been bitten, you had better hang them. If you suspect any, you had better separate them from the rest; and a short time, if you use no remedy, will determine whether they really were bitten or not. Should you, however, be desirous of trying a remedy, the following prescription, I am told, is a very good one:

> Of Turbith's mineral, eight grains,
> Ditto, sixteen grains,
> Ditto, thirty-two grains.

This is to be given for three mornings successively; beginning the first day with eight grains, and increasing it according to the above direction. The dog should be empty when he takes it, and should have been bled the day before. The dose should be given early in the morning, and the dog may have some thin broth, or pot-liquor, about two or three o'clock, but nothing else during the time he takes the medicine; he should also be kept from water. The best way to give it is in butter, and made up into balls with a little flour. Care must be taken that he does not throw it up again. After the last day of the medicine, he may be fed as usual. Various are the drenches and medicines which are given for this disorder, and all said to be infallible:

this last, however, I prefer. The whole pack belonging to a gentleman in my neighbourhood were bitten; and he assures me, he never knew an instance of a dog who went mad that had taken his medicine. The caution which I have recommended to you, I flatter myself will preserve you from this dreadful malady; a malady for which I know not how to recommend a remedy. Several years ago I had a gamekeeper much bitten in the fleshy part of his thigh: a horse that was bitten at the same time died raving mad: the man was cured by Sir George Cobb's medicine. I have heard that the Ormskirk medicine is also very good. I have given it to several people in my neighbourhood, and, I believe, with success; at least I have not, as yet, heard anything to the contrary. Though I mention these as the two most favourite remedies, I recommend neither. Somerville's advice, which I have already given, is what I recommend to you: if properly attended to, it will prevent the want of any remedy.

P.S.—A Treatise on Canine Madness, written by Dr. James, is worth your reading. You will find that he prescribes the same remedy for the cure of madness in dogs as I have mentioned here, but in different quantities. I have, however, taken the liberty of recommending the quantities above mentioned, as they have been known to succeed in my neighbourhood, and as the efficacy of them has been very frequently proved.

LETTER IX

THE variety of questions which you are pleased to ask concerning the huntsman, will perhaps be better answered when we are on the subject of hunting. In the meantime, I will endeavour to describe what a good huntsman should be. He should be young, strong, active, bold and enterprising; fond of the diversion and indefatigable in the pursuit of it: he should be sensible and good-tempered; he ought also to be sober: he should be exact, civil, and cleanly; he should be a good horseman and a good groom: his voice should be strong and clear; and he should have an eye so quick, as to perceive which of his hounds carries the scent when all are running; and should have so excellent an ear, as always to distinguish the foremost hounds when he does not see them: he should be quiet, patient, and without conceit. Such are the excellences which constitute a good hunstman: he should not, however, be too fond of displaying them till necessity calls them forth: he should let his hounds alone whilst they *can hunt*, and he should have genius to assist them *when they cannot*.

With regard to the whipper-in, as you keep two of them (and no pack of fox-hounds is complete without), the first may be considered as a second huntsman, and should have nearly the same good qualities. It is necessary, besides, that he should be attentive, and obedient to the huntsman; and, as his horse will probably have most work to do, the lighter he is, the better; though, if he be a good horseman, the objection of his weight will be sufficiently overbalanced. He must not be conceited. I had one formerly, who, instead of stopping hounds as he ought, would try to kill a fox by himself. This fault is unpardonable: he should always maintain to the huntsman's halloo, and stop such hounds as divide from it. When stopped, he should get forward with them after the huntsman.

He must always be contented to act an under part, except when circumstances may require that he should act otherwise;[1] and the moment they cease, he must not fail to resume his former station. You have heard me say, that where there is much riot, I prefer an excellent whipper-in to an excellent huntsman. The opinion, I believe, is new; I must, therefore, endeavour to explain it. My meaning is this: That I think I should have better sport, and kill more foxes, with a moderate huntsman, and an excellent whipper-in, than with the best of huntsmen without such an assistant. You will say, perhaps, that a good huntsman will make a good whipper-in; not such, however, as I mean; his talent must be born with him. My reasons are, that good hounds (and bad I would not keep) oftener need the one than the other; and genius, which, in a whipper-in, if attended by obedience, his first requisite, can do no hurt— in a huntsman is a dangerous, though a desirable, quality; and if not accompanied with a large share of prudence, and, I may say, humility, will oftentimes spoil your sport, and hurt your hounds. A gentleman told me, that he heard the famous Will Dean, when his hounds were running hard in a line with Daventry, from whence they were at that time many miles distant, swear exceedingly at the whipper-in, saying, *"What business have you here?"* The man was amazed at the question. *"Why, don't you know,"* said he, *"and be d—d to you, that the great earth at Daventry is open?"* The man got forward, and reached the earth just time enough to see the fox go in. If, therefore, whippers-in be left at liberty to act as they shall think right, they are much less confined that the huntsman himself, who must follow his hounds; and consequently, they have greater scope to exert their genius, if they have any.

I had a dispute with an old sportsman, who contended, that the whipper-in should always attend the huntsman, to obey his orders (a stable-boy, then, would make as good

---

[1] When the huntsman cannot be up with the hounds, the whipper-in should; in which case, it is the business of the huntsman to bring on the tail hounds along with him.

a whipper-in as the best); but this is so far from being the case, that he should be always on the opposite side of the cover from him, or I am much mistaken in my opinion: if within hearing of his halloo, he is near enough; for that is the hunting signal he is to obey. The station of the second whipper-in may be near the huntsman: for which reason, any boy that can halloo, and make a whip smack, may answer the purpose.

Your first whipper-in being able to hunt the hounds occasionally, will answer another good purpose; it will keep your huntsman in order. They are very apt to be impertinent, when they think you cannot do without them.

When you go from the kennel, the place of the first whipper-in is before the hounds; that of the second whipper-in should be some distance behind them; if not, I doubt if they will be suffered even to empty themselves, let their necessities be ever so great; for as soon as a boy is made a whipper-in, he fancies that he is to whip the hounds whenever he can get at them, whether they deserve it or not.

I have always thought a huntsman a happy man: his office is pleasing, and at the same time flattering: we pay him for that which diverts him, and he is enriched by his greatest pleasure;[1] nor is a general after a victory, more proud than is a huntsman who returns with his fox's head.

I have heard that a certain duke, who allowed no vails to his servants, asked his huntsman what he generally made of his field-money, and gave him what he asked instead of it. This went on very well for some time, till at last the huntsman desired an audience. "Your grace," said he, "is very generous, and gives me more than ever I got from field-money in my life; yet I come to beg a favour of your grace—that you would let me take field-money again; for I have not half the pleasure now in killing a fox that I had before."

As you ask my opinion of scent, I think I had better give it you before we begin on the subject of hunting.

---

[1] The *field-money* which is collected at the death of a fox.

I must, at the same time, take the liberty of telling you, that you have puzzled me exceedingly; for scent is, I believe, what we sportsmen know least about; and, to use the words of a great classic writer:—

Hoc sum contentus, quod etiam si quo quidque fiat ignorem, quid fiat intelligo."—
CIC. de Div.

Somerville, who, as I have before observed, is the only one that I know of who has thrown any light on the subject of hunting, says, I think, but little about scent. I send you his words: I shall afterwards add a few of my own.

Should some more curious sportsmen here inquire,
Whence this sagacity, this wond'rous power
Of tracing step by step or man or brute?
What guide invisible points out their way
O'er the dank marsh, bleak hill, and sandy plain?
The courteous Muse shall the dark cause reveal.
The blood that from the heart incessant rolls
In many a crimson tide, then here and there
In smaller rills disparted, as it flows
Propell'd, the serous particles evade,
Thro' th' open pores, and with the ambient air
Entangling mix. As fuming vapours rise,
And hang upon the gently-purling brook,
There, by the incumbent atmosphere compress'd.
The panting chase grows warmer as he flies,
And thro' the network of the skin perspires;
Leaves a long—steaming—trail behind; which by
The cooler air condens'd, remains, unless
By some rude storm dispers'd, or rarefied
By the meridian sun's intenser heat
To every shrub the warm effluvia cling,
Hang on the grass, impregnate earth and skies.
With nostrils opening wide, o'er hill, o'er dale
The vig'rous hounds pursue, with ev'ry breath
Inhale the grateful steam, quick pleasures sting
Their tingling nerves, while they their thanks repay,
And in triumphant melody confess
The titillating joy. Thus, on the air
Depend the hunter's hopes.

I cannot agree with Mr. Somerville, in thinking that scent depends on the air only: it depends also on the soil.

Without doubt, the best scent is that which is occasioned by the effluvia, as he calls it, or particles of scent, which are constantly perspiring from the game as it runs, and are strongest and most favourable to the hound, when kept by the gravity of the air to the height of his breast; for then it neither is above his reach, nor is it necessary that he should stoop for it. At such times, scent is said to lie *breast-high*.[1] Experience tells us, that difference of soil occasions difference of scent; and on the richness and moderate moisture of the soil does it also depend, I think, as well as on the air. At the time when leaves begin to fall, and before they are rotted, we know that the scent lies ill in cover. This alone would be a sufficient proof that scent does not depend on the air only. A difference of scent is also occasioned by difference of motion: the faster the game goes, the less scent it leaves. When game has been ridden after, and hurried on by imprudent sportsmen, the scent is less favourable to hounds: one reason of which may be, that the particles of scent are then more dissipated: but if the game should have been run by a dog not belonging to the pack, seldom will any scent remain.

I believe it is very difficult to ascertain exactly what scent is: I have known it alter very often in the same day. I believe, however, that it depends chiefly on two things— *"the condition the ground is in, and the temperature of the air;"* both of which, I apprehend, should be moist, without being wet. When both are in this condition, the scent is then perfect; and *vice versâ*, when the ground is hard and the air dry, there seldom will be any scent. It scarcely ever lies with a north, or an east wind: a southerly wind without rain, and a westerly wind that is not rough, are the most favourable. Storms in the air are great enemies to scent, and seldom fail to take it entirely away. A fine sunshiny day is not often a good hunting day; but what the French call *jours des dames*, warm without sun, is generally a perfect one: there are not many such in a whole season. In some

[1 We know as little about scent now as they did a hundred years ago, but it is generally safe to assume that it will never be first class with a falling barometer.]

fogs, I have known the scent lie high; in others, not at all; depending, I believe, on the quarter the wind is then in. I have known it lie very high in a mist, when not too wet; but if the wet should hang on the boughs and bushes, it will fall upon the scent, and deaden it. When the dogs roll, the scent, I have frequently observed, seldom lies; for what reason, I know not: but, with permission, if they smell strong when they first come out of the kennel, the proverb is in their favour; and that smell is a prognostic of good luck. When cobwebs hang on the bushes, there is seldom much scent. During a white frost the scent lies high; as it also does when the frost is quite gone. At the time of its going off, scent never lies: it is a critical minute for hounds, in which their game is frequently lost. In a great dew, the scent is the same. In healthy countries, where the game brushes as it goes along, scent seldom fails. Where the ground carries, the scent is bad, for a very evident reason, which hare-hunters, who pursue their game over greasy fallows and through dirty roads, have great cause to complain of. A wet night frequently produces good chases, as then the game neither like to run the cover nor the roads. If has been often remarked, that scent lies best in the richest soils; and countries which are favourable to horses, are seldom so to hounds. I have also observed, that, in some particular places, let the temperature of the air be as it may, scent never lies.

Take not out your hounds on a very windy or bad day.[1]

> These inauspicious days, on other cares
> Employ thy precious hours; th' improving friend
> With open arms embrace, and from his lips
> Glean science, season'd with good-natur'd wit;
> But if th' inclement skies, and angry Jove,
> Forbid the pleasing intercourse, thy books
> Invite thy ready hand; each sacred page
> Rich with the wise remarks of heroes old.

[1 This familiar quotation is about all the man who hunts to ride knows of Beckford, and because the advise is not practicable in these days, he condemns the rest of the work as not worth reading. Because it occasionally happens that there is

The sentiments of Mr. Somerville always do him honour, but on no occasion more than on this.

In reading over my Letter, I find that I have used the word *smell*, in a sense that, perhaps, you will criticize. A gentleman, who, I suppose, was not the sweetest in the world, sitting in the front boxes at the playhouse on a crowded night, his neighbour very familiarly told him that he *smelt strong*. "No, Sir." replied he, with infinite good humour, "it is you that smell—I *stink*."

a good scent in a high wind, Beckford must necessarily be a fool. If the book is carefully read, it will be seen Beckford only hunted two days a week, and as the weekly fixtures were not published he had the choice of days. The advice was given in the interest of hounds, not with any reference to the likelihood of a gallop, and it holds good to this day. A windy day may do young hounds a lot of harm, and will sometimes make old ones unsteady.]

LETTER X

I THOUGHT that I had been writing all this time to a fox-hunter; and hitherto my Letters have had no other object. I now receive a letter from you, full of questions about hare-hunting; to all of which you expect an answer. I must tell you, at the same time, that, though I kept harriers many years, it was not my intention, if you had not asked it, to have written on the subject. By inclination I was never a hare-hunter: I followed this diversion more for air and exercise than for amusement; and if I could have persuaded myself to ride on the turnpike-road to the three-mile stone, and back again, I should have thought that I had had no need of a pack of harriers. Excuse me, brother hare-hunters! I mean not to offend; I speak but relatively to my own particular situation in the country, where hare-hunting is so bad, that it is more extraordinary that I should have persevered in it so long, than that I should forsake it now. I respect hunting in whatever shape it appears: it is a manly and a wholesome exercise, and seems by Nature designed to be the amusement of a Briton.

You ask, How many hounds a pack of harriers should consist of? and, What kind of hound is best suited to that diversion? You should never exceed twenty couple in the field: it might be difficult to get a greater number to run well together; and a pack of harriers cannot be complete if they do not:[1] besides, the fewer hounds you have, the less you foil the ground, which you otherwise would find a great hindrance to your hunting. Your other question is not easily answered. The hounds, I think, most likely to show you sport, are between the large slow-hunting

---

[1] A hound that runs too fast for the rest, ought not to be kept. Some huntsmen load them with heavy collars; some tie a long strap round their necks; a better way would be, to part with them. Whether they go too slow, or too fast, they ought to be drafted.

BEAGLES AND HARRIER

From a painting at Steepleton

harrier and the little fox-beagle:[1] the former are too dull, too heavy, and too slow; the latter too lively, too light, and too fleet.[2] The first species, it is true, have most excellent noses, and, I make no doubt, will kill their game at last if the day be long enough; but you know the days are short in winter, and it is bad hunting in the dark: the other, on the contrary, fling and dash, and are all alive; but every cold blast affects them; and if your country be deep and wet, it is not impossible that some of them may be drowned. My hounds were a cross of both these kinds, in which it was my endeavour to get as much bone and strength in as small a compass as possible. It was a difficult undertaking. I bred many years, and an infinity of hounds, before I could get what I wanted: I at last had the pleasure to see them very handsome; small, yet bony; they ran remarkably well together; ran fast enough; had all the alacrity that you could desire; and would hunt the coldest scent. When they were thus perfect, I did as many others do—I parted with them.

[1 This fox-beagle referred to is probably the progenitor of the foot-beagle of the present day, but which in Beckford's time and long before that date, was used for hunting the fox on foot. The fox was looked on as a thief where no regular pack was kept, was hunted to earth with foot-beagles and terriers, then dug out and killed. In the *Essay on Hunting* (see introduction to 1820 edition of this work), the author, writing in 1733, and describing different kinds of hounds, says: "The North-country beagle is nimble and vigorous, and does his business as furiously as Jehu himself could wish." This hound was probably used for hunting both hare and fox. The same writer then mentions another sort, and says: "These, as their noses are very tender and not far from the ground, I have often seen to make tolerable sport; but without great care they are flirting and maggotty" (whimsical, capricious), "and very apt to chaunt and chatter on any or on no occasion."]

[2 Probably Beckford was unacquainted with hare-hunting on foot, which is the only sportsmanlike way of hunting that animal. Foot-beagles should never be over 15½ inches or under 12. The country they have to hunt must determine the size within those limits. A plough country, or one where there are many large dykes, as in the fens and some parts of Yorkshire, require the hound of the larger type. The little beagle will, however, generally be found able to get over or through most obstacles, provided he combines strength with activity, and is built on the right lines. Backs and loins should always be there, but a good shoulder is a necessity. A miniature foxhound, only with rather shorter legs in comparison, is an ideal beagle wherewith to hunt the hare.

Hunting on foot is splendid exercise, and affords a means of enjoying sport to those whose purse or inclination does not allow them to keep a horse. Harriers are only permissible in a country that is not hunted by foxhounds. From ten to fifteen couple of hounds are enough to hunt a hare.]

It may be necessary to unsay (now that I am turned hare-hunter again) many things that I have been saying as a fox-hunter; as I hardly know any two things of the same genus (if I may be allowed the expression) that differ so entirely. What I said in a former Letter, about the huntsman and whipper-in, is in the number. As to the huntsman, he should not be young: I should, most certainly, prefer one, as the French call it, *d'un certain âge*, as he is to be quiet and patient; for patience, he should be a very Grizzle; and the more quiet he is, the better. He should have infinite perseverance; for a hare should never be given up while it is possible to hunt her: she is sure to stop, and therefore may always be recovered. Were it usual to attend to the breed of our huntsman as well as to that of our hounds, I know no family that would furnish a better cross than that of the *silent gentleman* mentioned by the Spectator: a female of his line, crossed with a knowing huntsman, would probably produce a perfect hare-hunter.

The whipper-in also has little to do with him whom I before described: yet he may be like the second whipper-in to a pack of fox-hounds; the stable-boy who is to follow the huntsman: but I would have him still more confined, for he should not dare even to stop a hound or smack a whip, without the huntsman's order. Much noise and rattle is directly contrary to the first principles of hare-hunting, which is, to be perfectly quiet, and to let your hounds alone. I have seen few hounds so good as town packs, that have no professed huntsman to follow them. If they have no one to assist them, they have at the same time no one to interrupt them; which, I believe, for this kind of hunting is still more essential. I should, however, mention a fault that I have observed, and which such hounds must of necessity sometimes be guilty of; that is, *running back the heel*.[1] Hounds are naturally fond of scent; if they

[1 Hares will often run their foil for some distance, and then go off at a tangent. The old hounds, if left alone, will carry the line back, and therefore it must not be taken for granted they are running heel because they go back. This is one excellent reason why no one should follow directly behind hare-hounds; but it is one of the first rules of hunting never to follow directly in the wake of a pack, be they after either fox or hare.]

cannot carry it forward, they will turn, and hunt it back again: hounds that are left to themselves, make a fault of this; and it is, I think, the only one they commonly have. Though it be certainly best to let your hounds alone, and thereby to give as much scope to their natural instinct as you can; yet, in this particular instance, you should check it mildly; for, as it is almost an invariable rule in all hunting to make the head good, you should encourage them to try forward first; which may be done without taking them off their noses, or without the least prejudice to their hunting. If trying forward should not succeed, they may then be suffered to try back again, which you will find them all ready enough to do; for they are sensible how far they brought the scent, and where they left it. The love of scent is natural to them, and they have infinitely more sagacity in it than we ought to pretend to: I have no doubt that they often think us very obstinate, and very foolish.

Harriers, to be good, like all other hounds, must be kept to their own game: if you run fox with them, you spoil them. Hounds cannot be perfect, unless used to one scent, and one style of hunting. Harriers run fox in so different a style from hare, that it is of great disservice to them when they return to hare again: it makes them wild, and teaches them to skirt. The high scent which a fox leaves, the straightness of his running, the eagerness of the pursuit, and the noise that generally accompanies it, all contribute to spoil a harrier.

I hope you agree with me, that it is a fault in a pack of harriers to go too fast; for a hare is a little timorous animal, which we cannot help feeling some compassion for at the very time when we are pursuing her destruction: we should give scope to all her little tricks, nor kill her foully, and over-matched.[1] Instinct instructs her to make a good defence,

---

[1] The critic terms this, "a mode of destruction somewhat beyond brutal" (vide *Monthly Review*). I shall not pretend to justify that conventional cruelty, which seems so universally to prevail—neither will I ask the gentleman, who is so severe on me, why he feeds the lamb, and afterwards cuts his throat; I mean only to consider cruelty under the narrow limits which concern hunting—if it may be defined to be, a pleasure which results from giving pain; then, certainly, a sportsman is much less cruel than he is thought.

when not unfairly treated, and I will venture to say, that, as far as her own safety is concerned, she has more cunning than the fox, and makes many shifts to save her life far beyond all his artifice. Without doubt, you have often heard of hares, who, from the miraculous escapes they have made, have been thought *witches*; but, I believe, you never heard of a fox that had cunning enough to be thought a *wizzard*.

They who like to rise early, have amusement in seeing the hare trailed to her form. It is of great service to hounds: it also shows their goodness to the huntsman more than any other hunting, as it discovers to him those who have the most tender noses. But I confess I seldom judged it worth while to leave my bed a moment sooner on that account. I always thought hare-hunting should be taken as a ride, after breakfast, to get us an appetite to our dinner. If you make a serious business of it, you spoil it. Hare-finders, in this case, are necessary: it is agreeable to know where to go immediately for your diversion, and not beat about, for hours perhaps, before you find. It is more material with regard to the second hare than the first; for if you are warmed with your gallop, the waiting long in the cold afterwards is, I believe, as unwholesome as it is disagreeable. Whoever does not mind this, had better let his hounds find their own game: they will certainly hunt it with more spirit afterwards; and he will have a pleasure himself in expectation, which no certainty can ever give. Hare-finders make hounds idle: they also make them wild. Mine knew the men as well as I did myself; could see them almost as far; and would run, full cry, to meet them. Hare-finders are of one great use: they hinder your hounds from chopping hares, which they otherwise could not fail to do. I had in my pack one hound in particular, that was famous for it: he would challenge on a trail very late at noon, and had a good knack at chopping a hare afterwards: he was one that liked to go the shortest way to work; nor did he choose to take more trouble than was necessary. Is it not wonderful that the trail of a hare should lie after so many hours, when the scent of her dies away so soon?

Hares are said (I know not with what truth) to foresee a change of weather, and to seat themselves accordingly. This is, however, certain, that they are seldom found in places much exposed to the wind. In inclosures, they more frequently are found near to a hedge than in the middle of a field. They who make a profession of hare-finding (and a very advantageous one it is in some countries) are directed by the wind where to look for their game. With good eyes and nice observation, they are enabled to find them in any weather. You may make forms, and hares will sit in them. I have heard that it is a common practice with shepherds on the Wiltshire downs; and, by making them on the side of hills, they can tell at a distance off, whether there are hares in them or not. Without doubt, people frequently do not find hares from not knowing them in their forms. A gentleman coursing with his friends, was shown a hare that was found sitting. *"Is that a hare?"* he cried. *"Then by Jove, I found two this morning as we rode along!"*

Though the talent of hare-finding is certainly of use, and the money collected for it, when given to shepherds, is money well bestowed by a sportsman, as it tends to the preservation of his game—yet I think, that when it is indiscriminately given, hare-finders often are too well paid. I have known them frequently get more than a guinea for a single hare. I myself have paid five shillings in a morning, for hares found sitting. To make our companions pay dearly for their diversion, and oftentimes so much more than it is worth; to take from the pockets of men, who oftentimes can ill afford it, as much as would pay for a good dinner afterwards, is, in my opinion, an ungenerous custom; and this consideration induced me to collect but once, with my own hounds, for the hare-finders. The money was afterwards divided amongst them; and if they had less than half-a-crown each, I myself supplied the deficiency. An old miser who had paid his shilling, complained bitterly of it afterwards; and said, "*He had been made to pay a shilling for twopennyworth of sport.*"

When the game is found, you cannot be too quiet. The hare is an animal so very timorous, that she is frequently headed back, and your dogs are liable to over-run the scent at every instant. It is best, therefore, to keep a considerable way behind them, that they may have room to turn, as soon as they perceive they have lost the scent; and, if treated in this manner, they will seldom over-run it much. Your hounds, through the whole chase, should be left almost entirely to themselves; nor should they be hallooed much. When the hare doubles, they should hunt through those doubles; nor is a hare hunted fairly when hunted otherwise.[1] They should follow her every step she takes, as well over greasy fallows as through flocks of sheep; nor should they ever be cast, but when nothing can be done without it. I know a gentleman, a pleasant sportsman, but a very irregular hare-hunter, who does not exactly follow the method here laid down. As his method is very extraordinary, I will relate it to you:—His hounds are large and fleet: they have at times hunted every thing; red deer, fallow deer, fox, and hare; and must in their nature have been most excellent; since, notwithstanding the variety of their game, they are still good. When a hare is found sitting, he seldom fails to give his hounds a view; and as the men all halloo, and make what noise they can, she is half frightened to death immediately. This done, he then sends his whipper-in to ride after her, with particular directions not to let her get out of his sight: and he has found out that this is the only proper use of a whipper-in. If they come to a piece of fallow, or a flock of sheep, the hounds are not suffered to hunt any longer, but are capped and hallooed as near to the hare as possible: by this time the poor devil is near her

[1 This, of course, refers to harriers and hounds that are big enough to ride to, but foot-beagles may be handled like a pack of fox-hounds, and it is quite fair to take advantage of any holloa that will put you on better terms with your hare. It is, however, not advisable to lift hounds when they are running well, as there is always the possibility of changing hares and also of losing time by their not settling at once to the scent.]

end, which the next view generally finishes; the strongest
hare, in this manner, seldom standing twenty minutes.
But my friend says, a hare is good eating, and he therefore
thinks that he cannot kill too many of them. By what Martial
says, I suppose *he* was of the same opinion:

Inter quadrupedes gloria prima lepus.

A-propos to eating them—I must tell you, that in the
Encyclopédie, a book of universal knowledge, where, of
course, I expected to find something on hunting, which it
might be of service to you, as a sportsman, to know, I
found the following advice about the dressing of a hare,
which may be of use to your cook; and the regard I have
for your health will not suffer me to conceal it from you:—
"*On mange le levraut rôti dans quelques provinces du royaume,
en Gascogne et en Languedoc, par exemple, avec une sauce composée
de vinaigre at de sucre, qui est mauvaise, malsaine en soi essentielle-
ment, mais qui est surtout abominable pour tous ceux qui n'y
sont pas accoutumés.*" You, without doubt, therefore, will
think yourself obliged to the authors of the *Encyclopédie*
for their kind and friendly information.

Having heard of a small pack of beagles to be disposed
of in Derbyshire, I sent my coachman (the person whom
I could at that time best spare) to fetch them. It was a long
journey, and, not having been used to hounds, he had
some trouble in getting them along; besides which, as
ill-luck would have it, they had not been out of the kennel
for many weeks before, and were so riotous, that they ran
after everything they saw: sheep, cur-dogs, and birds of
all sorts, as well as hares and deer, I found, had been his
amusement all the way along. However, he lost but one
hound; and when I asked him what he thought of them,
he said, "they could not fail of being good hounds, for they
would hunt *anything*."

In your answer to my last Letter, you ask, Of what
service it can be to a huntsman to be a good groom? and,
Whether I think he will hunt hounds the better for it? I

wonder you did not rather ask, Why he should be *cleanly?* I should be more at a loss how to answer you. My huntsman has always the care of his own horses; I never yet knew one who did not think himself capable of it: it is for that reason I wish him to be a *good groom.*

You say, that you cannot see how a huntsman of genius can spoil your sport, or hurt your hounds. I will tell you how: by too much foul play he frequently will catch a fox before he is half tired; and by lifting his hounds too much, he will teach them to shuffle. An improper use of the one may spoil your sport; too frequent use of the other must hurt your hounds.

LETTER XI

I HAVE already observed, that a trail in the morning is of great service to hounds; and that, to be perfect, they should always find their own game; for the method of hare-finding, though more convenient, will occasion some vices in them, which it will be impossible to correct.

Mr. Somerville's authority strengthens my observation; that, when a hare is found, all should be quiet; nor should you ride near your hounds till they are well settled to the scent.

> Let all be hush'd,
> No clamour loud, no frantic joy be heard;
> Lest the wild hound run gadding o'er the plain
> Untractable, nor hear thy chiding voice.

The natural eagerness of the hounds will, at such a time, frequently carry even the best of them wide of the scent; which too much encouragement, or pressing too close upon them, may continue beyond all possibility of recovery: this should be always guarded against. After a little while you have less to fear. You may then approach them nearer, and encourage them more; leaving, however, at all times, sufficient room for them to turn, should they over-run the scent. On high roads, and dry paths, be always doubtful of the scent;[1] nor give them much encouragement; but when a hit is made on either side, you may halloo as much as you please; nor can you then encourage your hounds too much. A hare generally describes a circle as she runs; larger, or less, according to her strength and the openness of the country. In inclosures, and where there is much cover, the circle is, for the most part, so small, that it is a constant puzzle to the hounds. They have a Gordian

[1 Hares are very fond of running roads, and many are lost thereby. A good road hound is invaluable, but it is very few that develop this instinct, and then not before the fourth or fifth season.]

knot, in that case, ever to unloose; and though it may afford matter of speculation to the philosopher, it is always contrary to the wishes of the sportsman:—such was the country that I hunted in for many years.

> Huntsman! her gait observe: if in wide rings
> She wheel her mazy way, in the same round
> Persisting still, she'll foil the beaten track.
> But if she fly, and with the fav'ring wind
> Urge her bold course, less intricate thy task:
> Push on thy pack.—SOMERVILLE.

Besides running the foil, they frequently make doubles; which is going forward, to tread the same steps back again, on purpose to confuse their pursuers; and the same manner in which they make the first double, they generally continue, whether long or short. This information, therefore, if properly attended to by the huntsman, may be of use to him in his casts.

When they make their double on a high road, or dry path, and then leave it with a spring, it is often the occasion of a long fault. The spring which a hare makes on these occasions is hardly to be credited, any more than is her ingenuity in making it: both are wonderful.

> Let cavillers deny
> That brutes have reason; sure 'tis something more;
> 'Tis Heav'n directs, and strategems inspires,
> Beyond the short extent of human thought.—SOMERVILLE.

She frequently, after running a path a considerable way, will make a double, and then stop till the hounds have passed her; she will then steal away as secretly as she can, and return the same way she came. This is the greatest of all trials for hounds. It is so hot a foil, that, in the best packs, there are not many hounds that can hunt it; you must follow these hounds that can, and try to hit her off where she breaks her foil, which, in all probability, she will soon do, as she now flatters herself she is secure. When the scent

"I wish, Sir, with all my heart, that your cough was better"

lies bad in cover, she will sometimes seem to hunt the hounds.

> The covert's utmost bound
> Slily she skirts; behind them cautious creeps,
> And in that very track, so lately stain'd
> By all the steaming crowd, seems to pursue
> The foe she flies.—SOMERVILLE.

When the hounds are at a check, make your huntsman stand still, nor suffer him to move his horse one way or the other; hounds lean naturally towards the scent, and, if you say not a word to them, will soon recover it. If you speak to a hound at such a time, calling by his name, which is too much the practice, he seldom fails to look up in your face, as much as to say, *what the deuce do you want?*—when he stoops to the scent again, is it not probable that he means to say, *you fool you, let me alone?*

When your hounds are at fault, let not a word be said: let such as follow them ignorantly and unworthily, stand all aloof—*Procul, O procul este profani!*—for whilst such are chattering, not a hound will hunt. *A-propos*, Sir, a politician will say: "What news from America?" *A-propos*, "Do you think both the admirals will be tried?" or, *à-propos*, "Did you hear what has happened to my grandmother?" Such questions are, at such a time, extremely troublesome, and very *mal-à-propos*. Amongst the ancients, it was reckoned *an ill omen* to speak in hunting: I wish it were thought so now. *Hoc age,* should be one of the first maxims in hunting, as in life: and I can assure you, when I am in the field I never wish to hear any other tongue than that of a hound. A neighbour of mine was so truly a hare-hunter in this particular, that he would not suffer any body to speak a word when his hounds were at fault. A gentleman happening to cough—he rode up to him immediately, and said, "*I wish, Sir, with all my heart, that your cough was better.*"

In a good day, good hounds seldom give up the scent at head; if they do, there is generally an obvious reason for it: this observation a huntsman should always make; it will direct his cast. If he be a good one, he will attend as he goes, not only to his hounds (nicely observing which have the lead, and the degree of scent that they carry), but also to the various circumstances that are continually happening from change of weather and difference of ground: he will likewise be mindful of the distance which the hare keeps before the hounds, and of her former doubles: he will also remark what point she makes to. All these observations will be of use, if a long fault make his assistance necessary; and, if the hare should have headed back, he will carefully observe whether she met with anything in her course to turn her, or turned of her own accord. When he casts his hounds, let him begin by making a small circle: if that will not do, then let him try a larger: he afterwards may be at liberty to persevere in any cast that he shall judge most likely. As a hare generally re-visits her old haunts, and returns to the place where she was first found; if the scent be quite gone, and the hounds can no longer hunt—*that* is as likely a cast as any to recover her. Let him remember in all his casts, that the hounds are not to follow his horse's heels; nor are they to carry their heads high, and noses in the air. At these times they must try for the scent, or they will never find it; and he is either to make his cast quick or slow, as he perceives his hounds try, and as the scent is either good or bad.

Give particular directions to your huntsman to prevent his hounds, as much as he can, from chopping hares. Huntsmen like to get blood at any rate; and, when hounds are used to it, it would surprise you to see how attentive they are to find opportunities. A hare must be very wild, or very nimble, to escape them. I remember, in a furzy country, that my hounds chopped three hares in one morning; for it is the nature of those animals either to leap up before the hounds come near them, and *steal away*, as it is called; or else to lie close till they put their very noses upon them. Hedges also are very dangerous: if the huntsman beat the hedge himself, which is the usual practice, the hounds are always upon the watch; and a hare must have good luck to escape them all. The best way to prevent it, is

LIBRARY
BISHOP BURTON COLLEGE
BEVERLEY HU17 8QG

to have the hedge well beaten at some distance before the hounds.

Hares seldom run so well as when they do not know where they are. They run well in a fog, and generally take a good country. If they set off down the wind, they seldom return: you then cannot push on your hounds too much. When the game is sinking, you will perceive your old hounds get forward: they then will run at head.

> Happy the man who with unrivall'd speed
> Can pass his fellows, and with pleasure view
> The struggling pack; how in the rapid course
> Alternate they preside, and, jostling, push
> To guide the dubious scent; how giddy youth,
> Oft babbling, errs, by wiser age reprov'd;
> How, niggard of his strength, the wise old hound
> Hangs in the rear, till some important point
> Rouse all his diligence, or till the Chase
> Sinking he finds; then to the head he springs,
> With thirst of glory fir'd, and wins the prize.—SOMERVILLE.

Keep no babblers; for though the pack soon find them out, and mind them not, yet it is unpleasant to hear their noise; nor are such fit companions for the rest.

Though the *Spectator* may make us laugh at the oddity of his friend Sir Roger, for returning a hound which he said was an excellent *bass*, because he wanted a *counter-tenor;* yet I am of opinion, that if we attended more to the variety of notes frequently to be met with in the tongues of hounds, it might greatly add to the harmony of the pack. I do not know that a complete concert could be attained; but it would be easy to prevent discordant sounds.

Keep no hound that runs false: the loss of one hare is more than such a dog is worth.

It is but reasonable to give your hounds a hare sometimes: I always give mine the last they killed, if I thought they deserved her.

It is too much the custom, first to ride over a dog, and then cry, *'ware horse!* Take care not to ride over your hounds: I have known many a good dog spoiled by it. In open ground, caution them first; you may afterwards ride over them, if you please; but, in roads and paths, they frequently cannot get out of your way: it surely, then, is your business, either to stop your horse, or break a way for them; and the not doing it, give me leave to say, is not less absurd than cruel, nor can that man be called a good sportsman, who thus wantonly destroys his own sport. Indeed, good sportsmen seldom ride on the line of the tail hounds.

An acquaintance of mine, when he hears any of his servants say, *'ware horse!* halloos out, "*'ware horse! 'ware dog!* and be hang'd to you!"

You ask, How my warren-hares are caught? It shall be the subject of my next Letter.

You wish to know, How my warren-hares are caught? They are caught in traps, not unlike to the common rat-traps. I leave mine always at the meuses; but they are *set* only when hares are wanted: the hares, by thus constantly going through them, have no mistrust, and are easily caught. These traps should be made of old wood; and even then it will be some time before they will venture through them. Other meuses must be also left open, lest a distaste should make them forsake the place. To my warren I have about twenty of these traps; though, as the stock of hares is great, I seldom have occasion to set more than five or six, and scarcely ever fail of catching as many hares. The warren is paled in; but I found it necessary to make the meuses of brick; that is, where the traps are placed. Should you at any time wish to make a hare-warren, it will be necessary for you to see one first, and examine the traps, boxes, and stoppers; to all which there are particularities not easy to be described. Should you perceive the hares, toward the end of the season, to become shy of the traps, from having been often caught, it will be necessary to drive them in with spaniels. Should this be the case, you will find them very thick round the warren; for the warren-hares will be unwilling to leave it, and, when disturbed by dogs, will immediately go in.

If you turn them out before greyhounds, you cannot give them too much law; if before hounds, you cannot give them too little; for reasons which I will presently add. Though hares, as I told you before, never run so well before hounds, as when they do not know where they are; yet, before greyhounds, it is the reverse: and your trap-hares, to run well, should always be turned out within their knowledge: they are naturally timid; and are easily disheartened, when they have no point to make to for safety.

If you turn out any before your hounds (which, if it be not your wish, I shall by no means recommend), give them not much time, but lay on your hounds as soon as they are out of view: if you do not, they will be likely to stop, which is oftentimes fatal. Views are at all times to be avoided, but particularly with trap-hares; for, as these know not where they are, the hounds have too great an advantage over them. It is best to turn them down the wind: they hear the hounds better, and seldom turn again. Hounds for this business should not be too fleet. These hares run straight, and make no doubles: they leave a strong scent, and have other objections, in common with animals turned out before hounds: they may give you a gallop; they will, however, show but little hunting. The hounds are to be hunted like a pack of fox-hounds, as a trap-hare runs very much in the same manner, and will even top the hedges. What I should prefer to catching the hares in traps, would be a warren in the midst of an open country, which might be stopped close on hunting-days. This would supply the whole country with hares, which, after one turn round the warren, would most probably run straight at end. The number of hares that a warren will supply, is hardly to be conceived: I seldom turned out less, in one year, than thirty brace of trap-hares, besides many others killed in the environs, of which no account was taken. My warren is a wood of near thirty acres: one of half the size would answer the purpose perhaps as well. Mine is cut out into many walks: a smaller warren should have only *one*, and *that* round the outside of it. No dog should ever be suffered to go into it; and traps should be constantly set for stoats and pole-cats. It is said, that parsley makes hares strong; they certainly are very fond of eating it; it therefore cannot be amiss to sow some within the warren, as it may be a means of keeping your hares more at home.

I had once some conversation with a gentleman about the running of my trap-hares, who said he had been told that catching a hare, and tying *a piece of ribbon to her ear*, was a sure way to make her run *straight*—I make no doubt of it; and so would *a canister tied to her tail*.

I am sorry that you should think I began my first Letter on the subject of hare-hunting in a manner that might offend any of my brother-sportsmen. It was not hare-hunting that I meant to depreciate, but the country I had hunted hare in. It is good diversion in a good country: you are always certain of sport; and if you really love to see your hounds hunt, the hare, when properly hunted, will show you more of it than any other animal.

You ask me, What is the right time to leave off hare-hunting? You should be guided in that by the season: you should never hunt after March; and, if the season be forward, you should leave off sooner.

Having now so considerably exceeded the plan that I first proposed, you may wonder if I omit to say anything of *stag-hunting*. Believe me, if I do, it will not be for want of respect; but because I have seen very little of it. It is true, I hunted two winters at Turin; but their hunting, you know, is no more like ours than is the hot meal we *there* stood up to eat, to the English breakfast that we sit down to *here*. Were I to describe their manner of hunting, their infinity of dogs, their number of huntsmen, their relays of horses, their great saddles, great bitts, and jack-boots—it would be no more to our present purpose than the description of a wild-boar chase in Germany, or the hunting of jackals in Bengal—*C'est une chasse magnifique, et voilà tout*. However, to give you an idea of their huntsmen, I must tell you that one day the stag, which is very unusual, broke cover, and left the forest; a circumstance which gave as much pleasure to me as displeasure to all the rest: it put everything into confusion. I followed one of the huntsmen, thinking he knew the country best; but it was not long before we were separated: the first ditch we came to stopped him: I, eager, to go on, hallooed out to him, "*Allons, Piqueur, sautez donc.*" "*Non pardi,*" replied he, very coolly," *c'est un double fossé—je ne saute pas les doubles fossé.*" There was also an odd accident the same day, which, as it happened to a great man, even to the king himself, you may think interesting; besides, it was the occasion of a *bon mot* worth your hearing:—The king, eager in the pursuit, rode into a bog, and was dismounted: he was not hurt: he was soon on his legs, and we were all standing round him. One of his old generals, who was at some distance behind, no sooner saw the king off his horse, than he rode up full gallop to know the cause. "*Qu'est-ce que c'est?—qu'est-ce que c'est?*" cries the good old general, and in he tumbles into the same bog. Count Kevenhuller, with great humour, replied, pointing to the place, "*Voilà ce que c'est!—voilà ce que c'est!*"

With regard to the stag-hunting in this country, as I have already told you that I know but little of it, you will, without doubt, think it a sufficient reason for my being silent concerning it.

LETTER XIII

IN some of the preceding Letters, we have, I think, settled the business of the kennel in all its parts; and determined what should be the number, and what the qualifications, of the attendants on the hounds: we also agree in opinion, that a pack should consist of about twenty-five couple: I shall now proceed to give some account of the use of them. You desire that I would be as particular as if you were to hunt the hounds yourself. To obey you, therefore, I think I had better send you a description of an imaginary chase; in which I shall be at liberty to describe such events as probably may happen, and to which your present inquiries seem most to lead: a further and more circumstantial explanation of them will necessarily become the subject of my future Letters. I am, at the same time, well aware of the difficulties attending such an undertaking. A fox-chase is not easy to be described; yet, as even a faint description of it may serve, to a certain degree, as an answer to the various questions which you are pleased to make concerning that diversion, I shall prosecute my attempt in such a manner as I think may suit your purpose best. As I fear it may read ill, it shall not be long. A gentleman, to whose understanding Nature had most evidently been sparing of her gifts, as often as he took up a book and met with a passage which he could not comprehend, was used to write in the margin opposite, *matière embrouillée*, and gave himself no further concern about it. As different causes have been known to produce the same effects, should *you* treat *me* in like manner, I shall think it the severest censure that can be passed upon me. Our friend Somerville, I apprehend, was no great fox-hunter; yet all that he says on the subject of hunting is so sensible and just, that I shall turn to his account of fox-hunting, and quote it where I can. The hour most favourable to the diversion, is certainly an early one; nor do I think I can fix

it better than to say, the hounds should be at the cover
at sun-rising. Let us suppose that we are arrived at the
cover-side.

> Delightful scene!
> Where all around is gay, men, horses, dogs;
> And in each smiling countenance appears
> Fresh blooming health, and universal joy.—SOMERVILLE.

Now let your huntsman throw in his hounds as quietly
as he can, and let the two whippers-in keep wide of him
on either hand, so that a single hound may not escape them;
let them be attentive to his halloo, and be ready to encourage,
or rate, as that directs; he will, of course, draw up the wind,
for reasons which I shall give in another place. Now, if
you can keep your brother-sportsmen in order, and put
any discretion into them, you are in luck; they more
frequently do harm than good. If it be possible, persuade
those who wish to halloo the fox off, to stand quiet under
the cover-side, and on no account to halloo him too soon:
if they do, he most certainly will turn back again. Could
you entice them all into the cover, your sport, in all probability, would not be the worse for it.

How well the hounds spread the cover! the huntsman,
you see, is quite deserted, and his horse, who so lately had
a crowd at his heels, has not now one attendant left. How
steadily they draw! you hear not a single hound; yet none
are idle. Is not this better than to be subject to continual
disappointment, from the eternal babbling of unsteady
hounds?

> See! how they range
> Dispers'd, how busily this way and that
> They cross, examining with curious nose
> Each likely haunt. Hark! on the drag I hear
> Their doubtful notes, preluding to a cry
> More nobly full, and swell'd with every mouth.—SOMERVILLE.

How musical their tongues! and as they get nearer to
him, how the chorus fills! Hark, he is found! Now, where
are all your sorrows, and your cares, ye gloomy souls!

or where your pains and aches, ye complaining ones!
one halloo has dispelled them all. What a crash they make!
and echo seemingly takes pleasure to repeat the sound.
The astonished traveller forsakes his road, lured by its
melody: the listening ploughman now stops his plough;
and every distant shepherd neglects his flock, and runs to
see him break—what joy, what eagerness, in every face!

> How happy art thou, Man, when thou'rt no more
> Thyself! when all the pangs that grind thy soul,
> In rapture and in sweet oblivion lost,
> Yield a short interval and ease from pain.—SOMERVILLE.

Mark how he runs the cover's utmost limits, yet dares not
venture forth: the hounds are still too near! That check is
lucky. Now, if our friends head him not, he will soon be
off. Hark, they halloo! by G—d he's gone.

> Hark! what loud shouts
> Re-echo through the groves! he breaks away:
> Shrill horns proclaim his flight. Each straggling hound
> Strains o'er the lawn to reach the distant pack.
> 'Tis triumph all, and joy.—SOMERVILLE.

Now, huntsman, get on with the head hounds; the whipper-
in will bring on the others after you: keep an attentive eye
on the leading hounds, that, should the scent fail them,
you may know at least how far they brought it.

Mind *Galloper*, how he leads them! It is difficult to
distinguish which is first, they run in such a style; yet *he* is
the foremost hound: the goodness of his nose is not less
excellent than his speed. How he carries the scent! and,
when he loses it, see how eagerly he flings to recover it
again! There, now he's at head again! See how they top
the hedge! Now, how they mount the hill! Observe what
a head they carry; and show me, if thou canst, one shuffler
or skirter amongst them all. Are they not like a parcel of
brave fellows, who, when they engage in an undertaking,
determine to share its fatigue and its dangers equally
among them.

> Far o'er the rocky hills we range,
> And dangerous our course; but in the brave
> True courage never fails. In vain the stream
> In foaming eddies whirls; in vain the ditch,
> Wide gaping, threatens death. The craggy steep,
> Where the poor dizzy shepherd crawls with care,
> And clings to ev'ry twig, gives us no pain;
> But down we sweep, as stoops the falcon bold
> To pounce his prey. Then up th' opponent hill,
> By the swift motion slung, we mount aloft:
> So ships, in winter seas, now sliding sink
> Adown the steepy wave, then toss'd on high,
> Ride on the billows, and defy the storm.—SOMERVILLE.

It was then the fox I saw, as we came down the hill: those crows directed me which way to look, and the sheep ran from him as he passed along. The hounds are now on the very spot; yet the sheep stop them not, for they dash beyond them. Now see with what eagerness they cross the plain! *Galloper* no longer keeps his place. *Brusher* takes it: see how he flings for the scent, and how impetuously he runs; how eagerly he took the lead and how he strives to keep it! yet *Victor* comes up apace: he reaches him! Observe what an excellent race it is between them! it is doubtful which will reach the cover first. How equally they run! how eagerly they strain! Now *Victor, Victor!* Ah, *Brusher*, thou art beaten, *Victor* first tops the hedge! See there; see how they all take it in their strokes! The hedge cracks with their weight, so many jump at once!

Now hastes the whipper-in to the other side of the cover: he is right, unless he head the fox.

> Heav'ns! what melodious strains! how beat our hearts
> Big with tumultuous joy! the loaded gales
> Breathe harmony; and as the tempest drives
> From wood to wood, thro' ev'ry dark recess
> The forest thunders, and the mountains shake.—SOMERVILLE.

Listen! the hounds have turned: they are now in two parts. The fox has been headed back, and we have changed at last.

Now, my lad, mind the huntsman's halloo, and stop to those hounds which he encourages. He is right! that, doubtless, is the hunted fox. Now they are off again.

> What lengths we pass! where will the wand'ring Chase
> Lead us bewilder'd! Smooth as swallows skim
> The new-shorn mead, and far more swift, we fly.
> See my brave pack! how to the head they press,
> Jostling in close array, then more diffuse
> Obliquely wheel, while from their op'ning mouths
> The vollied thunder breaks.
>   Look back and view
> The strange confusion of the vale below,
> When sour vexation reigns;
>   Old age laments
> His vigour spent: the tall, plump, brawny youth
> Curses his cumbrous bulk; and envies now
> The short pygmean race, he whilome kenn'd
> With proud insulting leer. A chosen few
> Alone the sport enjoy, nor droop beneath
> Their pleasing toils.—SOMERVILLE.

Ha! a check. Now for a moment's patience! We press too close upon the hounds! Huntsman, stand still! as yet they want you not. How admirably they spread! how wide they cast! Is there a single hound that does not try? If there be, ne'er shall he hunt again. There, *Trueman*, is on the scent: he feathers, yet still is doubtful. 'Tis right! how readily they join him! See those wide-casting hounds, how they fly forward to recover the ground they have lost! Mind *Lightning*, how she dashes; and *Mungo*, how he works! Old *Frantic*, too, now pushes forward: she knows as well as we the fox is sinking.

>   Ha! yet he flies, nor yields
> To black despair. But one loose more and all
> His wiles are vain. Hark! through yon village now
> The rattling clamour rings. The barns, the cots,
> And leafless elms, return the joyous sounds.
> Thro' ev'ry homestall, and thro' ev'ry yard,
> His midnight walks, panting, forlorn, he flies.—
>   SOMERVILLE.

Huntsman! at fault at last? How far did you bring the scent? Have the hounds made their own cast? Now make yours. You see that sheep-dog has coursed the fox:[1] get forward with your hounds, and make a wide cast.

Hark! that halloo is indeed a lucky one. If we can hold him on, we may yet recover him; for a fox so much distressed must stop at last. We shall now see if they will hunt as well as run; for there is but little scent, and the impending cloud still makes that little less. How they enjoy the scent! See how busy they all are, and how each in his turn prevails!

Huntsman, be quiet! Whilst the scent was good, you press'd on your hounds: it was well done: when they came to a check, you stood still and interrupted them not: they were afterwards at fault; you made your cast with judgment, and lost no time. You now must let them hunt. With such a cold scent as this you can do no good: they must do it all themselves. Lift them now, and not a hound will stoop again. Ha! a high road at such a time as this, when the tenderest-nosed hound can hardly own the scent! Another fault! That man at work, then, had headed back the fox. Huntsman! cast not your hounds now; you see they have over-run the scent: have a little patience, and let them, for once, try back.

We now must give them time. See where they bend towards yonder furze brake! I wish he may have stopped there! Mind that old hound, how he dashes o'er the furze; I think he winds him! Now for a fresh *entapis*! Hark! they halloo! Aye, there he goes!

It is nearly over with him: had the hounds caught view, he must have died. He will hardly reach the cover. See how they gain upon him at every stroke! It is an admirable race! yet the cover saves him.

Now be quiet, and he cannot escape us: we have the wind of the hounds, and cannot be better placed. How short he runs! He is now in the very strongest part of the cover.

[1 When a fox is coursed by a sheep-dog, which, alas! often happens in these days, the scent is entirely changed, and the pack should be held forward at once. Whether the loss of scent is caused by the smell of the dog or by the fox being frightened is not certain, but probably it is a little of both.]

What a crash! every hound is in, and every hound is running for him. That was a quick turn! Again another! he's put to his last shifts.   Now *Mischief* is at his heels, and death is not far off. Ha! they all stop at once: all silent, and yet no earth is open.   Listen! now they are at him again! Did you hear that hound catch view?   They over-ran the scent, and the fox had laid down behind them.   Now, Reynard, look to yourself!   How quick they all give their tongues! Little *Dreadnought*, how he works him! The terriers, too, they now are squeaking at him.   How close *Vengeance* pursues! how terribly she presses!   It is just up with him! Gods! what a crash they make! the whole wood resounds! That turn was very short!   There! now—aye, now they have him! Who-hoop!

LETTER XIV

FOX-HUNTING, however lively and animating it may be in the field, is but a dull, dry subject to write upon; and I can now assure you from experience, that it is much less difficult to follow a fox-chase than to describe one. You will easily imagine, that to give enough of variety to a single action, to make it interesting, and to describe in a few minutes the events of, perhaps, as many hours; though it pretend to no merit, has at least some difficulty and trouble; and you will as easily conclude that I am glad they are over.

You desire me to explain that part of my last Letter, which says, *if we can hold him on, we may now recover him.* It means, if we have scent to follow on the line of him, it is probable that he will stop, and we may hunt up to him again. You also object to my saying, *catch* a fox: you call it a bad expression, and say that it is not *sportly.* I believe that I have not often used it; and when I have, it has been to distinguish between the hunting a fox down as you do a hare, and the killing of him with hard running. You tell me, I should always *kill* a fox: I might answer, I must *catch* him first.

You say, that I have not enlivened my chase with many halloos: it is true, I have not; and, what is worse, I fear I am never likely to meet your approbation in that particular; for should we hunt together, then I make no doubt you will think that I halloo too much; a fault which every one is guilty of, who really loves this animating sport, and is eager in the pursuit of it. Believe me, I never could halloo in my life, unless after hounds; and the writing a halloo appears to me almost as difficult as to *pen a whisper.*

Your friend A——, you say, is very severe on us fox-hunters: no one is more welcome. However, even he might have known, that the profession of fox-hunting is much altered since the time of Sir John Vanbrugh; and the

intemperance, clownishness, and ignorance of the old fox-
hunter, are quite worn out: a much truer definition of
one might now be made than that which he has left. Fox-
hunting is now become the amusement of *gentlemen*; nor
need any gentleman be ashamed of it.

I shall now begin to answer your various questions as
they present themselves. Though I was glad of this expe-
dient to methodize, in some degree, the variety that we have
to treat of, yet I was well aware of the impossibility of
sufficiently explaining myself in the midst of a fox-chase,
whose rapidity, you know wery well, brooks no delay.
Now is the time, therefore, to make good that deficiency:
what afterwards remains on the subject of hunting, will
serve as a supplement to the rest; in which I shall still have
it in my power to introduce whatever may be now forgotten,
or give a further explanation of such parts as may seem
to you to require it; for, since my principal view in writing
these Letters is, to make the instruction that they contain
of some use to you, if you should want it; if not, to others—
the being as clear and as explicit as I can, will be far beyond
all other considerations. Repetitions, we know, are shocking
things; yet, in writing so many Letters on the same subject,
I fear it will be difficult to avoid them.

First, then, as to the early hour recommended in my
former Letter—I agree with you, that it requires explanation: but you will please to consider, that you desired me
to fix the hour most favourable to the sport, and, without
doubt, it is *an early one*.[1] You say, that I do not go out
so early myself. It is true, I do not. Do physicians always
follow their own prescriptions? Is it not sufficient that
their prescriptions be good? However, if my hounds
should be out of blood, I go out early; for then it becomes
necessary to give them every advantage. At an early hour,
you are seldom long before you find. The morning is the
part of the day that generally affords the best scent; and
the animal himself, which, in such a case, you are more than
ever desirous of killing, is then least able to run away from

[1] An early hour is only necessary where you are not likely to find without a drag.

you. The want of rest, and perhaps a full belly, give hounds a great advantage over him.   I expect, my friend, that you will reply to this, "a fox-hunter, then, is not a *fair sportsman.*" He certainly is not; and, what is more, would be very sorry to be mistaken for one.   He is otherwise from principle. In his opinion, a fair sportsman, and a foolish sportsman, are synonymous: he therefore takes every advantage that he can of the fox.   You will think, perhaps, that he may sometimes spoil his own sport by this: it is true, he sometimes does, but then he *makes* his hounds; the whole art of fox-hunting being to keep the hounds well in blood. Sport is but a secondary consideration with a true fox-hunter.   The first is *the killing of the fox*: hence arises the eagerness of pursuit—chief pleasure of the chase.   I confess, I esteem blood so necessary to a pack of fox-hounds, that, with regard to myself, I always return home better pleased with but an indifferent chase, with death at the end of it, than with the best chase possible, if it end with the loss of the fox.   Good chases, generally speaking, are long chases; and, if not attended with success, never fail to do more harm to hounds than good.   Our pleasures, I believe, for the most part, are greater during the expectation than the enjoyment.   In this case, reality itself warrants the idea, and your present success is almost a sure fore-runner of future sport.[1]

I remember to have heard an odd anecdote of the late Duke of R——, who was very popular in his neighbourhood: A butcher at Lyndhurst, a lover of the sport, as often as he heard the hounds return from hunting, came out to meet them, and never failed to ask the duke, "What sport

[1 The whole of the foregoing paragraph is full of wisdom, and it would be impossible to call attention to any particular point. Most people who are connected with hounds are quite aware of the necessity for blood, but there are some men who have hunted for years and never like a fox to be killed. These men want their gallop, and would be the first to find fault if hounds grew slack, but they either don't care or don't realize the means that are necessary to provide them with sport. One pack will have good sport when at the same time another equally good pack will never run for twenty minutes consecutively, and never carry a run to a definite end. The reason for this is that one pack is in blood and the other is not. Nothing succeeds like success in hunting, and a pack of hounds in blood will carry all before them.]

he had?" "Very good, I thank you, honest friend." "Has your grace killed a fox?" "*No:* we have had a good run, but we have not killed." "*Pshaw!*" cried the butcher, looking archly, and pointing at him with his finger. This was so constantly repeated, that the duke, when he had not killed a fox, was used to say, that *he was afraid to meet the butcher.*

You ask, Why the huntsman is to draw so quietly? and, Why up the wind? With regard to his drawing quietly, that may depend on the kind of cover before him, and also on the season of the year. If your covers be small, or such from which a fox cannot break unseen, then noise can do no hurt; if you draw at a late hour, and when there is no drag, then the more the cover is disturbed the better—the more likely you are to find. Late in the season, foxes are wild, particularly in covers that are often hunted. If you do not draw quietly, he will sometimes get too much the start of you. When you have any suspicion of this, send on a whipper-in to the opposite side of the cover, before you throw in your hounds. With regard to the drawing up the wind—*that* is much more material. You never fail to give the wind to a pointer and setter—why not to a hound?[1] Besides, the fox, if you draw up the wind, does not hear you coming; and your hounds, by this means, are never out of your hearing: besides, should he turn down the wind, as most probably he will, it lets them all in. Suppose yourself acting directly contrary to this, and then see what is likely to be the consequence.

You think I am too severe on my brother-sportsmen: if more so than they deserve, I am sorry for it. I know many gentlemen who are excellent sportsmen; yet I am sorry to say, the greater number of those who ride after hounds are not: and it is those only to whom I allude. Few gentlemen will take any pains; few of them will stop a hound,

[1 It is quite right to draw up wind all large woodlands, but small coverts should be drawn down wind, otherwise foxes are very likely to be chopped. If several coverts are near together, those down wind should be drawn first unless they are a mile or two apart, when it is the best plan to begin drawing those furthest from home and work towards the kennels.]

though he should run riot close beside them; or will stand quiet a moment, though it be to halloo a fox. It is true, they will not fail to halloo if he should come in their way; and they will do the same to as many foxes as they see. Some will encourage hounds which they do not know: this is a great fault. Were every gentleman who follows hounds to fancy himself a huntsman, what noise, what confusion would ensue! I consider many of them as gentlemen riding out; and I am never so well pleased, as when I see them ride home again. You may perhaps have thought that I wished them all to be huntsmen—most certainly not: but the more assistants a huntsman has, the better, in all probability, his hounds will be. Good sense, and a little observation, will soon prevent such people from doing amiss; and I hold it as an almost invariable rule in hunting, that those who do not know how to do good, are always liable to do harm.[1] There is scarcely an instant during a whole chase, when a sportsman ought not to be in one particular place; and I will venture to say, that if he be not *there*, he might as well be in his bed.

I must give you an extraordinary instance of a gentleman's *knowledge* of hunting: He had hired a house in a fine hunting country, with a good kennel belonging to it, in the neighbourhood of two packs of fox-hounds, of which mine was one; and, that he might not offend the owner of either, intended, as he said, to hunt with both. He offered me the use of his kennel, which, for some reasons, I chose to decline: it was afterwards offered to the other gentleman, who accepted it. The first day that the hounds hunted his country, he did not appear: the second day, the hounds were no sooner at the cover-side, than my friend saw an odd figure, strangely accoutred, riding up, with

---

[1] This is a better reason, perhaps, why gentlemen ought to understand this diversion, than for the good they may do in it; since a pack of hounds that are well manned will seldom need any other assistance. A gentleman, perceiving his hounds to be much confused by the frequent halloos of a stranger, rode up to him, and thanked him with great civility for the trouble he was taking; but at the same time, acquainted him, that the two men he saw in green coats, were paid so much a-year *on purpose to halloo*; it would be needless for him, therefore, to give himself any *further* trouble.

a *spaniel* following him. "Sir," said he, "it gave me great concern not to be able to attend you when you was here before: I hope you was not offended at it; for, to show you how well I am inclined to assist your hunt, you see, *I have brought my little dog.*"

I will now give you an instance of another gentleman's *love* of hunting:—We were returning from hunting over a very fine country; and, upon its being remarked that we had a pleasant ride, he replied—"The best part of the *sport*, in my opinion, is the riding home to dinner afterwards." He is, without doubt, of the same opinion with a fat old gentleman that I one day overtook upon the road, who, after having asked me, "How many foxes we usually killed in one day?" and "Why I did not hunt hare rather than fox, as she was better to eat?" concluded with saying, "There is but one part of hunting I likes—*it makes one very hungry.*"

There are two things which I particularly recommend to you;—the one is, to make your hounds steady; the other, to make them all draw. Many huntsmen are fond of having them at their horse's heels; but, believe me, they never get so well, or so soon, together, as when they spread the cover: besides, I have often known, when there have been only a few finders, that they have found their fox, gone down the wind, and been heard of no more that day.

Never take out an unsteady old hound: young ones properly awed from riot, and that will stop at a rate, may be put into the pack, a few at a time; but an old hound that is vicious should not escape hanging: let him be ever so good in other respects, I will not excuse him; for a pack must be wretched indeed, that can stand in need of such assistance.

There is infinite pleasure in hearing a fox well found. When you get up to his kennel with a good drag, the chorus increasing as you go, it inspires a joy, more easy to be felt than described. With regard to my own sensations, I would rather hear one fox found in this lively manner, than ride the best hare-chase that was ever run.

Much depends on the first finding of your fox; *dimidium*

"I have brought my little dog."

facti, qui bene cœpit, habet, which we learned at Westminster, is verified here; for I look upon a fox well found to be half killed. I think people generally are in too great a hurry on this occasion. There is an enthusiasm attending this diversion, which, in this instance in particular, ought always to be restrained.[1] The hounds are always mad enough when they find their fox: if the men be also mad, they make mad work of it indeed. A gentleman of my acquaintance, who hunts his own hounds, and is not less eager then the rest of us, yet very well knows the bad consequences of being so—to prevent this fault in himself, always begins by taking a pinch of snuff; he then sings part of an old song, *"Some say that care killed the cat,"* &c. By this time his hounds get together, and settle to the scent. He then halloos, and rides as if the d—l drove.

If the fox break cover, you will sometimes see a young sportsman ride after him. He never fails to ask such a one, *"Do you think you can catch him, Sir?"* "No." "Why, then, be so good as to let my hounds try *if they can.*"

---

[1] There are but few instances where sportsmen are not too noisy and too fond of encouraging their hounds, which seldom do the business so well as when little is said to them.

LETTER XV

I LEFT off just as I had found the fox: I now, therefore, with your leave, will suppose that the hounds are running him. You desire that I would be more particular with regard to the men: it was always my intention. To begin, then—The huntsman ought certainly to set off with his foremost hounds, and I should wish him to keep as close to them afterwards as he conveniently can; nor can any harm arise from it, unless he should not have common sense. No hounds then can slip down the wind, and get out of his hearing: he will also see how far they carry the scent; necessary requisite;—for, without it, he can never make a cast with any certainty.

You will find it not less necessary for your huntsman to be active in pressing his hounds forward,[1] while the scent is good, than to be prudent in not hurrying them beyond it when it is bad. Yours, you say, is a good horseman: it is of the utmost consequence to your sport; nor is it possible for a huntsman to be of much use who is not; for the first thing, and the very *sine quâ non*, of a fox-hunter, is to ride up to his headmost hounds. It is his business to be ready at all times to lend them that assistance which they so frequently need, and which, when they are first at a fault, is then most critical. A fox-hound at that time will exert himself most: he afterwards cools, and becomes more indifferent about his game. Those huntsmen who do not get forward enough to take advantage of this eagerness and impetuosity, and direct it properly, seldom know enough of hunting to be of much use to them afterwards.

[1] Pressing hounds on, is perhaps a dangerous expression; as more harm may be done by pressing them beyond the scent, when it is good, than when it is bad. However, it means no more than to get forward the tail hounds, and to encourage the others to push on as fast as they can while the scent serves them.

You will perhaps find it more difficult to keep your whipper-in back, than to get your huntsman forward; at least, I always have found it so.[1] It is, however, necessary; nor will a good whipper-in leave a cover while a single hound remains in it: for this reason there should be two; one of whom should always be forward with the huntsman. You cannot conceive the many ills that may happen to hounds that are left behind.[2] I do not know that I can enumerate one half of them; but of this you may be certain, that the keeping them together is the surest means to keep them steady. When left to themselves, they seldom refuse any blood they can get; they acquire many bad habits; they become conceited; a terrible fault in any animal;— —and they learn to tie upon the scent; an unpardonable fault in a fox-hound:—besides this, they frequently get a trick of hunting by themselves; and they seldom are worth much afterwards. The lying out in the cold, perhaps the whole night, can do no good to their constitutions; nor will the being worried by sheep-dogs, or mastiffs, be of service to their bodies:—all this, however, and much more, they are liable to do. I believe I mentioned in my fourth Letter, that the straw-house door should be left open when any hounds are missing.

Every country is soon known; and nine foxes out of ten, with the wind in the same quarter, will follow the same track. It is easy, therefore, for the whipper-in to cut short, and catch the hounds again; at least, it is so in the country where I hunt. With a high scent, you cannot push on hounds too much. Screams keep the fox forward, at the same time that they keep the hounds together, or let

---

[1] Though a huntsman cannot be too fond of hunting, a whipper-in easily may. His business will seldom allow him to be forward enough with the hounds to see much of the sport. His only thought, therefore, should be to keep the hounds together, and to contribute as much as he can to the killing of the fox.

[2 Hounds should never be waited for unless they have not had a chance of hearing the horn. Hounds are very much like children; they hate being left behind or lost, and if they find no one waits, they will take care to get on, but if they see that there is a nursemaid waiting outside the covert until they choose to come out, they often won't hurry themselves.]

in the tail hounds;[1] they also enliven the sport, and, if discreetly used, are always of service; but, in cover, they should be given with the greatest caution.

Most fox-hunters wish to see their hounds run in a good style. I confess I am myself one of those. I hate to see a string of them; nor can I bear to see them creep where they can leap. It is the dash of the fox-hound which distinguishes *him*, as truly as the motto of William of Wickham distinguishes *us*. A pack of harriers, if they have time, may kill a fox; but I defy them to kill him in the style in which a fox ought to be killed: they must hunt him down. If you intend to tire him out, you must expect to be tired also yourself. I never wish a chase to be less than one hour, or to exceed two:[2] it is sufficiently long, if properly followed: it will seldom be longer, unless there be a fault somewhere; either in the day, in the huntsman, or in the hounds. What Lord Chatham once said of a battle, is particularly applicable to a fox-chase: it should be *short, sharp,* and *decisive.*

There is, I believe, but little difference in the speed of hounds of the same size: the great difference is in the head they carry; and, in order that they may run well together, you should not keep too many old hounds: after five or six seasons, they generally do more harm than good. If they tie upon the scent, and come hunting after, hang them up immediately, let their age be what it may: there is no getting such conceited devils on; they will never come to a halloo, which every hound that is off the scent, or behind the rest, should not fail to do; and they are always more likely to draw you back than help you forward.[3]

[1] Halloos seldom do any hurt, when you are running up the wind; for then, none but the tail hounds can hear you: when you are running down the wind, you should halloo no more than may be necessary to bring the tail hounds forward; for a hound that knows his business seldom wants encouragement when he is upon a scent.

[2 Now that horses and hounds are faster than in Beckford's time, we might say not less than thirty-five minutes or more than one hour and forty minutes, at least, in a grass country.]

[3] From this passage, the critic endeavours to prove the sportsman's ingratitude; and yet common sense, I believe, induces most men to rid themselves of that, which, if kept, would be prejudicial to them. The critic seems to allude to a well-known fable of Æsop, but is not very happy in the application. He has also misquoted the

You think me too severe on skirters. I must confess, that I have but one objection to them, and it is *this*—I have constantly seen them do more *harm* than *good*.

Changing from the hunted fox to a fresh one, is as bad an accident as can happen to a pack of fox-hounds, and requires all the observation and all the ingenuity that man is capable of, to guard against it. Could a fox-hound distinguish a hunted fox as the deer-hound does the deer that is blown, fox-hunting would then be perfect.[1] There are certain rules that ought to be observed by huntsmen. A huntsman should always listen to his hounds while they are running in cover; he should be particularly attentive to the headmost hounds, and should be constantly on his guard against a skirter; for, if there be two scents, he must be wrong. Generally speaking, the best scent is least likely to be that of the hunted fox; and as a fox seldom suffers hounds to run up to him as long as he is able to prevent it, so nine times out of ten, when foxes are hallooed early in the day, they are all fresh foxes. The hounds most likely to be right, are the hard-running line-hunting hounds, or such as the huntsman knows had the lead before there arose any doubt of changing. With regard to the fox, if he break over an open country, it is no sign that he is hard-run; for they seldom at any time will do that, unless they be a great way before the hounds; also, if he run up the wind; as they seldom or ever do that when they have been long hunted and grow weak; and when they run their foil, *that* also may direct him. All this, as you will perceive, requires a good

passage—the author does not say *tire*, but *tie* upon the scent.—Good hounds, when they become aged, are liable to the first; bad ones only, are guilty of the last. In either case, death is not meant as a punishment, nor is it considered as a misfortune. —Vide *Monthly Review*.

[1 This is a point on which we cannot quite agree with the author. Some hounds can and undoubtedly do distinguish between the scent of the run fox and that of a fresh one. It is a very delicate power of perception, and is often lost by a pack being continually holloaed on to fresh foxes. There is also no doubt that a fox's scent changes as he becomes tired, and the hounds to know this must be those that have had continual experience in catching their foxes. When a fox is getting tired and the scent is growing weaker, a pack that is out of blood will not persevere and try without considerable encouragement.]

THE PICK OF THE KENNEL—ALL BECKFORD'S BREEDING

CRAZY
BY LORD STAMFORD'S HERMIT
DAM COMELY
HERMIT BY FURRIER
DAM DEBORAH BY MR. NEAL'S
BACCHUS BY DAM DUMPISH
BY LORD GRANBY'S DOCTOR

BLAMELESS AND BRILLIANT
BY BRUSHER DAM LIVELY
BRUSHER BY LORD CASTLEHAWEN'S
TIPSTER
LIVELY BRED BY LORD EGMONT

PILLAGER
BY PANTALOON
DAM PRIESTLY BY BACCHUS
PANTALOON BY PUSHPIN
DAM RUBY BY MR. BARRY'S
BLUECAP

From a painting at Steepleton by Sartorius

ear and nice observation; and, indeed, in that consists the chief excellence of a huntsman.

When the hounds divide and are in two parts, the whipper-in, in stopping, must attend to the huntsman, and wait for his halloo, before he attempts to stop either; for want of proper management in this particular, I have known the hounds stopped at both places, and both foxes lost by it. If they have many scents, and it is quite uncertain which is the hunted fox, let him stop those that are farthest down the wind, as they can hear the others, and will reach them soonest: in such a case, there will be little use in stopping those that are up the wind.

When hounds are at a check, let every one be silent and stand still: but as I have already said so much on that head in my eleventh Letter, on hare-hunting, I beg leave to refer you to it. Whippers-in are frequently at this time coming on with the tail hounds: they should never halloo to them when the hounds are at fault: the least thing does hurt at such a time, but a halloo more than any other. The huntsman, at a check, had better let his hounds alone, or content himself with holding them forward, without taking them off their noses. Hounds that are not used to be cast, à tout bout de champ, will of themselves acquire a better cast than it is in the power of any huntsman to give them; will spread more, and try better for the scent; and, if in health and spirits, will want no encouragement.

Should they be at fault, after having made their own cast (which the huntsman should always first encourage them to do), it is then his business to assist them farther; but, except in some particular instances, I never approve of their being cast, as long as they are inclined to hunt. The first cast I bid my huntsman make, is generally a regular one; not choosing to rely entirely on his judgment: if that should not succeed, he is then at liberty to follow his own opinion, and proceed as observation and genius may direct. When such a cast is made, I like to see some mark of good sense and meaning in it; whether down the wind, or towards some likely cover, or strong earth: however,

as it is, at best, uncertain, and as the huntsman and the fox
may be of different opinions, I always wish to see a regular
cast before I see a knowing one; which as a last resource,
should not be called forth till it be wanted. The letting
hounds alone is but a negative goodness in a huntsman;
whereas, it is true, this last shows real genius, and, to be
perfect, it must be born with him. There is a fault, however,
which a knowing huntsman is too apt to commit:—he
will find a fresh fox, and then claim the merit of having
recovered the hunted one. It always is dangerous to throw
hounds into a cover to retrieve a lost scent, and, unless they
hit him in, is not to be depended on. Driven to the last
extremity, should a knowing cast not succeed, your huntsman is in nowise blamable. Mine, I remember, lost me
a good chase, by persevering too long in a favourite cast;
but he gave me so many good reasons why the fox *ought*
to have gone that way, that I returned perfectly well
satisfied, telling him at the same time, that, *if the fox was
a fool, he could not help it.*

Gentlemen, when hounds are at fault, are too apt themselves to prolong it: they should always stop their horses
some distance behind the hounds; and, if it be possible
to remain silent, this is the time to be so: they should be
careful not to ride before the hounds, or over the scent;
nor should they ever meet a hound in the face, unless with
a design to stop him. Should you at any time be before the
hounds, turn your horse's head the way they are going,
get out of their track, and let them pass by you.

In dry weather, foxes, particularly in healthy countries,
will run the roads. If gentlemen, at such times, will ride
close upon the hounds, they may drive them miles without
any scent.[1] High-mettled fox-hounds are seldom inclined
to stop while horses are close at their heels.

An acquaintance of mine, a good sportsman, but a very
warm one, when he sees the company pressing too close
upon his hounds, begins with crying out as loud as he can,

[1] No one should ever ride in a direction which, if persisted in, would carry him
amongst the hounds, unless he be at a great distance behind them.

hold hard! If any one should persist after that, he begins moderately at first, and says, *I beg, Sir, you will stop your horse—Pray, Sir, stop—God bless you, Sir, stop!—God d—n your blood, Sir, stop your horse!*

I am now, as you may perceive, in a very violent passion; so I will e'en stop the continuation of this subject till I be cool again.

LETTER XVI

I ENDED my last Letter, I think, in a violent passion. The hounds, I believe, were at fault also. I shall now continue the further explanation of my thirteenth Letter from that time

The first moment that hounds are at fault, is a critical one for the sport: people then should be very attentive. Those who look forward, perhaps, may see the fox; or the running of sheep, or the pursuit of crows, may give them some tidings of him. Those who listen, may sometimes take a hint which way he is gone, from the chattering of a magpie, or perhaps be at a certainty from a distant halloo: nothing, that can give any intelligence at such a time, is to be neglected. Gentlemen are too apt to ride all together: were they to spread more, they might sometimes be of service, particularly those who, from a knowledge of the sport, keep down the wind: it would then be difficult for either hounds or fox to escape their observation.[1]

You should, however, be cautious how you go to a halloo. The halloo itself must, in a great measure, direct you; and though it afford no certain rule, yet you may frequently guess by it whether it may be depended on or not. At the sowing time, when boys are bird-keeping, if you be not very much on your guard, their halloo will sometimes deceive you. It is best, when you are in doubt, to send on a whipper-in to know: the worst, then, that can befall you, is the loss of a little time; whereas, if you gallop away with the hounds to the halloo, and are obliged to return, it is a chance if they try for the scent afterwards: on the other hand, if, certain of the halloo, you intend going to it, then the sooner you get to it the better. I have been more angry with my huntsman for being slow at a time like this, than for any other fault whatsoever.

[1] Those sportsmen only who wish to be of service to the hounds, and know how, should ride wide of them.

Huntsmen who are slow at getting to a halloo, are void of common sense.

They frequently commit another fault, by being in too great a hurry when they get there. It is hardly credible how much our eagerness is apt, at such a time, to mislead our judgment; for instance, when we get to the halloo, the first questions are natural enough—Did you see the fox? Which way did he go? The man points with his finger, perhaps, and then away you all ride as fast as you can, and in such a hurry, that not one will stay to hear the answer to the question which all were so ready to ask: the general consequence of which is, you mistake the place, and are obliged to return to the man for better information. Depend upon it, the less you hurry on this occasion, the more time you save; and wherever the fox was seen for a certainty, whether near or distant, that will not only be the surest, but also the best, place to take the scent; and, besides the certainty of going right, you probably will get on faster than you would by any other means.

That halloos are not always to be depended on, will be sufficiently evinced by the following instances:

My hounds being at a long fault, a fellow halloo'd to them from the top of a rick at some distance off. The huntsman, as you may believe, stuck spurs to his horse, halloo'd till he was almost hoarse, and got to the man as quickly as he could: the man still kept hallooing; and, as he hounds got near him, "*Here*," said he—"*here—here the fox is gone.*" "Is he far before us?" cried the huntsman. "How long ago was it that you saw him?" "No, master, I have not *seen him;* but *I smelt him* here this morning, when I came to serve my sheep."

Another instance was this:—We were trying with some deer-hounds for an out-lying stag, when we saw a fellow running towards us in his shirt: we immediately concluded that we should hear some news of the stag, and set out joyfully to meet him. Our first question was, If he had seen the stag? "No, Sir, I have not seen him, *but my wife dreamt as how she saw him t'other night.*"

Once a man halloo'd us back a mile, only to tell us *that we were right before*, and we lost the fox by it.

A gentleman, seeing his hounds at fault, rode up to a man at plough, and with great eagerness asked him, If he had seen the fox. "The fox, Sir?" "Yes, d—n you, the fox!—did you never see a fox?" "Pray, Sir, if I may be so bould, what sort of a looking creature may he be? Has he *short ears* and a *long tail?*" "*Yes.*" "Why, then, I can assure you, Sir, I have seen *no such thing.*"

We are agreed, that hounds ought not to be cast, as long as they are able to hunt; and though the idea, that a hunted fox never stops, is a very necessary one to a fox-hunter, that he may be active and may lose no time; yet tired foxes will stop, if you can hold them on; and I have known them stop, even in wheel-ruts on the open down, and leap up in the midst of the hounds.   A tired fox ought not to be given up; for he is killed sometimes very unexpectedly. If hounds have ever pressed him, he is worth your trouble: perseverance may recover him, and, if recovered, he most probably will be killed; nor should you despair whilst any scent remains. The business of a huntsman is only difficult when the scent dies quite away; and it is then that he may show *his* judgment, when the hounds are no longer able to show *theirs.* The recovering a lost scent, and getting nearer to the fox by a long cast, requires genius, and is therefore what few huntsmen are equal to. When hounds are no longer capable of feeling the scent, it all rests with the huntsman: either the game is entirely given up, or is only to be recovered by him, and is the effect of real genius, spirit, and observation.

When hounds are at cold hunting with a bad scent, it may then be a proper time to send a whipper-in forward: if he can see the fox, a little mobbing, at such a time as this, may reasonably be allowed.

When hounds are put to a check on a high road, by the fox being headed back, if, in that particular instance, you suffer them to try back, it gives them the best chance of hitting off the scent again, as they may try on both sides at once.

When hounds are running in cover, you cannot be too quiet. If the fox be running short, and the hounds are catching him, not a word should then be said: it is a difficult time for hounds to hunt him, as he is continually turning, and will sometimes lie down and let them pass him.

I have remarked, that the greatest danger of losing a fox is at the first finding of him, and when he is sinking; at both of which times he frequently will run short; and the eagerness of the hounds is too apt to carry them beyond the scent. When a fox is first found I wish every one would keep behind the hounds till they are well settled to the scent; and when the hounds are catching him, I wish them to be as silent as they can.

When he is caught, I like to see hounds eat him eagerly. In some countries, I am told, they have a method of *treeing* him: [1] it is of use to make the hounds eager; it lets them all in; they recover their wind, and eat him more readily. I should advise you, at the same time, not to keep him too long, as I do not imagine the hounds have any appetite to eat him, longer than whilst they are angry with him.

When two packs of fox-hounds run together, and they kill the fox, the pack that found him is entitled to the head. Should both have found, how is it to be determined then? The huntsman who gets in first, seems, in my opinion, to have the best right to it; yet, to prevent a dispute (which, of course, might be thought a wrong-headed one), would he not do well to cut off the head, and present it to the other huntsman?

The same author, whom I quoted in my tenth Letter, and who tells us how we should *not eat a hare*, is also kind enough to tell us when we *should eat a fox;* I wish he had also added the best manner of *dressing him.* We are obliged to him, however, for the following information:—"*La chair du renard est moins mauvaise que celle du loup; les chiens et même les Hommes en mangent en automne, surtout lorsqu'il*

---

[1] The intention of it is, to make the hounds more eager, and to let in the tail hounds. The fox is thrown across the branch of a tree, and the hounds are suffered to bay at him for some minutes before he is thrown amongst them.

s'est nourri et engraissé de raisins." You would have been better pleased, I make no doubt, if the learned gentleman had instructed you *how to hunt him*, rather than *when to eat him*.

I shall end this Letter with an anecdote of a late huntsman of mine, who was a great slip-slop, and always called successively *successfully:*—One day, when he had been out with the young hounds, I sent for him in, and asked him, What sport he had had? and, How the hounds behaved? "Very great sport, Sir, and no hounds could behave any better." "Did you run him long?" "They ran him, and please your honour upwards of three hours *successfully.*" "So, then, you *did* kill him?" "*Oh, no, Sir, we lost him at last.*"

LETTER XVII

FOX-HUNTING, an acquaintance of mine says, is only
to be followed because you can ride hard, and do less harm
in that than any other kind of hunting. There may be some
truth in the observation; but, to such as love the riding
part only of hunting, would not a trail-scent be more
suitable? Gentlemen who hunt for the sake of a ride,
who are indifferent about the hounds, and know little of
the business, if they do no harm, fulfil as much as we have
reason to expect from them; whilst those of a contrary
disposition do good, and have much greater pleasure.
Such as are acquainted with the hounds, and can at times
assist them, find the sport more interesting, and frequently
have the satisfaction to think, that they themselves contribute to the success of the day.[1] This is a pleasure that
you often enjoy; a pleasure without any regret attending it.
I know not what effect it may have on you; but I know that
my spirits are always good after good sport in hunting;
nor is the rest of the day ever disagreeable to me. What
are other sports, compared with this, which is full of enthusiasm! Fishing is, in my opinion, a dull diversion, shooting,
though it admit of a companion, will not allow of many:
both, therefore, may be considered as selfish and solitary
amusements, compared with hunting; to which as many
as please are welcome: the one might teach patience to
a philosopher; and the other, though it occasion great
fatigue to the body, seldom affords much occupation to
the mind; whereas fox-hunting is a kind of warfare; its
uncertainties, its fatigues, its difficulties, and its dangers,
rendering it interesting above all other diversions. That
you may more readily pardon this digression, I return to
answer your letter now before me.

[1] It is not by a foolish attempt to hunt the hounds that gentlemen can be of
service. It is not by riding close upon them, but by keeping wide of them; when
by so doing they may hear a halloo, or view the fox.

I am glad to hear that your men have good voices; mine, unluckily, have not. There is a friend of mine who hunts his own hounds: his voice is the strangest, and his halloos the oddest, I ever heard. He has, however, this advantage— no dog can possibly mistake his halloo for another's. Singularity constitutes an essential part of a huntsman's halloo: it is for that reason alone, I prefer the horn, to which I observe, hounds fly more readily than to the huntsman's voice. Good voices certainly are pleasing; yet it might be as well, perhaps, if those who have them were less fond of exerting them. When a fox is halloo'd, those who under-stand this business and get forward may halloo him again;[1] yet let them be told, if the hounds go the contrary way, or do not seem to come upon the line of him, to halloo on more. With regard to its being the hunted fox—the fox which every man halloos, is the hunted fox in his own opinion, though he seldom has a better reason for it than because *he* saw him. Such halloos as serve to keep the hounds together, and to get on the tail hounds, are always of use: halloos of encouragement to the leading hounds, if injudi-ciously given, may spoil your sport. I am sorry to say, view halloos frequently do more harm than good: they are pleasing to sportsmen, but prejudicial to hounds. If a strong cover be full of foxes, and they be often halloo'd, hounds seldom take much pains in hunting them: hence arises that indifference which sometimes is to be perceived in fox-hounds while pursuing their game.

You ask me, If I would take off my hounds to a halloo? If they be running with a good scent, I most certainly would not; if otherwise, and I could depend upon the halloo, in some cases I would; for instance, when the fox is a great way before them, or persists in running his foil; for such foxes are difficult to kill, unless you endeavour to get

[1] Should a fox be halloo'd in cover, while the hounds are at fault; if they be long in coming, by getting forward, you may halloo the fox again; perhaps, before the hounds are laid on; by which means you will get nearer to him. In cases like this, a good sportsman may be of great use to hounds. There are days, when hounds will do their business best if left quite alone; and there are days, when they can do nothing without assistance. Let them be assisted at no other time. On a bad scent-ing day, or when hounds may be over-matched, you cannot assist them too much.

nearer to them by some means or other. When you hunt after them it will frequently happen, that the longer you run, the farther you will be behind.

If hounds be out of blood, and a fox run his foil, you need not scruple to stop the tail hounds, and throw them in at head; or, if the cover have any ridings cut in it, and the fox be often seen, your huntsman, by keeping some hounds at his horse's heels, at the first halloo that he hears, may throw them in close at him.[1] This will put him out of his pace, and, perhaps, put him off his foil. It will be necessary, when you do this, that the whipper-in should stop the pack from hunting after, and get forward with them to the huntsman. I have already given it as my opinion, that hounds may be halloo'd too much. If they should have been often used to a halloo, they will expect it, and may trust perhaps to their ears and eyes, more than to their noses. If they be often taken from the scent, it will teach them to shuffle, and probably will make them slack in cover: it should be done, therefore, with great caution; not too often; and always should be well-timed. Famous huntsmen, I think, by making too frequent a use of this, sometimes hurt their hounds. I have heard of a sportsman who never suffers his hounds to be lifted: he lets them pick along the coldest scent, through flocks of sheep: this is a particular style of fox-hunting, which, perhaps, may suit the country in which that gentleman hunts. I confess to you, I do not think that it would succeed in a bad-scenting country, or, indeed, in any country where foxes are wild. While hounds can get on with the scent, it cannot be right to take them off from it; but when they are stopped for want of it, it cannot then be wrong to give them every advantage in your power.

It is wrong to suffer hounds to hunt after others that

---

[1] Nothing is meant more than this—"that the huntsman should get the tail hounds off the line of the scent (where they do more harm than good), and encourage them forward; if he should hear a halloo whilst these hounds are off the scent, he should lay them on to it; if he should not, the tail hounds, by this means, may still stand a chance of getting to the head hounds by the *ear*, which they never could do, if they continued to run by the *nose*."

are gone on with the scent, particularly in cover; for how are they to get up to them with a worse scent? Besides, it makes them tie on the scent, teaches them to run dog, and destroys that laudable ambition of getting forward which is the chief excellence of a fox-hound. A good huntsman will seldom suffer his head hounds to run away from him; if it should so happen, and they be still within his hearing, he will sink the wind with the rest of the pack, and get to them as fast as he can. Though I suffer not a pack of fox-hounds to hunt after such as may be a long way before the rest, for reasons which I have just given; yet, when a single hound is gone on with the scent, I send a whipper-in to stop him. Were the hounds to be taken off the scent to get to him, and he should no longer have any scent when they find him, the fox might be lost by it. This is a reason why, in large covers, and particularly such as have many roads in them, skirting hounds should be left at home on windy days.

Skirters, I think, you may find hurtful, both in men and dogs. Such as skirt to save their horses, often head the fox. Good sportsmen never quit hounds but to be of service to them: with men of this description, skirting becomes a necessary part of fox-hunting, and is of the greatest use. Skirters, beware of a furze-brake! If you head back the fox, the hounds, most probably, will kill him in the brake. Such as ride after the hounds, at the same time that they do no good, are least likely to do harm: let such only as understand the business, and mean to be of service to the hounds, ride wide of them. I cannot, however, allow, that the riding close up to hounds is always a sign of a good sportsman; if it were, a *monkey*, upon a good horse, would be the best sportsman in the field. Here must I censure (but with respect) that eager spirit which frequently interrupts and sometimes is fatal to, sport in fox-hunting; for though I cannot subscribe to the doctrine of my friend ****, "that a pack of fox-hounds, would do better without a huntsman than with one, and that, if left to themselves, they would never lose a fox;" yet, allowing them their

"a leap which you do not choose to take"

usual attendants, had he objected only to the sportsmen
who follow them, I must have joined issue with him.
Whoever has followed hounds, must have seen them
frequently hurried beyond the scent; and whoever is con-
versant in hunting, cannot but know, that the steam of
many horses, carried by the wind, and mixed with a cold
scent, is prejudicial to it.[1]

It sometimes will happen, that a good horseman is not
so well in with hounds as an indifferent one; because he
seldom will condescend to get off his horse. I believe, that
the best way to follow hounds across a country, is to keep
on the line of them, and to dismount at once, when you
come to a leap which you do not choose to take; for
in looking about for easier places, much time is lost.
In following hounds, it may be useful to you to know,
that when in cover they run up the wind, you cannot in
reason be too far behind them, as long as you have a
perfect hearing of them, and can command them; and on
the contrary, when they are running down the wind, you
cannot keep too close to them.

You complain that foxes are in too great plenty: believe
me, it is a good fault. I should as soon have expected to
have heard our old acquaintance, Jack R——, complain
of having too much money: however, it is not without a
remedy—hunt the same covers constantly, and you will
soon disperse them. If your pack be strong enough, divide
it; hunt every day, and you will catch many tired foxes.
I remember to have killed a brace in one morning in the
strongest season; the first in ten minutes, the second in
half an hour. If your own pack be not strong enough to
hunt more than every other day, get a pack of harriers
to hunt hare in the cover the intermediate day. Foxes, thus
disturbed, will shift their quarters; they know their enemies,
and smell in the night where they have been in the day,
and will not stay where they are likely to be disturbed by

[1 No one should ride directly behind the pack, and at the first sign of a check
they should stop at once. It should be remembered that the smell of perspiring
horses and human beings is much stronger than the scent from a fox. Overriding
hounds is evidently not a sin of recent growth.]

them. Follow them for one week in this manner, and I do not think you will have any reason, afterwards, to complain that they are in too great plenty.

When covers are much disturbed, foxes will sometimes break as soon as they hear a hound. Where the country round is very open, the fox least likely to break, is that which you are hunting: *he* will be very unwilling to quit the cover, if it be a large one, unless he can get a great distance before the hounds. Should you be desirous to get a run over such a country, the likeliest means will be to post a quiet and skilful person to halloo one off, and lay on to him. The further he is before you, the less likely he will be to return. The best method, however, to hunt a cover like this, is to stick constantly to it, not suffering the hounds to break, so long as one fox shall remain: do this two or three hunting days following; foxes will then fly, and you will have good chases.

Nothing is more hurtful to hounds, than the frequent changing of their country: should they change from a good-scenting country to a bad one, unless they have luck on their sides, they may be some time without killing a fox; whereas, hounds have always a great advantage in a country which they are used to: they not only know better where to find their game, but they will also pursue it with more alacrity afterwards.

This Letter began by a digression in favour of hunting; it will end with the opinion of a Frenchman, not so favourable to it. This gentleman was in my neighbourhood, on a visit to the late Lord Castlehaven, who, being a great sportsman, thought he could not oblige his friend more, than by letting him partake of an amusement which he himself was so fond of; he therefore mounted him on one of his best horses, and showed him a fox-chase. The Frenchman, after having been well shaken, dirtied, tired, run away with, and thrown down, was asked on his return, *"Comment il avait trouvé la chasse?"* *"Morbleu! Milord!"* said he, shrugging up his shoulders, *"votre chasse est une chasse diabolique."*

LETTER XVIII

BEFORE I proceed on my subject, give me leave to set you right in one particular, where I perceive you have misunderstood me. You say, that you little expected to see the abilities of a huntsman degraded beneath those of a whipper-in. This is a serious charge against me, as a sportsman; and, though I cannot admit that I have put the cart before the horse in the manner you are pleased to mention, yet you have made it necessary for me to explain myself farther.

I must therefore remind you, that I speak of my own country only; a country full of riot, where the covers are large, and where there is a chase full of deer and full of game. In such a country as this, you that know so well how necessary it is for a pack of fox-hounds to be steady, and to be kept together, ought not to wonder that I should prefer an excellent whipper-in to an excellent huntsman. No one knows better than yourself, how essential a good adjutant is to a regiment: believe me, a good whipper-in is not less necessary to a pack of fox-hounds: but I must beg you to observe, I mean only, *that I could do better with mediocrity in the one than in the other*. If I have written any thing in a former Letter that implies more, I beg leave to retract it in *this*. Yet I must confess to you, that a famous huntsman I am not very ambitious to have, unless it necessarily followed that he must have *famous hounds*; a conclusion that I cannot admit, as long as these so famous gentlemen will be continually attempting themselves to do, what would be much better done if left to their hounds: besides, they seldom are good servants, are always conceited, and sometimes impertinent. I am very well satisfied if my huntsman be acquainted with his country and his hounds; if he ride well up to them; and if he have some knowledge of the nature of the animal which he is in pursuit of: but so far am I from wishing him to be famous, that I hope he will still continue to think his hounds know best how to hunt a fox.

You say you agree with me, that a huntsman should stick close to his hounds. If, then, his place be fixed, and that of the first whipper-in (where you have two) be not; I cannot but think genius may be at least as useful in one as in the other: for instance, while the huntsman is riding to his head-most hounds, the whipper-in, if he have genius, may show it in various ways: he may clap forwards to any great earth that may, by chance, be open; he may sink the wind to halloo, or mob a fox, when the scent fails; he may keep him off his foil; he may stop the tail hounds, and get them forward; and has it frequently in his power to assist the hounds, without doing them any hurt, provided he should have sense to distinguish where he may be chiefly wanted. Besides, the most essential part of fox-hunting, the making and keeping the pack steady, depends entirely upon him; as a huntsman should seldom rate, and never flog, a hound. In short, I consider the first whipper-in as a second hunts-man; and, to be perfect, he should be not less capable of hunting the hounds than the huntsman himself.

You cannot too much recommend to your whipper-in to get to the head of his hounds before he attempts to stop them. The rating behind is to little purpose, and, if they should be in cover, may prevent him from knowing who the culprits are. When your hounds are running a fox, he then should content himself with stopping such as are riotous, and should get them forward. They may be condemned upon the spot; but the punishment should be deferred till the next day, when they may be taken out on purpose to commit the fault, and suffer the punishment. I agree with you, that young hounds cannot be awed too much; yet suffer not your punishment of them to exceed their offence. I could wish to draw a line betwixt justice and barbarity.[1]

---

[1] I am sorry that it should be necesary to explain what I mean by *barbarity*. I mean *that* punishment which is either unnecessarily inflicted, which is inflicted with severity, or from which no possible good can arise. Punishment, when properly applied, is not cruelty, is not revenge—it is justice, it is even mercy. The intention

A whipper-in, while breaking-in young hounds, sometimes will rate them before they commit the fault: this may
perhaps, prevent them for that time; but they will be just
as ready to begin the next opportunity. Had he not better
let them quite alone, till he see what they would be at?
The discipline then may be proportioned to the degree of
the offence. Whether a riotous young hound run little
or much, is of small consequence, if he be not encouraged:
it is the blood only that signifies, which in every kind of
riot should carefully be prevented.[1]

My general orders to my whipper-in are, if, when he
rate a hound, the hound does not mind him, to take him
up immediately, and give him a severe flogging. Whippers-
in are too apt to continue rating, even when they find that
rating will not avail. There is but one way to stop such
hounds, which is, to get to the heads of them. I also tell
him, never, on any account, to strike a hound, unless the
hound be at the same time sensible what it is for. What
think you of the whipper-in who struck a hound as he was
going to cover, because he was likely to be noisy afterwards
—saying, *"you will be noisy enough by and bye, I warrant you?"*
Whippers-in, when left to themselves, are rare judges of
propriety. I wish they would never strike a hound that
does not deserve it, and would strike those hard that do.
They seldom distinguish sufficiently the degrees of offence
which a dog may have committed, to proportion their
punishment accordingly; and such is their stupidity, that,
when they turn a hound after the huntsman, they will rate
him as severely as if he had been guilty of the greatest fault.

It is seldom necessary to flog hounds to make them
obedient, since obedience is the first lesson that they are
taught; yet, if any should be more riotous than the rest,

of punishment is to prevent crimes, and consequently to prevent the necessity of
punishing.

[1] It is not meant that hounds should be suffered to continue on a wrong scent
longer than may be necessary to know that the scent *is* a wrong one. This passage
refers to page 58, where the author's meaning is more fully explained. It is introduced here more strongly, to mark the danger of encouraging hounds on a wrong
scent, and indulging them afterwards in the blood of it.

they may receive a few cuts in the morning, before they leave the kennel.

When hounds prove unsteady, every possible means should be taken to make them otherwise: a hare, or a deer, put into the kennel amongst them, may then be necessary. Huntsmen are too fond of kennel-discipline: you already know my opinion of it: I never allow it but in cases of great necessity: I then am always present myself, to prevent excess. To prevent an improper and barbarous use of such discipline, I have already told you, is one of the chief, objects of these Letters. If what Montaigne says be true, "that there is a certain general claim of kindness and benevolence which every creature has a right to from us," surely we ought not to suffer unnecessary severity towards an animal to whom we are obliged for so much diversion: and what opinion must we have of the huntsman who inflicts it on one to whom *he* owes his daily bread?[1]

If any of my hounds be very riotous, they are taken out by themselves on the days when they do not hunt, and properly punished; and this is continued whilst my patience lasts, which, of course, depends on the value of the dog. It is a trial between the whipper-in and the dog, which will tire first, and the whipper-in, I think, generally prevails. If this method will not make them steady, no other can; they then are looked upon as incorrigible, and are put away.

Such hounds as are notorious offenders, should also feel the lash, and hear a rate, as they go to the cover; it may be a useful hint to them, and may prevent a severer flogging afterwards. A sensible whipper-in will wait his opportunity to single out his hound; he will then hit him

---

[1] "Perhaps it is not the least extraordinary circumstance in these flogging lectures, that they should be given, with Montaigne, or any other moral author whatever, in recollection at the same instant!" (vide *Monthly Review*.) Perhaps it is not the least extraordinary circumstance in these criticisms, that this passage should have been quoted as a proof of the author's inhumanity. The critic ends his strictures with the following exclamation :—"Of a truth, a sportsman is the most uniform consistent character, from his own representation, that we ever contemplated!" and yet, perhaps, there are sportsmen to be found, possessed of as tender feelings of humanity as any critic whatsoever. The motto prefixed to these Letters, if it had been attended to, might have entitled the author to more candour than the critic has thought fit to bestow upon him.

hard, and rate him well; whilst a foolish one will often hit a dog that he did not intend to strike; will ride full gallop into the midst of the hounds; will, perhaps, ride over some of the best of them, and put the whole pack into confusion: this is a manœuvre that I cannot bear to see.

Have-a-care! are words which seldom do any harm; since hounds, when they are on a right scent, will not mind them.   Let your whipper-in be careful how he *encourage* the hounds; that, improperly done, may spoil your pack.

A whipper-in will rate a hound, and then endeavour to flog him. A dog, after having been rated, will naturally avoid the whip. Tell your whipper-in whenever a hound shall deserve the lash, to hit him first and rate him afterwards.

When there are two whippers-in, one ought always to be forward; when there is only *one*, he, to be perfect, should be a very Mungo, *here*, *there*, and *everywhere*.

You will find it difficult to keep your people in their proper places: I have been obliged to stop back myself, to bring on hounds which my servants had left behind. I cannot give you a greater proof how necessary it is that a whipper-in should bring home all his hounds, than by telling you that I had lost an old hound for ten days, and sent all the country over to inquire after him; and at last, when I thought no more about him, in drawing a large cover in the country where he had been lost, he joined the pack; he was exceedingly emaciated, and it was a long time before he recovered. How he subsisted all that time, I cannot imagine. When any of your hounds may be missing, you should send the whipper-in back immediately to look for them: it will teach him to keep them more together.

The getting forward the tail hounds is a necessary part of fox-hunting, in which you will find a good whipper-in of the greatest use. He must also get forward himself at times, when the huntsman is not with the hounds; but the second whipper-in (who frequently is a young lad, ignorant

of his business) on no account ought to encourage or
rate a hound, but when he is quite certain that it is right
to do it; nor is *he* ever to get forward, so long as a single
hound remains behind.

Halloo forward, is certainly a necessary and a good halloo
but is it not used too indiscriminately? it is forever in the
mouth of a whipper-in. If your hounds be never used to
that halloo till after a fox be found, you will see them fly
to it. At other times, other halloos will answer the purpose
of getting them on as well. *Halloo forward* being used as
soon as the game is on foot, it seems as if another halloo
were necessary, to denote the breaking cover. *Away! Away!*
might answer that purpose. Gentlemen who are kind enough
to stop back to assist hounds, should have notice given
them when the hounds leave the cover.

Most huntsmen, I believe, are jealous of the whipper-in:
they frequently look on him as a successor, and therefore
do not very readily admit him into the kennel; yet, in my
opinion, it is necessary that he should go thither; for he
ought to be well acquainted with the hounds, who should
know and follow him, as well as the huntsman.

To recapitulate what I have already said. If your whipper-
in be bold and active; be a good and careful horseman;
have a good ear, and a clear voice; if, as I said, he be a very
Mungo, having, at the same time, judgment to distinguish
where he can be of most use; if, joined to these, he be above
the foolish conceit of killing a fox without the huntsman;
but, on the contrary, be disposed to assist him all he can—he
then is a perfect whipper-in.

I am sorry to hear that your hounds are so unsteady. It
is scarcely possible to have sport with unsteady hounds:
they are half tired before the fox is found, and are not to be
depended upon afterwards. It is a great pleasure, when a
hound challenges, to be certain that he is right: it is a cruel
disappointment to hear a rate immediately succeed it, and
the smacking of whips instead of halloos of encouragement.
A few riotous and determined hounds do a deal of mischief
in a pack. Never, when you can avoid it, put them among

the rest; let them be taken out by themselves, and well chastised; and if you find them incorrigible, hang them. The common saying, *Evil communications corrupt good manners*, holds good with regard to hounds; they are easily corrupted. The separating of the riotous ones from those which are steady, answers many good purposes: it not only prevents the latter from getting the blood which they should not, but it also prevents them from being overawed by the smacking of whips, which is too apt to obstruct drawing and going deep into cover. A couple of hounds, which I received from a neighbour last year, were hurtful to my pack: they had run with a pack of harriers, and, as I soon found, were never afterwards to be broken from hare. It was the beginning of the season; covers were thick, hares in plenty, and we seldom killed less than five or six in a morning. The pack, at last, got so much blood, that they would hunt them as if they were designed to hunt nothing else. I parted with that couple of hounds; and the others, by proper management, are become as steady as they were before. You will remind me, perhaps, that they were draft-hounds: it is true, they were so; but they were three or four years hunters; an age when they might be supposed to have known better. I advise you, unless a known good pack of hounds are to be disposed of, not to accept old hounds. I mention this, to encourage the breeding of hounds, and as the likeliest means of getting a *handsome, good,* and *steady pack*. Though I give you this advice, it is true, I have accepted draft-hounds myself, and they have been very good; but they were the gift of the friend mentioned by me in a former Letter,[1] to whom I have already acknowledged many obligations; and unless you meet with such a one, old hounds will not prove worthy your acceptance: besides, they may bring vices enough along with them to spoil your whole pack. If old hounds should be unsteady, it may not be in your power to make them otherwise; and I can assure you

---

[1] The Hon. Mr. Booth Grey, brother to the Earl of Stamford. The hounds here alluded to, were from Lord Stamford's kennel.

from experience, that an unsteady old hound will give you more trouble than all your young ones: the latter will at least stop; but an obstinate old hound will frequently run mute, if he find that he can run no other way: besides, old hounds that are unacquainted with your people, will not readily hunt for them as they ought; and such as were steady in their own pack may become unsteady in yours. I once saw an extraordinary instance of this, when I kept harriers. Hunting one day on the downs, a well-known fox-hound of a neighbouring gentleman came and joined us; and as he both ran faster than we did, and skirted more, he broke every fault, and killed many hares. I saw this hound often in his own pack afterwards, where he was perfectly steady; and though he constantly hunted in covers where hares were in great plenty, I never remember to have seen him run one step after them.

A change of country, also, will sometimes occasion a difference in the steadiness of hounds. My hounds hunt frequently in Cranborn Chase, and are steady from deer; yet I once knew them run an outlying deer, which they unexpectedly found in a distant country.

I am sorry to hear that so bad an accident has happened to your pack, as that of killing sheep; but I apprehend from your account of it, that it proceeded from idleness, rather than vice. The manner in which the sheep were killed, may give you some insight into it; old practitioners generally seizing by the neck, and seldom, if ever, behind. This, like other vices, sometimes runs in the blood: in an old hound it is, I believe, incorrigible: the best way, therefore, will be to hang all those which, after two or three whippings, cannot be cured of it. In some countries, hounds are more inclined to kill sheep than they are in others. Hounds may be steady in countries where the covers are fenced, and sheep are only to be seen in flocks, either in large fields or on open downs; and the same hounds may be unsteady in forests and heathy countries, where the sheep are not less wild than the deer. However, hounds, should they stir but a step after them, should undergo the severest discipline: if young hounds do it from idleness, *that*, and plenty of work, may reclaim them: for old hounds guilty of this vice, I know, as I said before, of but one sure remedy —*the halter*.

Though I so strongly recommend to you to make your hounds steady, from having seen unsteady packs, yet I must also add that I have frequently seen the men even more unsteady than the hounds. It is shocking to hear hounds halloo'd one minute and rated the next: nothing offends a good sportsman so much, or is in itself so hurtful. I will give you an instance of the danger of it:—My beagles were remarkably steady: they hunted hare in Cranborn Chase, where deer are in great plenty, and would draw for hours, without taking the least notice of them. When tired of hare-hunting, I was inclined to try if I could find any diversion in hunting of fallow deer. I had been told that it would be impossible to do it with those hounds that had been made steady from them; and, to put it to the trial, I took them into a cover of my own, which has many ridings cut in it, and where are many deer. The first deer that we saw we halloo'd; and, by great encouragement and constant hallooing, there were but few of these steady hounds but would run the scent. They hunted deer constantly from that day, and never lost one afterwards. Dogs are sensible animals: they soon find out what is required of them, when we do not confuse them by our own heedlessness: when we encourage them to hunt a scent which they have been rated from, and perhaps severely chastised for hunting, they must needs think us cruel, capricious, and inconsistent.[1]

If you know any pack that is very unsteady, depend upon it, either no care has been taken in entering the young hounds to make them steady, or else the men afterwards,

[1] Though all hounds ought to be made obedient, none require it so much as fox-hounds, for, without it, they will be totally uncontrollable; yet not all the chastisement that cruelty can inflict, will render them obedient, unless they be made to understand what is required of them: when that is effected, many hounds will not need chastisement, if you do not suffer them to be corrupted by bad example. Few packs are more obedient than my own, yet none, I believe, are chastised less; for, as those hounds that are guilty of an offence *are never pardoned;* so those that are innocent, being by this means less liable to be corrupted, *are never punished.*

by hallooing them on improperly, and to a wrong scent, have forced them to become so.

The first day of the season, I advise you to take out your pack where you have least riot, and where you are most sure to find; for, notwithstanding their steadiness at the end of the last season, long rest may have made them otherwise. If you have any hounds more vicious than the rest, they should be left at home a day or two, till the others are well in blood. Your people, without doubt, will be particularly cautious, at the beginning of the season, what hounds they halloo to: should they be encouraged on a wrong scent, it will be a great hurt to them.

The first day that you hunt in the forest, be equally cautious what hounds you take out. All should be steady from deer: you may afterwards put others to them, a few at a time. I have seen a pack draw steadily enough, and yet, when running hard, fall on a weak deer, and rest as contented as if they had killed their fox. These hounds were not chastised, though caught in the fact, but were suffered to draw on for a fresh fox: I would rather they had undergone severe discipline. The finding of another fox with them afterwards, might then have been of service; otherwise, in my opinion, it could only serve to encourage them in the vice, and make them worse and worse.

I must mention an instance of extraordinary sagacity in a fox-beagle that once belonged to the Duke of Cumberland. I entered him at hare, to which he was immediately so steady, that he would run nothing else. When a fox was found by the beagles, which sometimes happened, he would instantly come to the heels of the huntsman's horse. Some years afterwards I hunted fox *only*, and, though I parted with most of the others, I kept *him*. He went out constantly with the pack; and, as hares were scarce in the country that I then hunted, he did no hurt: the moment a fox was found, he came to the horse's heels. This continued some time, till, catching view of a fox that was sinking, he ran in with the rest, and was well blooded. He, from that time to the day of his death, was not only as steady a hound to *fox* as ever I knew, but became also our very best finder. I bred some buck-hounds from him, and they are remarkable for never changing from a hunted deer.

Your huntsman's weekly return is a very curious one: he is particularly happy in the spelling. The following letter, which is in the same style, may make you laugh, and is, perhaps, no unsuitable return for yours.

SIR.

Honored[1] . . . I have been out with the hounds this day to ayer the frost is very bad the hounds are all pure well at present and horses shepard has had a misfortin with his mare she hung harself with the holter and throd har self and broak har neck and frac tard skul so we was forsd to nock har In the head from your ever dutyful Humbel Sarvant

**** ******

Wednesday evening.

[1] The lines omitted were not upon the subject of hunting.

LETTER XIX

FINDING, by your last letter, that an early hour does not suit you, I will mention some particulars which may be of use to you when you hunt late:—An early hour is only necessary where covers are large and foxes scarce: where they are in plenty, you may hunt at any hour you please. When foxes are weak, by hunting late you have better chases: when they are strong, give me leave to tell you, you must hunt early, or you will not always kill them. I think, however, when you go out late, you should go immediately to the place where you are most likely to find, which generally speaking, is the cover that hounds have been least in. If the cover be large, you should draw only such parts of it as a fox is likely to kennel in: it is useless to draw any other at a late hour: besides though it be always right to find as soon as you can, yet it can never be so necessary as when the day is far advanced. If you do not find soon, a long and tiresome day is generally the consequence. Where the cover is thick, you should draw it as exactly as if you were trying for a hare, particularly if it be furzy; for when there is no drag, a fox, at a late hour, will lie till the hounds come close upon him. Having drawn one cover, let your huntsman stay for his hounds, and take them along with him to another: I have known hounds find a fox after the huntsman had left the cover. The whippers-in are not to be sparing of their whips or voices on this occasion, and are to come through the middle of the cover, to be certain that they leave no hounds behind.

A huntsman will complain of hounds, for staying behind in cover: it is a great fault, and makes the hound addicted to it of but little value; yet this fault frequently is occasioned by the huntsman's own mismanagement. Having drawn one cover, he hurries away to another, and leaves the whipper-in to bring on the hounds after him; but the whipper-in is seldom less desirous of getting forward than the huntsman; and, unless they come off easily, it is not often that he will give himself much concern about them.   Hounds also that are left too long at their walks, will acquire this trick from hunting by themselves, and are not easily broken of it.   Having said all that I can at present recollect of the duty of a whipper-in, I shall now proceed to give you a further account of *that* of a huntsman.   What has already been said on the subject of *drawing* and *casting*, related to the fox-chase described in a former Letter. Much, without doubt, is still left to say: and I will endeavour, as well as I am able, to supply the deficiency, by considering, first, in what manner he should draw; and, afterwards, how he should cast his hounds.

The fixing, a day or two before-hand, upon the cover in which you intend to hunt, is a great hindrance to sport in fox-hunting.   You, that have the whole country to yourself, and can hunt on either side of your house, as you please, should never (when you can help it) determine on your place of hunting till you see what the weather is likely to be.[1]   The most probable means to have good chases, it to choose your country according to the wind.

It will also require some consideration to place hounds to the greatest advantage, where foxes either are in great plenty, or very scarce.

Hounds that lie idle are always out of wind, and are easily fatigued.[2]   The first day you go out after a long frost, you cannot expect much sport; take, therefore, considerably more than your usual number of hounds, and throw them into the largest cover that you have: if any foxes be in the country, it is *there* that you will find them.   After once or twice going out in this manner, you should reduce your number.[3]

[1] When the scent lies badly, small covers, or those in which a fox cannot move unseen, are most favourable to hounds.   In such covers, good sportsmen will kill foxes in almost any weather.

[[2] Hounds cannot have too much exercise during a long frost, and if this is done thoroughly they will be neither out of wind nor easily fatigued when the thaw comes.]

[3] During a frost, hounds may be exercised on downs, or the turnpike roads; nor will it do any material injury to their feet.   Prevented from hunting, they should

Before a huntsman goes into the kennel to draft his hounds, let him determine within himself the number of hounds that it will be right to take out, as likewise the number of young hounds that he can venture in the country where he is going to hunt. Different countries may require different hounds: some may require more hounds than others. It is not an easy matter to draft hounds properly; nor can any expedition be made in it without some method.[1]

I seldom suffer many unsteady hounds to be taken out together; and when I do, I take care that none shall go with them but such as they cannot spoil.

When the place and time of meeting are fixed, every huntsman ought to be as exact to them as it is possible. On no account is he to be *before* the time; yet, on some occasions, it might be better, perhaps, for the diversion, were he permitted to be *after it*.[2] The course that your huntsman intends to take in drawing, ought also to be well understood before he leaves the kennel.

If your huntsman, without inconveniency, can begin drawing at the farthest cover down the wind, and so draw from cover to cover up the wind till you find, let him do it. It will have many advantages attending it: he will draw the same covers in half the time; your people cannot fail

be fed sparingly; and such as can do without flesh, should have none given them: a course of vegetables, sulphur, and thin meat, is the likeliest means to keep them healthy.

[1] No hound ought to be left at home, unless there be a reason for it; it is therefore that I say, great nicety is required to draft hounds *properly*. Many huntsmen, I believe, think it of no great consequence which they take out, and which they leave, provided they have the number requisite. A perfect knowledge in feeding and drafting hounds, are the two most essential parts of fox-hunting: good hounds will require but little assistance afterwards. By *feeding*, I mean the bringing the hound into the field in his highest vigour; by *drafting*, I particularly mean the taking out no unsteady hound, nor any that are not likely to be of service to the pack. When you intend to hunt two days following, it is then that the greatest nicety will be requisite to make the most of a small pack. Placing hounds to the greatest advantage, as mentioned page 148, may also be considered as a necessary part of fox-hunting.

Hounds that are intended to hunt the next day, and are drafted off into the hunting-kennel as soon as they are fed, should be let out again into the outer court in the evening: my hounds have generally some thin meat given them at this time, while the feeder cleans out their kennel. (*Vide* note, p. 30.) I have already said, that cleanliness is not less essential than food.

[2] When there is a white frost, for instance; at the going off of which the scent never lies.

of being in their proper places; you will have less difficulty in getting your hounds off; and, as the fox will most probably run the covers that have been already drawn, you are less likely to change.

If you have a string of small covers, and plenty of foxes in them, some caution may be necessary, to prevent your hounds from disturbing them all in one day. Never hunt your small covers till you have well rattled the large ones first; for, until the foxes be thinned and dispersed where they were in plenty, it must be bad policy to drive others there to increase the number. If you would thin your foxes you must throw off at the same cover as long as you can find a fox. If you come off with the first fox that breaks, you do not disturb the cover, and may expect to find there again the next day; but where they are scarce, you should never draw the same cover two days following.[1]

Judicious huntsmen will observe where foxes like best to lie. In chases and forests, where you have a great tract of cover to draw, such observation is necessary, or you will lose much time in finding. Generally speaking, I think they are fondest of such as lie high, and are dry and thick at bottom; such also as lie out of the wind, and such as are on the sunny side of hills.[2] The same cover where you find one fox, when it has remained quiet any time, will probably produce another.

It is to little purpose to draw hazel coppices at the time when nuts are gathering; furze-covers, or two or three years coppices, are then the only quiet places that a fox can kennel in: *they* also are disturbed when pheasant-shooting begins, and older covers are more likely. The season when foxes are most wild and strong, is about Christmas: a huntsman then must lose no time in drawing; he must draw up the wind, unless the cover be very large; in which case it may be better, perhaps, to cross it, giving the hounds a side-wind, lest he should be obliged to turn

[1 To find a good fox in a small covert it should have at least three weeks' rest.]

2 This must of course vary in different countries: a huntsman who has been used to a country, knows best where to find his game.

down the wind at last: in either case, let him draw as quietly as he can.

Young coppices, at this time of the year, are quite bare: the most likely places are, four or five-years coppices, and such as are furzy at bottom.

It is easy to perceive, by the account you give of your hounds, that they do not draw well; your huntsman, therefore, must be particularly attentive to them after a wet night. The best drawing hounds are shy of searching a cover when it is wet: yours, if care be not taken, will not go into it at all. Your huntsman should ride into the likeliest part of the cover; and, as it is probable there will be no drag, the closer he draws the better: he must not draw too much an end, but should cross the cover backwards and forwards, taking care, at the same time, to give his hounds as much the wind as possible.[1]

It is not often that you will see a pack perfectly steady where there is much riot, and yet draw well: some hounds will not exert themselves till others challenge, and are encouraged.[2]

I fear the many harriers that you have in your neighbourhood will be hurtful to your sport: by constantly disturbing the covers, they will make the foxes shy, and when the covers become thin, there will be but little chance of finding foxes in them: furze-covers are then the most likely places. Though I like not to see a huntsman to a pack of fox-hounds ever off his horse, yet, at a late hour, he should draw a furze-cover as slowly as if he were himself on foot. I am well convinced that huntsmen, by drawing in too great a hurry, leave foxes sometimes behind them. I once saw a remarkable instance of it with my own hounds: we had drawn (as we thought) a cover, which, in the whole, consisted of about ten acres; yet, whilst the huntsman was

---

[1] Hounds that are hunted constantly at an early hour, seldom, I think, draw well: they depend too much upon a drag, and it is not in the strongest part of the cover that they are accustomed to try for it.

[2] This relates to making hounds steady only, which always causes confusion, and interrupts drawing. When once a pack are become steady, they will be more likely to draw well than if they were not.

blowing his horn to get his hounds off, one young fox was halloo'd, and another was seen immediately after: it was a cover on the side of a hill, and the foxes had kennelled close together at an extremity of it, where no hound had been. Some huntsmen draw too quick, some too slow. The time of day, the behaviour of his hounds, and the covers that they are drawing, will direct an observing huntsman in the pace which he ought to go. When you try a furze-brake, let me give you one caution—never halloo a fox till you see that he is quite clear of it. When a fox is found in such places, hounds are sure to go off well with him; and it must be owing either to bad scent, bad hounds, bad management, or bad luck, if they fail to kill him afterwards.

It is usual, in most packs, to rate, as soon as a young hound challenges. Though young hounds are often wrong, yet, since it is not impossible that they may be sometimes right, is it not as well to have a little patience, in order to see whether any of the old ones will join, before anything is said to them? *Have-a-care!* is fully sufficient, till you are more certain that the hound is on a wrong scent. I mention this as a hint only: I am myself no enemy to a *rate*: I cannot think that a fox was ever lost, or a pack spoilt, by it: it is *improper encouragement* that I am afraid of most.

When a fox slinks from his kennel, gets a great way before the hounds, and you are obliged to hunt after him with a bad scent; if it be a country where foxes are in plenty, and you know where to find another, you had better do it.[1]

While hounds are drawing for a fox, let your people place themselves in such a manner, that he cannot go off unseen. I have known them lie in sheep's scrapes, on the sides of hills, and in small bushes, where huntsmen never think of looking for them; yet, when they hear a hound they generally shift their quarters, and make for closer covers. Gentlemen should take this necessary part of

[1] Yet, if this were practised often, it might make the hounds indifferent when upon a cold scent. Hounds should be made to believe they are to kill that game which they are first encouraged to pursue.

"under good command."

fox-hunting on themselves; for the whipper-in has other business to attend to.[1]

I approve not of long drags in large covers: they give too great an advantage to the fox; they give him a hint to make the best of his way; and he frequently will set off a long while before you. This may be prevented, by throwing your hounds into that part of the cover in which he is most likely to kennel: for want of this precaution, a fox sometimes gets so far the start of hounds, that they are not able to do anything with him afterwards. Also, when hounds first touch on a drag, some huntsmen are so careless, that, while they are going on with it the wrong way themselves, a single hound finds the fox, and is not caught any more by the pack, till he has lost him again.

Foxes are said to go down the wind to their kennel; but I believe they do not always observe that rule.

Huntsmen, while their hounds are drawing, or are at a fault, frequently make so much noise themselves, that they can hear nothing else: they should always have an ear to a halloo. I once saw an extraordinary instance of the want of it in my own huntsman, who was making so much noise with his hounds, which were then at fault, that a man halloo'd a long while before he heard him; and, when he did hear him, so little did he know whence the halloo came, that he rode two miles the wrong way, and lost the fox.

When hounds approach a cover which it is intended they should draw, and dash away towards it, whippers-in ride after them to stop them: it is too late, and they had better let them alone; it checks them in their drawing, and is of no kind of use: it will be soon enough to begin to rate when they have found, and hunt improper game. When a huntsman has his hounds under good command, and is attentive to them, they will not break off till he chooses that they should. When he goes by the side of a cover which he does not intend to draw, his whippers-in must be in their

---

[1] Upon these occasions, when you see two gentlemen *together*, you may reasonably conclude, that one of them, at least, knows nothing of the matter.

proper places; for if he should ride up to a cover with them unawed, uncontrolled; a cover where they have been used to find—they must be slack indeed, if they do not dash into it. It is, for that reason, better, not to come into a cover always the same way: hounds, by not knowing what is going forward, will be less likely to break off, and will draw more quietly. I have seen hounds so flashy, that they would break away from the huntsman as soon as they saw a cover; and I have seen the same hounds stop when they got to the cover-side, and not go into it. It is want of proper discipline which occasions faults like these. Hounds that are under such command, as never to leave their huntsman till he encourage them to do it, will then be so confident that they will not return to him again.

Were fox-hounds to stop, like stag-hounds, at the smack of a whip, they would not do their business the worse for it, and it would give you many advantages, very essential to your sport;—such as, when they have to wait under a cover-side; when they run riot; when they change scents; when a single hound is on before; and when a fox is headed back into a cover. Hounds that are not under good command, subject you to many inconveniencies; and you may, at times, be obliged to go out of your way, or be made to draw a cover against your will. A famous pack of hounds in my neighbourhood, I mean the late Lord C——n's, had no fault but what had its rise from bad management: nor is it possible to do any thing with a pack of fox-hounds, unless they be obedient: they should both love and fear the huntsman: they should fear him much, yet they should love him more. Without doubt, hounds would do more for the huntsman, if they loved him better. Dogs that are constantly with their masters, acquire a wonderful deal of penetration, and much may be done through the medium of their affections. I attribute the extraordinary sagacity of the buck-hound to the manner in which he is treated: he is the constant companion of his instructor and bene-factor; the man whom he was first taught to fear, and has since learned to love. Ought we to wonder that he should be obedient to him? Yet who can view without surprise, the hounds and the deer amusing themselves familiarly together upon the same lawn; living, as it were, in the most friendly intercourse; and know that a word from the keeper will dissolve the amity? The obedient dog, gentle when unprovoked, flies to the well-known summons: how changed from what he was! Roused from his peaceful state, and cheered by his master's voice, he is now urged on with a relentless fury, that only death can satisfy—the death of the *very deer* he is encouraged to pursue; and which the various scents that cross him in his way cannot tempt him to forsake. The business of the day over, see him follow, careless and contented, his master's steps, to repose upon the same lawn where the frightened deer again return, and are again indebted to *his* courtesy for their wonted pasture —wonderful proofs of obedience, sagacity, and penetration! The many learned dogs and learned horses, that so frequently appear and astonish the vulgar, sufficiently evince what education is capable of; and it is to education that I must chiefly attribute the superior excellence of the buck-hound, since I have seen high-bred fox-hounds do the same, under the same good masters. But, to return to my subject.

Young foxes that have been much disturbed, will lie at ground. I once found seven or eight in a cover, where, the next day, I could not find one; not were they to be found elsewhere: the earths, at such times, should be stopt three or four hours before day, or you will find no foxes.

The first day you hunt a cover that is full of foxes, and you want blood, let them not be checked back into the cover[1] (which is the usual practice at such times), but let some of them get off: if you do not, what with continual changing, and sometimes running the heel, it is probable

[1 This, it may be presumed, refers to cub-hunting, and authorities on the subject hold different opinions. What Beckford advises seems to be the best plan, that is, to let all go except the last, and hold him up until he is killed. Another litter may then be disturbed and the young hounds do not get disheartened by hunting on foiled ground. The practice of holding all up often results in the death of an old fox who would have given good sport later in the season.]

that you will not kill any. Another precaution, I think, may be also necessary—that is, to stop such earths only as you cannot dig. If some foxes should go to ground, it will be as well; and if you should be in want of blood at last, you will then know where to get it.

It is usual, when people are not certain of the steadiness of their hounds from deer, to find a fox in an adjacent cover, that they may be on their right scent when they come where deer are. I have my doubts of the propriety of this proceeding. If hounds have not been well awed from deer, it is not fit that they should come among them; but, if hounds be tolerably steady, I would rather find a fox with them among deer, than bring them afterwards into covers where deer are. By drawing amongst them, they will, in some degree, be awed from the scent, and possibly may stick to the fox when he is found; but should unsteady hounds, when high on their mettle, run into a cover where deer are in plenty, there is no doubt that, the first check they come to, they will all fall off. I always have found hounds most inclined to riot when most upon their mettle: such as are given to sheep will then kill sheep, and such as are not quite steady from deer, will then be most likely to break off after them. When hounds are encouraged on a scent, if they lose that scent, it is then that an unsteady hound is ready for any kind of mischief.

I have already said, that a huntsman ought never to flog a hound. When a riotous hound, conscious of his offence, may escape from the whipper-in, and fly to the huntsman, you will see him put his whole pack into confusion, by endeavouring to chastise him himself. This is the height of absurdity. Instead of flogging the hound, he ought to encourage him, who should always have some place to fly to for protection. If the offence be a bad one, let him get off his horse, and couple up the dog, leaving him to be chastised by the whipper-in, after he himself is gone on with the pack; the punishment over, let him again encourage the hound to come to him. Hounds that are riotous in cover, and will not come off readily to the huntsman's halloo, should be flogged in the cover, rather than out of it:—treated in this manner, you will not find any difficulty in getting your hounds off; otherwise, they will soon find that the cover will save them; from whence they will have more sense, when they have committed an offence, than to come to receive punishment. A favourite hound, that has acquired a habit of staying back in large covers, had better not be taken into them.

I am more particular than I otherwise should have been, upon a supposition that your hounds draw ill; however, you need not observe all the cautions that I have given, unless your hounds require them.

Some art may be necessary, to make the most of the country that you hunt. I would advise you not to draw the covers near your house, while you can find elsewhere: it will make them certain places to find in when you go out late, or may otherwise be in want of them: for the same reason, I would advise you not to hunt those covers late in the season: they should not be much disturbed after Christmas: foxes will then resort to them; will breed there; and you can preserve them with little trouble. This relates to the good management of a pack of hounds, which is a business distinct from hunting them.[1]

Though a huntsman ought to be as silent as possible at going into a cover,[2] he cannot be too noisy at coming out of it again; and, if at any time he should turn back suddenly, let him give as much notice of it as he can to his hounds, or he will leave many behind him; and, should he turn down the wind, he may see no more of them.

I should be sorry that the silence of my huntsman should proceed from either of the following causes:—A huntsman that I once knew (who, by the bye, I believe, is at this time

---

[1] Breeding, feeding, steadying, drafting, and placing, are the essential parts of fox-hunting; when these are properly attended to, the hounds will require but little assistance from the huntsman, whose chief business then will be to keep with them, say little, and do nothing.

[2 In drawing large woodlands a huntsman should not be too sparing of his voice, for unless the hounds can hear him every now and again they will not spread wide enough, will be listening for him instead of looking for a fox.]

a drummer in a marching regiment) went out one morning so very drunk, that he got off his horse in the midst of a thick cover, laid himself down, and went to sleep: he was lost; nobody knew what was become of him; and he was at last found in the situation that I have just described. He had, however, great good luck on his side; for, at the very instant he was found, a fox was halloo'd; upon which he mounted his horse, rode desperately, killed his fox handsomely, and was forgiven.

I remember another huntsman silent from a different cause: this was a sulky one. Things did not go on to please him: he therefore alighted from his horse in the middle of a wood, and, as quietly as he could, collected his hounds about him: he then took an opportunity, when the coast was clear, to set off silently, and by himself, for another cover. However, his master, who knew his tricks, sent others after him to bring him back: they found him running a fox most merrily; and, to his great astonishment, they stopped the hounds, and made him go back along with them. This fellow had often been severely beaten, but was stubborn and sulky to the last.

To give you an idea, before I quit this subject, how little some people know of fox-hunting, I must tell you, that, not long ago, a gentleman asked me, If I did not send people out *the day before*, to find where the foxes lay?

What relates to the casting of hounds, shall be the subject of my next Letter.

LETTER XX

IN my seventeenth Letter, I gave you the opinion of my friend ****—*"that a pack of fox-hounds, if left entirely to themselves, would never lose a fox."* I am always sorry when I differ from that gentleman in anything; yet I am so far from thinking they never would lose a fox, that I doubt much if they would ever kill one. There are times when hounds should be helped, and at all times they must be kept forward. Hounds will naturally tie on a cold scent, when stopped by sheep, or other impediments; and, when they are no longer able to get forward, will oftentimes hunt the old scent back again, if they find that they can hunt no other. It is the judicious encouraging of hounds to hunt, when they cannot run, and the preventing them from losing time by hunting too much when they might run, that distinguishes a good sportsman from a bad one.[1] Hounds that have been well taught, will cast forward to a hedge, of their own accord; but you may assure yourself that this excellence is never acquired by such as are left entirely to themselves. To suffer a pack of fox-hounds to hunt through a flock of sheep, when it is easy to make a regular cast round them, is, in my judgment, very unnecessary; it is wilfully losing time to no purpose. I have, indeed, been told, that hounds at no time should be taken off their noses: I shall only say, in answer to this, that a fox-hound who will not bear lifting, is not worth the keeping; and, I will venture to say, it should be made part of his education.

Though I like to see fox-hounds cast wide and forward, and dislike to see them pick a cold scent through flocks of sheep to no purpose; yet I must beg leave to observe, that I dislike still more to see that unaccountable hurry, which huntsmen will sometimes put themselves into the

---

[1] In hunting a pack of hounds, a proper medium should be observed; for though too much help will make them slack, too little will make them tie on the scent, and hunt back the heel.

moment their hounds are at fault. Time ought always to be allowed them to make their own cast; and, if a huntsman be judicious, he will take that opportunity to consider what part he himself has next to act: but, instead of this, I have seen hounds hurried away the very instant they came to a fault; a wide cast made; and the hounds at last brought back again to the very place from whence they were so abruptly taken; and where, if the huntsman could have had a minute's patience, they would have hit off the scent themselves. It is always great impertinence in a huntsman, to pretend to make *his* cast before the hounds have made *theirs*. Prudence should direct him to encourage, and I may say, humour, his hounds, in the cast they seem inclined to make, and either to stand still, or trot round with them, as circumstances may require.

I have seen huntsmen make their cast on bad ground, when they might as easily have made it on good; I have seen them suffer their hounds to try in the midst of a flock of sheep, when there was a hedge near, where they might have been sure to take the scent; and I have seen a cast made with every hound at their horse's heels. When a hound tries for the scent, his nose is to the ground; when a huntsman makes a cast, his eye should be on his hounds; and when he sees them spread wide, and try as they ought, his cast may then be quick.

When hounds are at fault, and the huntsman halloos them off the line of the scent, the whippers-in smacking their whips, and rating them after him; if he should trot away with them, may they not think that the business of the day is over? Hounds never, in my opinion (unless in particular cases, or when you go to a halloo), should be taken entirely off their noses; but, when lifted, should be constantly made to try as they go. Some huntsmen have a dull, stupid way of speaking to their hounds: at these times little should be said, and that should have both meaning and expression in it.

When your huntsman makes a cast, I hope he makes it perfect one way, before he tries another; as much time is lost in going backwards and forwards. You will see huntsmen, when a forward cast does not succeed, come slowly back again: they should return as fast as they can.

When hounds are at fault, and it is probable that the fox has headed back, your cast forward should be short and quick; for the scent is then likely to be behind you: too obstinate a perseverance forward, has been the loss of many foxes. In heathy countries, if there be many roads, foxes will always run them in dry weather: when hounds, therefore, over-run the scent, if your huntsman return to the first cross-road, he probably will hit off the scent again.

In large covers where there are several roads; in bad scenting days, when these roads are dry; or, after a thaw, when they carry—it is necessary that your huntsman should be near to his hounds, to help them, and hold them forward. Foxes will run the roads at these times, and hounds cannot always own the scent. When they are at fault on a dry road, let not your huntsman turn back too soon; let him not stop, till he can be certain that the fox is not gone on. The hounds should try on both sides the road at once: if he perceive that they try on one side only, let him try the other on his return.

When hounds are running in cover, if a huntsman should see a fox come into a road, and cannot see which way he turns afterwards, let him stand still, and say nothing: if he ride on, he must ride over the scent; and if he encourage the hounds, they most probably would run beyond it.

Wide ridings cut through large woods, render them less exceptionable to sportsmen than they otherwise might be; yet I do not think that they are of service to hounds: they are taught to shuffle; and, the fox being frequently headed back, they are put to many faults: the roads are foiled by the horses, and the hounds often interrupted by the horsemen: such ridings only are advantageous, as enable the servants belonging to the hounds to get to them.

If a fox should run up the wind when first found, and afterwards turn, he will seldom, if ever, turn again. The

observation may not only be of use to your huntsman
in his cast, but may be of use to yourself, if you should
lose the hounds.

When you are pursuing a fox over a country, the scent
being bad, and the fox a long way before, without ever
having been pressed; if his point should be for strong earths
that are open, or for large covers where game is in plenty—
it may be acting wisely to take off the hounds at the first
fault; for the fox will go many miles to your one, and
probably will run you out of all scent; and, if he should
not, you will be likely to change at the first cover you come
into. When a fox has been hard pressed, you have already
my opinion, that he never should be given up.

When you would recover a hunted fox, and have no
longer scent to hunt him by, a long cast to the first cover
which he seems to point for, is the only resource that you
have left. Get thither as fast as you can, and then let your
hounds try as slowly and as quietly as possible. If hunting
after him be hopeless, and a long cast do not succeed, you
had better give him up. I need not remind you, when the
scent lies badly, and you find it impossible for hounds to
run, that you had better return home; since the next day
may be more favourable. It surely is a great fault in a
huntsman to persevere in bad weather, when hounds
cannot run, and when there is not a probability of killing
a fox.[1] Some there are, who, after they have lost one fox,
for want of scent to hunt him by, will find another: this
makes their hounds slack, and sometimes vicious: it also
disturbs the covers to no purpose. Some sportsmen are
more lucky in their days than others. If you hunt every
other day, it is possible they may be all bad, and the intermediate days all good: an indifferent pack, therefore, by
hunting on good days, may kill foxes, without any merit:
and a good pack, notwithstanding all their exertion, may
lose foxes which they deserved to kill. Had I a sufficiency

---

[1] Though I would not go out on a very windy day, yet a bad-scenting day is
sometimes of service to a pack of fox-hounds: they acquire patience from it, and
method of hunting.

of hounds, I would hunt on every good day, and never on a bad one.[1]

A perfect knowledge of his country, certainly, is a great help to a huntsman: if yours, as yet, should have it not, great allowance ought to be made.   The trotting away with hounds, to make a long and knowing cast, is a privilege which a new huntsman cannot pretend to: an experienced one may safely say, A fox has made for such a cover—when he has known, perhaps, that nine out of ten, with the wind in the same quarter, have constantly gone thither.

In a country where there are large earths, a fox that knows the country, and tries any of them, seldom fails to try the rest.   A huntsman may take advantage of this: they are certain casts, and may help him to get nearer to his fox.

Great caution is necessary when a fox runs into a village: if he be halloo'd there, get forward as fast as you can. Foxes, when tired, will lie down anywhere, and are often lost by it.   A wide cast is not the best to recover a tired fox with tired hounds: they should hunt him out, inch by inch, though they are ever so long about it, for the reason I have just given, *that he will lie down anywhere.*

In chases and forests, where high fences are made to preserve the coppices, I like to see a huntsman put only a few hounds over, enough to carry on the scent, and get forward with the rest: it is a proof that he knows his business.

A huntsman must take care, where foxes are in plenty, lest he should run the heel; for it frequently happens, that hounds can run the wrong way of the scent better than they can the right, when one is up the wind, and the other down.

Fox-hunters, I think, are never guilty of the fault of

[1] On windy days, or such as are not likely to afford any scent for hounds, it is better, I think, to send them to be exercised on the turnpike-road; it will do them less harm than hunting with them might do; and more good than if they were to remain confined in their kennel; for though nothing makes hounds so handy as taking them out often, nothing inclines them so much to riot, as taking them out *to hunt* when there is little or no scent, and particularly on windy days, when they cannot hear one another.

trying up the wind before they have tried down: I have known them lose foxes, rather than condescend to try up the wind at all.

When a huntsman hears a halloo, and has five or six couple of hounds along with him, the pack not running, let him get forward with those which he has: when they are on the scent, the others will soon join them.

Let him lift his tail hounds, and get them forward *after the rest*: it can do no hurt: but let him be cautious in lifting any hounds, to get them forward *before the rest*: it always is dangerous, and foxes are sometimes lost by it.

When a fox runs his foil in cover, if you suffer all your hounds to hunt on the line of him, they will foil the ground, and tire themselves to little purpose. I have before told you that your huntsman, at such a time, may stop the tail hounds, and throw them in at head: I am almost inclined to say it is the only time when it should be done. While hounds run straight it cannot be of any use; for they will get on faster with the scent than they would without it.

When hounds are hunting a cold scent, and point towards a cover, let a whipper-in get forward to the opposite side of it: should the fox break before the hounds reach the cover, stop them, and get them nearer to him.

When a fox persists in running in a strong cover, lies down often behind the hounds, and they are slack in hunting him, let the huntsman get into the cover to them: it may make the fox break; it may keep him off his foil; or may prevent the hounds from giving him up.

It is not often that slow huntsmen kill many foxes: they are a check upon their hounds, which seldom kill a fox but with a high scent, when it is out of their power to prevent it. What avails it, to be told which way the fox is gone, when he is so far before that you cannot hunt him? A Newmarket boy, with a good understanding and a good voice, might be preferable, perhaps, to an indifferent and slack huntsman; he would press on his hounds while the scent was good, and the foxes that he killed he would kill handsomely. A perfect knowledge of the intricacies of

LIBRARY
BISHOP BURTON COLLEGE
BEVERLEY HU17 8QG

hunting is chiefly of use to slow huntsmen, and bad hounds; since they more often stand in need of it. Activity is the first requisite in a huntsman to a pack of fox-hounds: a want of it, no judgment can make amends for; while the most difficult of all his undertakings is the distinguishing between different scents, and knowing with any certainty the scent of his hunted fox. Much speculation is here required—the length of time that hounds remain at fault; difference of ground; change of weather;—all these contribute to increase the difficulty, and require a nicety of judgment, and a precision, much above the comprehension of most huntsmen.

When hounds are at fault, and cannot make it out of themselves, let the first cast be quick: the scent is then good; nor are the hounds likely to go over it:—as the scent gets worse, the cast should be slower, and be more cautiously made. This is an essential part of hunting, and which, I am sorry to say, few huntsmen attend to. I wish they would remember the following rules, viz. that, with a good scent, their cast should be *quick*; with a bad scent, *slow*; and that, when their hounds are picking along a cold scent, *they are not to cast them at all.*

When hounds are at fault, and staring about, trusting entirely to their eyes and their ears, the making a cast with them, I apprehend, would be to little purpose. The likeliest place for them to find the scent, is where they left it; and when the fault is evidently in the dog, a forward cast is least likely to recover the scent.[1]

When hounds are making a regular cast, trying for the scent as they go, suffer not your huntsman to say a word to them: it cannot do any good, and probably may make them go over the scent: nor should you suffer either the whip or the voice of your whipper-in to be now heard; his usual roughness and severity would ill suit the stillness and gentleness which are required at a time like this.

When hounds come to a check, a huntsman should

[1] Hounds know where they left the scent, and, if let alone, will try to recover it. Impatience in the huntsman, at such times. seldom fails, in the end, to spoil the hounds.

observe the tail hounds: they are least likely to over-run the scent; and he may see by them how far they brought it: in most packs there are some hounds that will show the point of the fox, and, if attended to, will direct his cast. When such hounds follow slowly and unwillingly, he may be certain that the rest of the pack are running without a scent.

When he casts his hounds, let him not cast wide, without reason; for, of course, it will take more time. Huntsmen, in general, keep too forward in their casts; or, as a sailor would say, keep too long *on one tack*: they should endeavour to hit off the scent, by crossing the line of it:—*two parallel lines, you know, can never meet.*[1]

When he goes to a halloo, let him be careful, lest his hounds run the heel, as much time is lost by it. I once saw this mistake made by a famous huntsman:—after we had left a cover which we had been drawing, a disturbed fox was seen to go into it: he was halloo'd, and we returned. The huntsman, who never inquired *where* the fox was seen, or on *which side* of the cover he entered, threw his hounds in at random, and, as it happened, on the opposite side: they immediately took the heel of him, broke cover, and hunted the scent back to his very kennel.

Different countries require different casts. Such huntsmen as have been used to a woodland and inclosed country, I have seen lose time in an open country, where wide casts are always necessary.

When you want to cast round a flock of sheep, the whipper-in ought to drive them the other way, lest they should keep running on before you.

A fox seldom goes over or under a *gate*, when he can avoid it.

Huntsmen are frequently very conceited, and very obstinate. Oftentimes have I seen them, when their hounds came to a check, turn directly back, on seeing hounds at head which they had no opinion of. They *supposed* the fox was gone another way; in which case, Mr. Bayes's remark in

---

[1] By attending to this, a huntsman cannot fail to make a good cast; for, if he observe the point of the fox, he may always cross upon the scent of him.

the *Rehearsal* always occurs to me, *"that, if he should not, what then becomes of their suppose."* Better, surely, would it be, to make a short cast forward first; they then might be *certain* the hounds were wrong, and, of course, could make their own cast with greater confidence:—the advantage, next to that of knowing whither the fox *is* gone, is that of knowing with certainty whither he is *not*.

Most huntsmen like to have all their hounds turned after them when they make a cast: I wonder not at them for it, but I am always sorry when I see it done; for, till I find a huntsman that is infallible, I shall continue to think the more my hounds spread the better: as long as they are within sight or hearing, it is sufficient. Many a time have I seen an obstinate hound hit off the scent, when an obstinate huntsman, by casting the wrong way, has done all in his power to prevent it. Two foxes I remember to have seen killed in one day by skirting hounds, while the huntsman was making his cast the contrary way.

When hounds, running in cover, come into a road, and horses are on before, let the huntsman hold them quickly on beyond where the horses have been, trying the opposite side as he goes along:—should the horsemen have been long enough there to have headed back the fox, let them then try back. Condemn me not for suffering hounds *to try back* when the fox *has been headed back*: I recommend it at no other time.

When your hounds divide into many parts, you had better go off with the first fox that breaks. The ground will soon get tainted; nor will hounds like a cover where they are often changing.

If a cover be very large, and you have many scents, be not in a hurry to get your hounds together; if your pack be numerous, let them run separate, only taking care that none get away entirely from the rest:—by this means many foxes will be equally distressed; the hounds will get together at last; and one fox, at the least, you may expect to kill.

The heading a fox back at first, if the cover be not a large one, is oftentimes of service to hounds, as he will not stop, and cannot go off unseen. When a fox has been hard-run, I have known it turn out otherwise; and hounds that would easily have killed him out of the cover, have left him in it.

If it be not your intention that a fox should break, you should prevent him, I think, as much as you can, from coming at all out of the cover; for, though you should head him back afterwards, it most probably would put the hounds to a fault. When a pack of fox-hounds once leave a cover after their game, they do not readily return to it again.

When a fox has been often headed back on one side of a cover, and a huntsman knows there is not anybody on the other side to halloo him, the first fault his hounds come to, let him cast that way, lest the fox should be gone off; and, if he be still in the cover, he may still recover him.

Suffer not your huntsman to take out a lame hound. If any be tender-footed, he will tell you, perhaps, that they will not mind it when they are out: probably they may not; but how will they be on the next day? A hound not in condition to run, cannot be of much service to the pack; and the taking him out at that time may occasion him a long confinement afterwards: put it not to the trial. Should any fall lame while they are out, leave them at the first house that you come to.

I have seen huntsmen hunt their young blood in couples. Let me beg of you not to suffer it. I know you would be sorry to see your hounds hanging across a hedge, grinning at each other, perhaps in the very agonies of death: yet it is an accident that often has happened; and it is an accident so likely to happen, that I am surprised any man of common sense will run the risk of it. If necessary, I would much rather they should be held in couples at the cover-side, till the fox be found.

The two principal things which a huntsman has to attend to, are the keeping of his hounds *healthy* and *steady*. The first is attained by cleanliness and proper food; the latter, by putting as seldom as possible any unsteady ones among them.

At the beginning of the season, let him be attentive to get his hounds well in blood. As the season advances, and foxes become stout, attention then should be given to keeping them as vigorous as possible. It is a great fault, when hounds are suffered to become too high in flesh at the beginning of the season, or too low afterwards.

When a fox is lost, the huntsman, on his return home, should examine into his *own conduct*, and endeavour to find in what he might have done better: he may, by this means, make the very loss of a fox of use to him.

Old tieing hounds, and a hare-hunter turned fox-hunter, are both as contrary to the true spirit of fox-hunting as anything could possibly be:—one is continually bringing the pack back again; the other as constantly does his best to prevent them from getting forward. The natural prejudices of mankind are such, that a man seldom alters his style of hunting, let him pursue what game he may; besides, it may be constitutional, as he is himself slow or active, dull or lively, patient or impatient. It is for that reason that I object to a hare-hunter for a pack of fox-hounds; for the same ideas of hunting will most probably stick by him as long as he lives.

Your huntsman is an old man; should he have been working hard all his life on wrong principles, he may be now incorrigible.

Sometimes you will meet with a good kennel-huntsman; sometimes an active and judicious one in the field: some are clever at finding a fox, others are better after he is found; while perfection in a huntsman, like perfection in anything else, is scarcely ever to be met with:—there are not only good, bad, and indifferent huntsmen, but there are, perhaps, a few others, who being, as it were, of a different species, should be classed apart;—I mean such as have *real genius*. It is this peculiar excellence, which I told you, in a former Letter, I would rather wish my first whipper-in to be possessed of than my huntsman; and one reason, among others, is, that he, I think, would have more opportunities of exercising it.

The keeping of hounds clean and healthy, and bringing them into the field in their fullest vigour, is the excellence of a good kennel-huntsman;[1] if, besides this, he make his hounds both love and fear him; if he be active, and press them on while the scent is good, always aiming to keep as near the fox as he can; if, when his hounds are at fault, he makes his cast with judgment, not casting the wrong way first, and only blundering upon the right at last, as many do; if, added to this, he be patient and persevering, never giving up a fox while there remains a chance of killing him —he then is a perfect huntsman.

Did I not know your love of this diversion, I should think, by this time, that I must have tired you completely. You are not singular, however, in your partiality to it; for, to show you the effect which fox-hunting has on those who are really fond of it, I must tell you what happened to me not long ago:—My hounds, in running a fox, crossed the great Western road, where I met a gentleman travelling on horseback, his servant, with a portmanteau, following him. He no sooner saw the hounds, than he rode up to me with the greatest eagerness. *"Sir,"* said he, *"are you after a fox?"* When I told him that we were, he immediately stuck spurs to his horse, took a monstrous leap, and never quitted us any more till the fox was killed. I suppose, had I said that we were after a *hare*, my gentleman would have pursued his journey.

---

[1] To make the most of a pack of hounds, and bring them into the field in their fullest vigour, is an excellence that huntsmen are very deficient in. To obtain a knowledge of the different constitutions of so many animals, requires more discernment than most of them are endowed with. To apply that knowledge, by making separate drafts when they feed them, would also take up more time than they choose to bestow: hence it is that they generally are fed all together:—they may be well fed, but I much doubt whether they are ever made the most of; such as require to be fed *a little at a time*, and *often*, must, I believe, be contented with *a little only*. Few huntsmen seem fond of their hounds:[2] one reason of it, perhaps, may be, that they are paid for looking after them.

[2] Beckford must have been singularly unfortunate in his huntsmen, or the breed has altered very much since that date, It would be very difficult now to find a huntsman who was not devoted to his hounds, and it always seems rather cruel, when a change is made, that the man should have to part with his four-footed friends.]

YOUR huntsman, you say, has hunted a pack of harriers: it might have been better, perhaps, had he never seen one; since fox-hunting and hare-hunting differ almost in every particular;—so much, that I think it might not be an improper negative definition of fox-hunting to say, it is, of *all* hunting, *that* which resembles hare-hunting the least. A good huntsman to a pack of harriers, seldom succeeds in fox-hunting:—like old hounds, they dwell upon the scent, and cannot get forward; nor do they ever make a bold cast; so much are they afraid of leaving the scent behind them. Hence it is, that they poke about, and try the same place ten times over, rather than leave it; and, when they do, are totally at a loss which way to go, for want of knowing the nature of the animal they are in pursuit of. As hare-hounds should scarcely ever be cast, halloo'd, or taken off their noses, hare-hunters are too apt to hunt their fox-hounds in the same manner; but it will not do; nor could it please you if it would. Take away the spirit of fox-hunting, and it is no longer fox-hunting: it is stale small-beer compared to brisk champagne. You would also find in it more fatigue than pleasure. It is said, *there is a pleasure in being mad, which only madmen know*; and it is the enthusiasm, I believe, of fox-hunting, that is its best support: strip it of that, and you had better leave it quite alone.

The hounds themselves also differ in their manner of hunting. The beagle, who has always his nose to the ground, will puzzle an hour on one spot, sooner than leave the scent; while the fox-hound, full of life and spirit, is always dashing and trying forward:—a high-bred fox-hound, therefore shows himself to most advantage when foxes are at their strongest, and run an end. A pack of harriers will kill *a cub* better, perhaps, than a pack of fox-hounds; but, when foxes are strong, they have not the method of getting on with the scent which fox-hounds have, and generally tire themselves before the fox. To kill foxes, when they are strong, hounds must run, as well as hunt: besides, catching a fox by hard running, is always preferred, in the opinion of a fox-hunter.[1] Much depends on the style in which it is done; and I think, without being sophistical, a distinction might be made betwixt hunting a fox and fox-hunting. Two hackneys become not racers by running round a course: nor does the mere hunting of a fox change the nature of the harrier. I have also seen a hare hunted by high-bred fox-hounds; yet, I confess to you, it gave me not the least idea of what hare-hunting ought to be. Certain ideas are necessarily annexed to certain words—this is the use of language—and when a fox-hound is mentioned, I should expect not only a particular kind of hound, as to make, size, and strength (by which the fox-hound is easy to be distinguished); but I should also expect by fox-hunting, a lively, animated, and eager pursuit, as the very essence of it.[2] Eagerness and impetuosity are such essential parts of this diversion, that I am never more surprised than when I see a fox-hunter without them. One *hold hard*, or reproof, *unnecessarily* given, would chill me more than a north-east wind; it would damp my spirits, and send me home. The enthusiasm of a fox-hunter should not be checked in its career; for it is the very life and soul of fox-hunting.[3] If it be the eagerness with which you pursue your game that makes the chief pleasure of the chase, fox-hunting surely should afford the greatest degree of it; since you pursue no animal with the same eagerness that you pursue a fox.

Knowing your partiality to hounds that run in a good style, I advise you to observe strictly your own, when a fox

[1 A capital definition of fox-hunting, and yet we often see a huntsman in these days hunt a fox as he would a hare. This method may occasionally result in the death of a fox after many weary hours, but, as Beckford says, it is not fox-hunting.]

[2 The six following lines may have a dangerous tendency. Only a good sportsman can know when a reproof is given *unnecessarily*, and only a bad one will be deserving of reproof. This passage, therefore, should be compared with pages 100, 127, 129, 138, where the meaning of the author is very clearly expressed.

[3 Masters should read this sentence, for they may often spoil a good sportsman's day by speaking harshly, and thereby chilling that enthusiasm which Beckford truly says is the life and soul of the sport. Strong language rarely does any good, for to the sensitive and those who are accidentally in the wrong, it is too severe, whilst to hardened offenders and those who hunt only for the ride, it makes no impression whatever.]

is sinking in a strong cover: *that* is the time to see the true spirit of a fox-hound. If they spread not the cover, but run tamely on the line of one another, I shall fear it is a sort that will not please you long. A fox-hound that has not spirit and ambition to get forward at a time like this, is at no other likely to do much good.

You mention, in your last Letter, pretty hounds: certainly I should not pretend to criticise others, who am so incorrect myself; yet, with your leave, I think I can set you right in that particular. Pretty is an epithet improperly applied to a fox-hound: we call a fox-hound handsome, when he is strong, bony, of a proper size, and of exact symmetry; and fitness is made essential to beauty. A beagle may be pretty; but, according to my idea of the word, a fox-hound cannot: but, as it is not to be supposed that you will keep a pack of fox-hounds for the pleasure of looking at them, without doubt, you will think goodness more necessary than beauty. Should you be ambitious to have a handsome pack of hounds, on no account ought you to enter an ugly dog, lest you be tempted to keep him afterwards.

I once heard an old sportsman say, that he thought a fox, to show sport, should run four hours at least; and I suppose he did not care how slow his hounds went after him. This idea, however, is not conceived in the true spirit of fox-hunting—which is not to walk down a fox, or starve him to death; but to keep close at him, and kill him as soon as you can. I am convinced that a fox-hound may hunt too much: if tender-nosed, and not over-hurried, he will always hunt enough; whilst the highest-bred hounds may be made to tie upon the scent, by improper management.[1]

It is youth, and good spirits, which suit best with fox-hunting: slackness in the men occasions slackness in the hounds; and one may see, by the manner in which hounds hunt, what kind of men they have been accustomed to. The speediest hounds may, by degrees, be rendered slow; and it is impossible for the best to do their business as they

---

[1] It more frequently is owing either to want of patience, or want of mettle, than to want of nose, that a hound does not hunt well.

"followed with life
    and spirit"

ought, unless followed with life and spirit. Men who are slack themselves, will be always afraid of hurrying their hounds too much; and, by carrying this humour too far, will commit a fault which has nothing to excuse it. The best method to hunt a fox, they say, is never, upon any account, to cast the hounds; but, on the contrary, to let them tie upon the scent as long as they will, and that they will hit it off at last.   I agree with them partly: it certainly must be the best method *to hunt a fox*; for, by this means, you may hunt him from morning till night; and, if you have the luck to find him, may hunt him again the next day: the likeliest method, however, to kill him, is to take every advantage of him that you can.

All hounds go fast enough with a good scent; but it is the particular excellence of a fox-hound, when rightly managed, to get on faster with an indifferent scent than any other hound:[1] it is the business of a huntsman to encourage this; *and here, most probably, the hare-hunter will fail.* He has been used to take his time; he has enjoyed a cold scent, like a southern hound; and has sitten patiently upon his horse, to see his hounds hunt. It is, to be sure, very pretty to see; and, when you consider that the hare is all the time, perhaps, within a few yards of you, and may leap up the next minute, you are perfectly contented with what you are about: but it is not so in fox-hunting: every minute that you lose is precious, and increases your difficulties; and while you are standing still, the fox is running miles.   It is a satisfaction to a hare-hunter to be told where his game was seen, though a long while before; but it is melancholy news to a fox-hunter, whose game is not likely to stop. I believe I mentioned to you, in a former Letter on hare-hunting, a great fault which I had observed in some harriers, from being let alone too much—that of *running back the heel.* I have seen a pack of high-bred fox-hounds do the same, for the same reasons.

When hounds flag, from frequent changes, and a long

---

[1] It is a quick method of hunting, that I mostly value in any hound: such as are possessed of it, are seldom long off the scent: it is the reverse of slackness.

day, it is necessary for a huntsman to animate them as much as he can: he must keep them forward, and press them on; for it is not likely, in this case, that they should over-run the scent. At these times the whole work is generally done by a few hounds, and he should keep close to them. *Here I also fear that the hare-hunter will fail.*[1] If they come to a long fault, it is over, and you had better then go home.

The many chances that are against you in fox-hunting: the changing frequently; the heading of the foxes; their being coursed by sheep-dogs; long faults; cold hunting; and the dying away of the scent; make it necessary to keep always as near to the fox as you can; which should be the first and invariable principle of fox-hunting. Long days do great hurt to a pack of fox-hounds. I set out one day last winter from the kennel at half-past seven, and returned home a quarter before eight at night, the hounds running hard the greatest part of the time: the huntsman killed one horse and tired another, and the hounds did not recover for more than a week:[2] we took them off at last, when they were running with a better scent than they had had the whole day. I also remember, after it was quite dark, to have heard a better view-halloo from *an owl*, than I ever heard from a sportsman in my life, though I hope that I shall never hear such another. A long day, nevertheless, *once* or *twice* in a season, is of use to a huntsman: it shows the real goodness and stoutness of his hounds.

When long days happen to hounds that are low in

[1] It is at a time like this that good sportsmen may be of great service to hounds: it is the only time when they want encouragement; and it is (I am sorry to say) almost the only time when they do not receive it. Those who ride too forward in the morning, will, in the evening, perhaps, be too far behind, and thereby lose an opportunity that is offered them of making some amends for the mischiefs they have already done. When hounds flag from frequent changes, and the hunts-man's horse sinks under the fatigue of a tiresome day, then it is that sportsmen may assist them. Such as know the hounds, should then ride up to them: they should endeavour, by great encouragement, to keep them *running*, and get those forward that may be behind; for when hounds that are tired once come to *hunting*, they tie upon the scent, and, by losing time, lose every chance they had of killing the fox: great encouragement, and proper and timely assistance, only can prevent it.

[2] Hounds, after every hard day, should have two clear days to rest: it does them less hurt to hunt two days following, when their work is easy, than to hunt, before they may be perfectly recovered, after having been hard-run.

flesh, nothing will get them up again so effectually as rest: it is for this reason, hounds, that are kept constantly hunted, ought always to be, as sportsmen call it, *above their work*. If your hounds, either from accident or inattention, should ever be in the low condition here alluded to, be not impatient to get them out of it: should you feed them high with *flesh*, the mange, most probably, would be the immediate consequence of it: it is rest, and wholesome meat, that will recover them best. It will surprise you to see how soon a dog becomes either fat or lean: a little patience, therefore, and some attention, will always enable you to get your hounds into proper condition; and I am certain that you can receive no pleasure in hunting with them, if they be not.

I forgot, in my Letter upon the feeding of hounds, to observe, that such hounds as have the mange actually upon them, or only a tendency towards it, should be fed separately from the rest; they should have no flesh; their meat should be mixed up rather thin than thick; and they should have vegetables in great plenty.[1] I must also add, that if my hounds return from hunting earlier than they were expected, I now order them to be shut up in the lodging-room till their meat be made ready for them. Hounds never rest contented till they have been fed; nor will they remain upon their benches, unless they be confined: yet, without doubt, lying upon the pavement, or even standing out in the cold after violent exercise, must be prejudicial to them.

I am glad to hear that your huntsman knows the country which he is to hunt: nothing in fox-hunting is more essential than *that*; and it may make amends for many faults. Foxes are not capricious: they know very well what they are about; are quick, I believe, at determining, and resolute in persevering: they generally have a point to go to; and, though headed and turned directly from it, seldom fail to make it good at the last: *this*, therefore, is a great help to an observing huntsman.

---

[1] Sulphur made into a ball with butter, or hog's-lard, and given two or three mornings following, may also be necessary.

Suffer not your huntsman to encourage his hounds too much on a bad-scenting day, particularly in covers where there is much riot. *Hark! hark! hark!* which injudicious huntsmen are so fond of upon every occasion, must often do mischief, and cannot do good: while hounds are near together, they will get sooner to the hound that challenges without that noise than with it. If it be a right scent, they will be ready enough to join; and if it be a wrong one, provided they be let alone, they will soon leave it: injudicious encouragement, on a bad day, might make them run something or other, right or wrong.

I know of no fault so bad in a hound as that of running false: it should never be forgiven. Such as are not stout, or are stiff-nosed, or have other faults, may at times do good, and, at their worst, may do no harm; but such as run false, most probably, will spoil your sport. A hound capable of spoiling one day's sport, is scarcely worth your keeping: indifferent ones, such as I have above described, may be kept till you have better to supply their places.

A huntsman should know how to marshal every hound in his pack, giving to each his proper rank and precedence; for, without this knowledge, it is not possible that he should make a large draft, as he ought. There are, in most packs, some hounds that assist but little in killing a fox; and it is the judicious drafting off of such hounds that is a certain sign of a good huntsman.

My huntsman is very exact: he always carries a list of his hounds in his pocket, and when in a distant country, he looks it over, to see if any of them be missing; he has also a book in which he keeps a regular account where every fox is found, and where he is killed.

Your huntsman, you say, knows perfectly the country that he has to hunt: let him then acquire as perfect a knowledge of his hounds: good sense and observation will do the rest; at least, will do as much as you seem to require of him; for I am glad to find, that you would rather depend upon the goodness of your hounds for sport, than the genius of your huntsman: it is, believe me, a much surer dependence.

LETTER XXII

ARE not your expectations somewhat too sanguine, when you think that you shall have no occasion for bag-foxes to keep your hounds in blood the first season? It may be as well, perhaps, not to turn them all out, till you can be more certain that your young pack will keep good and steady without them. When blood is much wanted, and they are tired with a hard day, one of these foxes will put them into spirits, and give them, as it were, new strength and vigour.

You desire to know, what I call *being out of blood*? In answer to which, I must tell you, that, in my judgment, no fox-hound can fail of killing more than three or four times following, without being visibly the worse for it. When hounds are out of blood, there is a kind of evil genius attending all that they do; and, though they may seem to hunt as well as ever, they do not get forward; while a pack of fox-hounds well in blood, like troops flushed with conquest, are not easily withstood. What we call *ill luck*, day after day, when hounds kill no foxes, may frequently I think, be traced to another cause, namely, *their being out of blood*; nor can there be any other reason assigned why hounds, which we know to be good, should remain so long as they sometimes do without killing a fox.[1] Large packs are least subject to this inconvenience: hounds that are quite fresh, and in high spirits, least feel the want of blood: the smallest packs, therefore, should be able to leave at least ten or twelve couple of hounds behind them, to be fresh against the next hunting day. If your hounds be much out of blood, give them rest: take this opportunity to hunt with other hounds; to see how they are managed; to observe what stallion hounds they have; and to judge yourself, whether they be such as it is fit for you to breed from. If what I have now recommended should not

---

[1] A pack of hounds that had been a month without killing a fox, at last ran one to ground, which they dug, and killed upon the earth: the next seven days that they hunted, they killed a fox each day.

succeed; if a little rest, and a fine morning, do not put your hounds into blood again, I know of nothing else that will; and you must attribute your ill success, I fear, to another cause.

You say, that you generally hunt at a late hour: after a tolerably good run, do not try to find another fox. Should you be long in finding, and should you not have success afterwards, it will hurt your hounds: should you try a long time, and not find, *that* also will make them slack. Never try to find a fox after one o'clock; you had better return home, and hunt again on the next day: not that I, in general, approve of hunting two days following with the same hounds: the trying so many hours in vain, and the being kept so long off their food, both contribute to make them slack; and nothing, surely, is more contrary to the true spirit of fox-hunting; for fox-hounds, I have already said, ought always to be above their work. This is another particular, in which hare-hunting and fox-hunting totally differ; for harriers cannot be hunted too much, as long as they are able to hunt at all: the slower they go, the less likely they will be to over-run the scent, and the sooner, in all probability, will they kill their game. I have a friend, who hunted his five days following, and assured me that he had better sport with them the last day than the first.

I remember to have heard, that a certain pack of fox-hounds, since become famous, were many weeks, from a mixture of indifferent hounds, bad management, and worse luck, without killing a fox; however, they killed one at last, and tried to find another:—they found him, and they lost him; and were then, as you may well suppose, another month without killing another fox:—this was ill-judged: they should have returned home immediately.

When hounds are much out of blood, some men proceed in a method that must necessarily keep them so: they hunt them every day, as if tiring them out were a means to give them strength and spirit:—this, however, proceeds more from ill-nature and resentment, than sound judgment.[1]

---

[1] It is not the want of blood only that is prejudicial to hounds: the trying long in vain to recover a lost scent, no less contributes to make them slack.

As I know your temper to be the reverse, without doubt, you will adopt a different method; and, should your hounds ever be in the state here described, you will keep them fresh for the first fine day; when, supposing them to be all perfectly steady, I do not question that they will kill their fox.

When hounds are in want of blood, give them every advantage; go out early, choose a good quiet morning, and throw off your hounds where they are likely to find, and are least likely to change:—if it be a small cover, or furze-brake, and you can keep the fox in, it is right to do it; for the sooner you kill him, when you are in want of blood, the better for the hounds.

When hounds are in want of blood, and you get a fox into a small cover, it must be your own fault if you do not kill him there: place your people properly, and he cannot get off again. You will hear, perhaps, that it is impossible to head back a fox. No animal is so shy; consequently, no animal is so easily headed back by those who understand it. When it is your intention to check a fox, your people must keep at a little distance from the cover side; nor should they be sparing of their voices; for, since you cannot keep him in (if he be determined to come out), prevent him, if you can, from being so inclined. All kind of mobbing is allowable, when hounds are out of blood;[1] and you may keep the fox in cover, or let him out, as you think the hounds will manage him best.

Though I am so great an advocate for blood, as to judge it necessary to a pack of fox-hounds, yet I by no means approve of it, so far as it is sometimes carried. I have known three young foxes chopped in a furze-brake in one day, without any sport; a wanton destruction of foxes, scarcely answering the purpose of blood; since that blood does hounds most good which is most dearly earned. Such sportsmen richly deserve blank days; and, without doubt, they often meet with them. Mobbing a fox, indeed, is only allowable when hounds are not likely to be a match for him

---

[1] Yet, how many foxes owe their lives to the too great eagerness of their pursuers?

SOME OF BECKFORD'S FAVOURITES

BELLMAN
BY LORD DONEGALL'S BLOOMER
DAM BEAUTY
BEAUTY BRED BY LORD EGMONT

MANNERLY
BY MR RIDGE'S MATCHERN
DAM BEAUTY BY SIR SIMON
STUART'S BRUSHER

BELMAID
BY LORD DONEGALL'S
BLOOMER DAM VIXEN
BY CROWNER DAM COMELY
BY CRUISER CROWNER
BY MR. SELBY'S PIFLER

GUIDER
BY SIR BAILY JENNING'S
BLUECAP DAM GAYLASS
BY MR. NEIL'S GUARDIAN
DAM RUTH BY MR.
PELHAM'S LOYAL DAM
GAILY BY MR. BARRY'S
FAMOUS BLUECAP

From a painting at Steepleton by Sartorius

without it.   One would almost be inclined to think blood as necessary to the men as to the hounds, since the best chase is flat, unless you kill the fox.   When you ask a fox-hunter, What sport he has had? and he replies, It was *good;* I think the next question generally is, *Did your hounds kill?* If he should say, They did *not*, the conversation ends; but if, on the contrary, he tell you that they did, you then ask a hundred questions, and seldom are satisfied till he has related every particular of the chase.

When there is snow on the ground, foxes will lie at earth.[1] Should your hounds be in want of blood, it will at that time be easy to dig one to turn out before them, when the weather breaks; but I seem to have forgotten a new doctrine which I lately heard, that blood is not necessary to a pack of fox-hounds.[2] If *you* also should have taken up that opinion, I have only to wish, that the goodness of your hounds may prevent you from changing it, or from knowing how far it may be erroneous.[3]

Before you have been long a fox-hunter, I expect to hear you talk of the ill-luck which so frequently attends this diversion.   I can assure you, it has provoked me often, and has made *even a parson swear*:—it was but the other day that we experienced an extraordinary instance of it: we found at the same instant a brace of foxes in the same cover; and they both broke at the opposite ends of it. The hounds soon got together, and went off very well with one of them; yet notwithstanding this, such was our ill-luck, that, though the hunted fox took a circle of several miles, he at last crossed the line of the other fox; the heel of which

[1] Earths should be watched when there is snow upon the ground; for foxes then will lie at earth. Those who are inclined to destroy them, can track them in, and may dig them out.

[[2] This doctrine has its advocates in these days, but it is generally amongst the lookers-on, and not those who have the management of hounds. Blood, as the author says, is all-important, and no pack will show good sport unless they get plenty of it.]

[3] Those who can suppose the killing of a fox to be of no service to a pack of fox-hounds, may suppose, perhaps, that it does them hurt: it is going but one step further.

we hunted back to the cover from whence we came: it is true, we perceived that our scent worsted, and were going to stop the hounds; but the going off of a white frost deceived us also in that.

Many a fox have I known lost by running into houses and stables. It is not long since my hounds lost one, when hunting in the New Forest:—after having tried the country round, they had given him up, and were gotten home; when in rode a farmer, full gallop, with news of the fox: he had found him, he said, in his stable, and had shut him in. The hounds returned: the fox, however, stood but a little while, as he was quite *run up* before.

Some years ago, my hounds running a fox across an open country in a thick fog, the fox scarcely out of view, three of the leading hounds disappeared all of a sudden; and the whipper-in, luckily, was near enough to see it happen. They fell into a dry well, near a hundred feet deep: they and the fox remained there together till the next day, when, with the greatest difficulty, we got them all four out.

Another time, having run a fox a burst of an hour and a quarter (the severest I ever remember), the hounds at last got up to him by the side of a river, where he had stayed for them. One hound seized him as he was swimming across, and they both went down together: the hound came up again, but the fox appeared no more. By means of a boat and a long pole, we got the fox out. Had he not been seen to sink, he would hardly have been tried for *under water*; and, without doubt, we should have wondered what had become of him.

Now we are in the chapter of accidents, I must mention another, that lately happened to me on crossing a river, to draw a cover on the other side of it:—The river Stower frequently overflows its banks, and is also very rapid and very dangerous. The flood that morning, though sudden, was extensive: the neighbouring meadows were all laid under water, and only the tops of the hedges appeared. There were posts to direct us to the bridge; but we had a great length of water to pass before we could get at it: it was, besides, so deep, that our horses almost swam; and the shortest-legged horses, and longest-legged riders, were worst off. The hounds dashed in as usual, and were immediately carried, by the rapidity of the current, a long way down the stream. The huntsman was far behind them; and, as he could advance but slowly, he was constrained to see his hounds wear themselves out in a useless contention with the current, from their efforts to get to him. It was a shocking scene! many of the hounds, when they reached the shore, had entirely lost the use of their limbs; for it froze, and the cold was intolerable: some lay as if they were dead, and others reeled as if they had been drinking wine. Our ill-luck was not yet complete: the weakest hounds, or such as were most affected by the cold, we now saw entangled in the tops of the hedges, and heard their lamentations. Well-known tongues! and such as I had never heard before without pleasure. It was painful to see their distress, and not know how to relieve it. A number of people, by this time, were assembled near the river-side; but there was not one amongst them that would venture in. However, a guinea, at last, tempted one man to fetch out a hound that was entangled in a bush, and would otherwise have perished. Two hounds remained upon a hedge all night; and, though at a considerable distance from each other when we left them, yet they got together afterwards; and the next morning, when the flood abated, they were found closely clasping each other: without doubt, it was the friendly warmth which they afforded each other that kept both alive. We lost but one hound by this unlucky expedition, but could not save any of our terriers. They were seen to sink, their strength not being sufficient to resist the two enemies they had to encounter (powerful when combined) the severity of the cold, and the rapidity of the stream.

You ask, At what time you should leave off hunting? It is a question which I know not how to answer; as it depends as much on the quantity of game that you have, as on the country that you hunt: however, in my opinion, no good country should be hunted after February; nor should there be any hunting at all after March. Spring-hunting is sad destruction of foxes: in one week you may destroy as many as would have shown you sport for a whole season. We killed a bitch-fox one morning, with seven young ones, which were all alive. I can assure you we missed them very much the next year, and had many blank days which we needed not to have had, but through our own fault. I should tell you, this notable feat was per-formed, *literally*, on the *first of April*. If you will hunt late in the season, you should at least leave your terriers behind you. I hate to kill any animal out of season. A hen-pheasant with egg, I have heard, is famous eating; yet, I can assure you I never mean to taste it; and the hunting a bitch-fox big with young, appears to me cruel and unnatural. A gentleman of my acquaintance, who killed most of his foxes at this season, was humorously called, *midwife to the foxes*.

Are not the foxes' heads, which are so pompously exposed to view, often prejudicial to sport in fox-hunting? How many foxes are wantonly destroyed, without the least service to the hounds or sport to the master; that the hunts-man may say he has killed so many brace! How many are digged out and killed, when blood is not wanted, for no better reason! foxes that, another day, perhaps, the earths well stopped, might have run hours, and died gallantly at last. I remember, myself, to have seen a pack of hounds kill three in one day; and, though the last ran to ground, and the hounds had killed two before, therefore could not be supposed to be in want of blood, the fox was digged out, and killed upon the earth.[1] However, it answered one purpose which you would little expect—it put a clergyman, who was present, in mind that he had *a corpse to bury*, which otherwise had been forgotten.

[1 It will be seen that though Beckford is such a great believer in *blood*, he yet strongly condemns killing foxes wantonly. The only excuse for wholesale butchery is when foxes are too numerous and farmers are complaining.]

I should have less objection to the number of foxes' heads that are to be seen against every kennel-door, did it ascertain with more precision the goodness of the hounds; which may more justly be known from the few foxes they lose, than from the number that they kill.   When you inquire after a pack of fox-hounds, whether they be good, or not, and are told they seldom miss a fox; your mind is perfectly satisfied about them, and you inquire no further: it is not always so, when you are told the number of foxes they have killed.   If you ask a Frenchman, What age he is of? he will tell you that he is *in good health*.   In like manner, when I am asked, How many brace of foxes my hounds have killed?   I feel myself inclined to say, the hounds *are good*; an answer which, in my opinion, goes more immediately to the spirit of the question than any other that I could give; since the number of foxes' heads is, at best, but a presumptive proof of the goodness of the hounds.   In a country neighbouring to mine, foxes are difficult to be killed, and not easy to be found; and the gentlemen who hunt that country, are very well contented when they kill a dozen brace of foxes in a season.   My hounds kill double that number: ought it to be inferred from thence that they are twice as good?

All countries are not equally favourable to hounds.   I hunt in three, all as different as it is possible to be; and the same hounds that behave well in one, sometimes appear to behave indifferently in another.   Were the most famous pack, therefore, to change their good country for the bad one I here allude to (though, without doubt, they would behave well), they certainly would meet with less success than they are at present used to: our cold flinty hills would soon convince them, that the difference of strength between one fox and another—the difference of goodness betwixt one hound and another—are yet but trifles, when compared with the more material difference of a good-scenting country and a bad one.[1]

[1] Great inequality of scent is very unfavourable to hounds. In heathy countries the scent always lies; yet, I have remarked, that the many roads which cross them, and the many inclosures of poor land that surround them, render hunting in such

I can hardly think you serious, when you ask me, If the same hounds can hunt both hare and fox? However, thus far you may assure yourself, that it cannot be done with any degree of consistency. As to your other question, of hunting the hounds yourself, *that* is an undertaking which, if you will follow my advice, you will let alone. It is your opinion, I find, that a gentleman might make the best huntsman: I have no doubt that he would, if he chose the trouble of it. I do not think there is any profession, trade, or occupation, to which a good education would not be of service; and hunting, notwithstanding it is at present exercised by such as have not had an education, might, without doubt, be carried on much better by those that have. I will venture to say, fewer faults would then be committed; nor would the same faults be committed over and over again, as they now are. Huntsmen never reason by analogy, nor are they much benefited by experience.

Having told you, in a former Letter, what a huntsman ought to be, the following, which I can assure you is a true copy, will show you, in some instances at least, what he ought not to be:

SIR,

Yours I received the 24th of this present Instant June and at your request I will give you an impartial account of my man John G——'s Character. He is a Shoemaker or Cordwainer which you please to call it by trade and now in our Town he is following the Carding Business for every one that wants him he served his Time at a Town called Brigstock in Northamptonshire and from thence in great Addington Journeyman to this Occupation as before mentioned and used to come to my house and found by riding my horses to water that he rode a horse

countries, at times, very difficult to hounds. The sudden change from a good scent to a bad one, puzzles their noses, and confuses their understandings; and many of them, without doubt, follow the scent unwillingly, owing to the little credit that they give to it. In my opinion, therefore, a scent which is less good, but more equal, is more favourable to hounds.

pretty well which was not at all mistaken for he rides a
horse well and he looks after a kennel of hounds very well
and finds a hare very well he hath no judgment in hunting
a pack of hounds now tho he rides well he dont with discretion for he dont know how to make the most of a horse
but a very harey starey fellow will ride over a church if in
his way tho may prevent the leap by having a gap within
ten yards of him and if you are not in the field with him
yourself when you are a hunting to tutor him about riding
he will kill all the horses you have in the stable in one
month for he hath killed downright and lamed so that will
never be fit for use no more than five horses since he hath
hunted my hounds which is two years and upwards he
can talk no dog language to a hound he hath no voice
speaks to a hound just as if his head were in a drum nor
neither does he know how to draw a hound when they are
at a loss no more than a child of two years old as to his
honesty I always found him honest till about a week ago
and have found him dishonest now for about a week ago
I sent my servant that I have now to fetch some sheep's
feet from Mr. Stanjan of Higham Ferrers where G—— used
to go for feet and I always send my money by my man that
brings the feet and Stanjan told my man that I have now
that I owed him money for feet and when the boy came
home he told me and I went to Stanjan and when I found
the truth of the matter G—— had kept my money in his
hands and had never paid Stanjan he had been along with
me once for a letter in order for his character to give him
one but I told him I could not give him a good one so I
would not write at all G—— is a very great drunkard cant
keep a penny in his pocket a sad notorious lyar if you send
him upon an errand a mile or two from Uppingham he
will get drunk stay all day and never come home while
the middle of the night or such time as he knows his master
is in bed he can nor will not keep any secret neither hath
he so much wit as other people for the fellow is half a fool
for if you would have business done with expedition if he
once gets out of the town or sight of you you shall see him

no more while the next morning he serves me so and so you must expect the same if you hire him I use you just as I would be used myself if I desired a character of you of a servant that I had designed to hire of yours as to let you know the truth of every thing about him.

I am Sir

Your most humble servant to command

* * * * *

P.S.—He takes good care of his horses with good looking after him as to the dressing e'm but if you dont take care he will fill the manger full of corn so that he will cloy the horses and ruin the whole stable of horses.

Great Addington June the 28th 1734.

LETTER XXIII

I TOLD you, I believe, at the beginning of our correspondence, that I disliked bag-foxes: I shall now tell you
what my objections to them are:—the scent of them is
different from that of other foxes: it is *too good*, and makes
hounds idle; besides, in the manner in which they generally
are turned out, it makes hounds very wild: they seldom fail
to know what you are going about before you begin; and,
if often used to hunt bag-foxes, will become riotous enough
to run any thing. A fox that has been confined long in a
small place, and carried out afterwards in a sack, many
miles perhaps, his own ordure hanging about him, must
needs stink extravagantly. You are also to add to this
account, that he most probably is weakened for want of his
natural food and usual exercise; his spirit broken by despair,
and his limbs stiffened by confinement: he then is turned
out in open ground, without any point to go to. He runs
down the wind, it is true; but he is so much at a loss all the
while, that he loses a deal of time, in not knowing what
to do; while the hounds, who have no occasion to hunt,
pursue as closely as if they were tied to him. I remember
once to have hunted a bag-fox with a gentleman, who,
not thinking these advantages enough, poured a whole
bottle of *aniseed* on the fox's back. I cannot say that I could
have hunted the fox, but I assure you I could very easily
have hunted the *aniseed*. Is it to be expected, that the same
hounds will have patience to hunt a cold scent the next day
o'er greasy fallows, through flocks of sheep, or on stony
roads? However capable they may be of doing it, I should
much doubt their giving themselves the trouble. If
notwithstanding these objections, you still choose to turn
one out, turn him into a *small* cover; give him what time
you judge necessary, and lay on your hounds as quietly
as you can; and, if it be possible, let them think they find
him. If you turn out a fox for blood, I should, in that case,

prefer the turning him into a *large* cover, first drawing it well, to prevent a change. The hounds should then find him themselves; and the sooner he is killed the better. Fifteen or twenty minutes is as long as I should ever wish a bag-fox to run, that is designed for blood: the hounds should then go home.

Bag-foxes always run down the wind: such sportsmen, therefore, as choose to turn them out, may at the same time choose what country they shall run. Foxes that are found, do not follow this rule invariably. Strong earths, and large covers, are great inducements; and it is no inconsiderable wind that will keep foxes from them. A gentleman who never hunts, being on a visit to a friend of his in the country, who hunts a great deal, heard him talk frequently of *bag-foxes*: as he was unwilling to betray his ignorance, his discretion and curiosity kept him for some time in suspense, till at last he could not refrain from asking, What kind of an animal a *bag-fox* was? and, If it was not *a species of fox peculiar to that country?*

A pack of hounds having run a fox to a ground immediately after they had found him, he was digged and turned out again; and, that the operation of turning him out might be better performed, the master of the hounds undertook it himself. You will hardly believe me when I tell you, that he forgot the place where he turned him out, and they never once could hit upon the scent.

If you breed up cubs, you will find a fox-court necessary: they should be kept there till they are large enough to care of themselves. It ought to be open at the top, and walled in. I need not tell you, that it must be every way well secured, and particularly the floor of it, which must be either bricked or paved. A few boards fitted to the corners will also be of use, to shelter and to hide them. Foxes ought to be kept very clean, and have plenty of fresh water:[1] birds and rabbits are their best food: horse-flesh might give them the mange; for they are subject to this

[1 Foxes in confinement should be kept on peat-moss, and their coats occasionally dusted with sulphur.]

disorder. I remember a remarkable instance of it:—Going out to course, I met the whipper-in returning from exercising his horses, and asked him, If he had found any hares? No, Sir, he replied; but I have caught a fox: I saw him sunning himself under a hedge, and, finding he could not run, I drove him up into a corner, got off my horse, and took him up; but he is since dead. I found him at the place he directed me to, and he was indeed a curiosity: he had not a single hair on his brush, and very few on his body.[1]

I have kept foxes too long; I also have turned them out too young. The safest way, I believe, will be to avoid either extreme. When cubs are bred in an earth near you, if you add two or three to the number, it is not improbable that the old fox will take care of them. Of this you may be certain, that if they live they will be good foxes; for the others will show them the country. Those which you turn into an earth, should be regularly fed: if they should be once neglected, it is probable they will forsake the place, wander away, and die through want of food. When the cubs leave the earth (which they may soon do), your gamekeeper should throw food for them, in parts of the cover where it may be most easy for them to find it; and, when he knows their haunt, he should continue to feed them there. Nothing destroys so much the breed of foxes as buying them[2] to turn out, unless care be taken of them afterwards.

Your country being extensive, probably it may not be all equally good: it may be worth your while, therefore,

[1 There is much yet to be learnt about mange in foxes, and until it has been more thoroughly investigated, it would be better not to advance here any opinions on the subject. The disease in some forms is identical with that which attacks dogs, but there are varieties which we believe no dog has ever been known to have. There are many instances of mangy foxes giving the disease to terriers. In one form of fox-mange the blood turns black, and a few drops of it applied externally to any animal is said to infect the skin with the disease. Foxes in confinement nearly always get the mange, and it is therefore likely in those cases that the cause is the want of some particular food which they get in a wild state. By inspecting the wild fox's billet it will be seen that blackbeetles form a large portion of his food. Whether that insect possesses medicinal properties for keeping the blood in order we do not know, but in that case it would explain much.]

[2 Foxes should be bought only from a country where there is no hunting.]

to remove some of the cubs from one part of it into the other: it is what I frequently do myself, and find it answer.[1] A fox-court is of great use: it should be airy, or I cannot advise you to keep them long in it. I turned out one year ten brace of cubs; most of which, by being kept till they were tainted before they were turned out, were found dead in the covers, with scarcely any hair upon them; whilst a brace which had effected their escape, by making a hole in the sack in which they were brought, lived, and showed excellent sport. Should the cubs be large, you may turn them out immediately:—a large earth will be best for that purpose; where they ought to be regularly fed with rabbit's, bird's, or sheep's henges, whichever you can most conveniently get. I believe when a fox is once tainted he never recovers. The weather being remarkably hot, those which I kept in my fox-court (and it at that time was a very close one) all died, one after the other, of the same disorder.

Where rabbits are plentiful, Nature will soon teach your cubs how to catch the young ones; and, till that period of abundance arrives, it may be necessary to provide food for them.[2] Where game is scarce, wet weather will be most favourable to them: they can then live on beetles, chaffers, worms, &c., which they will find great plenty of. I think the morning is the best time to turn them out: if turned out in the evening, they will be likely to ramble; but if turned out early, and fed on the earth, there is little doubt of their remaining there.[3] I also recommend to you, to turn them into large covers and strong earths:—out of

---

[1] Though turned-out foxes may sometimes answer the purpose of entering young hounds, yet they seldom show any diversion: few of those I have turned into my woods, have I ever seen again; besides, the turning out of foxes, and alarming the neighbourhood, may *hasten* their destruction. Foxes will be plentiful enough where traps are not set to destroy them: should they do any injury to the farmer, make satisfaction for it: encourage the neighbouring game-keepers to preserve them, by paying them handsomely for every litter of cubs that they take care of for you. If you act in this manner, you may not have occasion to turn any out.

[2] If a sheep die, let it be carried to the earth, and it will afford the cubs food for some time.

[3] A more certain method, perhaps, might be to pale in part of a copse which has an earth in it. It might be well stocked with rabbits; the young ones of which

small earths they are more liable to be stolen; and from
small covers are more likely to stray. Your game-keepers,
at this season of the year, having little to do, may feed,
and take care of them. When you stop any of these earths,
remember to have them opened again, as (I have reason to
think) I lost some young foxes one year by not doing it.
For your own satisfaction, put a private mark on every
fox which you turn out, that you may know him again.
Your cubs, though they may get off from the covers where
they were bred, when hunted will seldom fail to return to
them.

Gentlemen who buy foxes do great injury to fox-hunting;
for they encourage the robbing of neighbouring hunts:
in which case, without doubt, the receiver is as bad as the
thief. It is the interest of every fox-hunter to be cautious
how he behaves in this particular. Indeed, I believe most
gentlemen are; and it may be easy to retaliate on such as are
not. I am told, that in some hunts it is the constant employment of one person to watch the earths at the breeding
time, to prevent the cubs from being stolen. Furze-covers
cannot be too much encouraged, for that reason; for there
they are safe. They have also other advantages attending
them: they are certain places to find in: foxes cannot break
from them unseen; nor are you so liable to change as in
other covers.[1]

Acquainted as I am with your sentiments, it would be
needless to desire you to be cautious how you buy foxes.
The price that some men pay for them, might well encourage the robbing of every hunt in the kingdom, their own
not excepted. But you despise the *soi-disant* gentleman who
receives them, more than the poor thief who takes them.

the cubs would soon learn to catch. You might have meuses in the pale, and let
them out when capable of getting their own food. Foxes turned out answer best,
when left to breed.

[1] A fox, when pressed by hounds, will seldom go into a *furze-brake*. Rabbits,
which are the fox's favourite food, may also be encouraged *there*, and yet do little
damage. Were they suffered to establish themselves in your woods, it would be
difficult to destroy them afterwards. Thus far I object to them, as a farmer: I object
to them also, as a fox-hunter; since nothing is more prejudicial to the breeding of
foxes, than disturbing your woods late in the season, to destroy the rabbits.

Some gentlemen ask no questions, and flatter themselves they have found out that convenient *mezzo termino* for the easy accommodation of their consciences.

With respect to the digging of foxes that you run to ground—what I myself have observed in that business, I will endeavour to recollect. My people usually, I think, follow the hole, except when the earth is large, and the terriers have fixed the fox in an angle of it; for they then find it a more expeditious method to sink a pit as near to him as they can. You should always keep a terrier in at the fox; for, if you do not, he not only may move, but also, in loose ground, may dig himself further in. In digging, you should keep room enough; and care should be taken not to throw the earth where you may have to move it again. In following the hole, the surest way not to lose it is to keep below it. When your hounds are in want of blood, stop all the holes, lest the fox should bolt out unseen. It causes no small confusion when this happens: the hounds are dispersed about, and asleep in different places; the horses are often at a considerable distance; and many a fox, by taking advantage of the moment, has saved his life.

If hounds want blood, and have had a long run, it is the best way, without doubt, to kill the fox upon the earth; but, if they have not run long; if it be easy to dig out the fox, and the cover be such a one as they are not likely to change in—it is better for the hounds to turn him out upon the earth, and let them work for him. It is the blood that will do them most good, and may be serviceable to the hounds, to the horses, and to yourself. Digging a fox is cold work, and may require a gallop afterwards, to warm you all again. Before you do this, if there be any other earths in the cover, they should be stopped, lest the fox should go to ground again.

Let your huntsman try all around, and let him be perfectly satisfied that the fox is not gone on, before you try an earth:[1] for want of this precaution, I dug three hours to

---

[1 A fox will often go through a drain and out the other end, so that a huntsman should always make a cast forward to make certain.]

a terrier, that lay all the time at a rabbit. There was another circumstance, which I am not likely to forget—"*that I had twenty miles to ride home afterwards.*" A fox sometimes runs over an earth, and does not go into it: he sometimes goes in, and does not stay: he may find it too hot, or may not like the company that he meets with there. I make no doubt that he has good reasons for everything he does, though we are not always acquainted with them.

Huntsmen, when they get near the fox, will sometimes put a hound in to draw him. This is, however, a cruel operation, and seldom answers any other purpose than to occasion the dog a bad bite, the fox's head generally being towards him; besides, a few minutes' digging will render it unnecessary. If you let the fox first seize your whip, the hound will draw him more readily.[1]

You should not encourage badgers in your woods: they make strong earths, which will be expensive and troublesome to you, if you stop them; or fatal to your sport, if you do not. You, without doubt, remember an old Oxford toast:

> Hounds stout, and horses healthy,
> Earths well stopp'd, and foxes plenty.

All, certainly, very desirable to a fox-hunter; yet, I apprehend the *earths stopped* to be the most necessary; for the others, without *that*, would be useless. Besides, I am not certain that earths are the safest places for foxes to breed in; for frequently, when poachers cannot dig them, they will catch the young foxes in trenches dug at the mouth of the hole, which I believe they call *tunning* them. A few large earths near to your house, are certainly desirable, as they will draw the foxes thither, and, after a long day, will sometimes bring you home.

If foxes should have been bred in an earth which you think unsafe, you had better stink them out: *that*, or indeed any disturbance at the mouth of the hole, will make the old one carry them off to another place.

[1] You may draw a fox, by fixing a piece of whip-cord, made into a noose, at the end of a stick; which, when the fox seizes, you may draw him out by.

In open countries, foxes, when they are much disturbed, will lie at earth. If you have difficulty in finding, stinking the earths will sometimes produce them again. The method which I use to stink an earth, is as follows:—Three pounds of sulphur and one pound of asafœtida are boiled up together: matches are then made of brown paper, and lighted in the holes, which are afterwards stopped very close. Earths that are not used by badgers, may be stopped early, which will answer the same purpose; but, where badgers frequent, it would be useless; for they would open them again.

Badgers may be caught alive in sacks placed at the mouth of the hole: setting traps for them would be dangerous, as you might catch your foxes also: they may be caught by stinking them out of a great earth, and afterwards following them to a smaller one, and digging them.

Your country requires a good terrier. I should prefer the black or white terrier: some there are so like a fox, that awkward people frequently mistake one for the other. If you like terriers to run with your pack, large ones, at times, are useful; but in an earth they do little good, as they cannot always get up to a fox. You had better not enter a young terrier at a badger. Young terriers have not the art of shifting like old ones; and, should they be good for any thing, most probably will go up boldly to him at once, and get themselves most terribly bitten: for this reason, you should enter them at young foxes when you can. Before I quit this subject I must mention an extraordinary instance of sagacity in a bitch-fox that was digged out of an earth, with four young ones, and brought in a sack upwards of twenty miles to a gentleman in my neighbourhood, to be turned out the next day before his hounds. This fox, weak as she must have been, ran in a straight line back again to her own country, crossed two rivers, and was at last killed near to the earth out of which she had been digged the day before. Foxes that are bred in cliffs near the sea, seldom are known to ramble any great distance from them: and sportsmen, who know the country where this fox was turned out, will tell you, that there is not the least reason to think that she could have had any knowledge of it.

Besides the digging of foxes (by which method many young ones are taken, and old ones destroyed), traps, &c., too often are fatal to them:—farmers for their lambs (which, by the bye, few foxes ever kill); gentlemen for their game; and old women for their poultry—are their inveterate enemies. I must, however, give an instance of civility that I once met with from a farmer:—The hounds had found, and were running hard: the farmer came up in high spirits, and said, "I hope, Sir, you will kill him: he has done me much damage lately: he carried away all my ducks last week. I would not *gin* him though—too good a sportsman for that." So much for the honest farmer.

In the country where I live, most of the gentlemen are sportsmen; and even those who are not, show every kind of attention to those who are. I am sorry that it is otherwise with you; and that your old gouty neighbour should destroy your foxes, I must own, concerns me. I know some gentlemen, who, when a neighbour had destroyed all their foxes, and thereby prevented them from pursuing a favourite amusement, loaded a cart with spaniels, and went all together and destroyed his pheasants. I think they might have called this very properly, *lex talionis*; and it had the desired effect; for, as the gentleman did not think it prudent to fight them *all*, he took the wiser method—he made peace with them:—he gave an order, that no more foxes should be destroyed; and they never afterwards killed any of his pheasants.

LETTER XXIV

I AM now, my friend, about to take leave of you; and, at the same time that I give repose to you, let me entreat you to show the same favour to your hounds and horses. It is now the breeding season; a proper time, in my opinion, to leave off hunting; since it is more likely to be your servants' amusement than yours; and is always to the prejudice of two noble animals, which we sportsmen are bound in gratitude to take care of.

After a long and tiresome winter, surely the horse deserves some repose. Let him, then, enjoy his short-lived liberty; and, as his feet are the parts which suffer most, turn him out into a soft pasture. Some there are who disapprove of grass, saying, that, when a horse is in good order, the turning him out undoes it all again. It certainly does: yet, at the same time, I believe that no horse can be fresh in his limbs, or will last you long, without it. Can standing in a hot stable do him any good?—and can hard exercise, particularly in the summer, be of any advantage to him? Is it not soft ground and long rest that will best refresh his limbs, while the night air and morning dews will invigorate his body?[1] Some never physic their hunters; only observing, when they first take them up from grass, to work them gently: some turn out theirs all the year. It is not unusual for such as follow the latter method, to physic their horses at grass: they then are taken up, well fed, and properly exercised, to get them into order: this done, they are turned out for a few hours every day when they are not ridden. The pasture should be dry, and should have but little grass: there they will stretch their limbs, and cool their bodies, and will take as much exercise as is

[1 The question of summering hunters is still being debated, and each system has its advocates. We agree with Beckford that turning them out to grass is the best plan, and if they get a few old beans they won't lose much muscle. Even if when they come up from grass their legs are not so fine as those that have been standing in the stable, they will be found to stand their work better than the others.]

Let him then enjoy his short lived liberty.

necessary for them. I have remarked, that, thus treated, they catch fewer colds, have the use of their limbs more freely, and are less liable to lameness, than other horses. Another advantage attends this method, which, in the horses you ride yourself, you will allow to be very material: —Your horse, when once he is in order, will require less strong exercise than grooms generally give their horses; and his mouth, in all probability, will not be the worse for it.

The Earl of Pembroke, in his Military Equitation, is, I find, of the same opinion:—He tells us, "it is of the greatest consequence for horses to be kept clean, regularly fed, and as regularly exercised: but whoever chooses to ride in the way of ease and pleasure, without any fatigue on horseback; or, in short, does not like to carry his horse, instead of his horse's carrying him—must not suffer his horse to be exercised by a groom; standing up on his stirrups, holding himself on by means of the reins, and thereby hanging his whole dead weight on the horse's mouth, to the entire destruction of all that is good, safe, or pleasant, about the animal." And in another place he says: "Horses should be turned loose somewhere, or walked about every day, when they do not work, particularly after hard exercise: swelled legs, physic, &c., will be saved by these means, and many distempers avoided." He also observes, that "it is a matter of the greatest consequence, though few attend to it, to feed horses according to their work. When the work is hard, food should be in plenty; when it is otherwise, the food should be diminished immediately—the hay particularly."

I have no doubt that the noble author is perfectly right in these observations: I am also of opinion, that a handful or two of clean wheaten straw, chopped small, and mixed with their corn, would be of great service to your horses, provided that you have interest enough with your groom to prevail on him to give it them.

Such of my horses as are physicked at grass, have two doses given them when they are turned out, and three more before they are taken up. Grass-physic is of so mild a kind, that you will not find this quantity too much; nor have I ever known an accident happen from it, although it has been given in very indifferent weather. I should tell you, that my horses are always taken in the first night after their physic, though the printed directions, I believe, do not require it. Such horses as are full of humours should be physicked at house, since they may require stronger doses than grass-physic will admit of; which I think more proper to prevent humours than to remove them. The only use I know in physicking a horse that does not appear to want it, is to prevent, if possible, his requiring it at a time when you cannot so well spare him; I mean the hunting season. should an accident of this kind happen, Stibium's balls, of which I send you the receipt, will be found of use:—

Crocus metallorum, levigated . . .	2 ounces
Stibium's ditto	2 ,,
Flour of brimstone	1 ,,
Castile-soap	1 ,,
Liquorice-powder	1 ,,
Honey q. s. to make it into a paste.	

A ball (of one ounce weight) is to be given for three mornings successively. The horse must be kept fasting for two hours after he has taken it; he then may have a feed of corn, and soon after that, moderate exercise: the same should be repeated four days afterwards. These balls purify the blood, and operate on the body by insensible perspiration.

I frequently give nitre to such of my hunters as are not turned out to grass: it cools their bodies, and is of service to them: it may be given either in their water or in their corn: I sometimes give an ounce in each.

To such of my horses as are thick-winded, and such as carry but little flesh, I give *carrots*. In many stables they are given *at the time of feeding*, in the corn: I prefer giving them at any other time; for it is a food which horses are so fond of, that if by any accident you should omit the *carrots*, I doubt whether they would eat the *corn* readily without them.

I think you are perfectly in the right to mount your people well:—there is no good economy in giving them bad horses: they take no care of them, but wear them out as soon as they can, that they may have others.

The question that you ask me about shoeing, I am unable to answer: yet I am of opinion, that horses should be shod with more or less iron, according as the country wherein they hunt requires; but in this a good farrier will best direct you. Nothing, certainly, is more necessary to a horse than to be well shod:—the shoe should be a proper one, and it should fit his foot. Farriers are but too apt to make the foot fit the shoe.[1] My groom carries a false shoe, which just serves to save a horse's hoof, when he loses a shoe, till it can be put on again. In some countries you see them loaded with saws, hatchets, &c. I am glad that the country in which I hunt does not require them. In the book that I have just quoted, you will find the shoeing of horses treated of very much at large. I beg leave, therefore, if you want further information on that head, to refer you to it.

Having declared my disapprobation of summer hunting, on account of the horses, I must add, that I am not less an enemy to it on account of the hounds also: *they*, I think, should have some time allowed them to recover the strains and bruises of many a painful chase; and their diet, in which the adding to their strength has been, perhaps, too much considered, should now be altered. No more flesh should

---

[1] I venture to give the following rules on shoeing, in a short and decisive manner, as founded on the strictest anatomical and mechanical principles laid down by the best masters:—The shoe should be flat, and not turned up at the heel, or reach beyond *that* or the *toe*; but the middle part should extend rather beyond the outward edge of the hoof, that the hoof may not be contracted; the outward part of which may be pared, to bring it down to an even surface, to fit it for the fixing on of the shoe. If the foot be too long, the *toe* may be pared, or rasped down; which, in many cases, may even be necessary to preserve the proper shape of the hoof, and bring the foot to a stroke and bearing the most natural and advantageous. Neither the horny sole, or frog (meant by Nature for the guard of the foot and safety of the horse), are upon any account to be pared, or cut away. The small, loose ragged parts that at times appear, should be cut off with a pen-knife; but that destructive instrument called the *butteris*, which, in the hands of stubborn ignorance, has done more injury to the feet of horses than all the chases of the world, should be banished for ever.

they now eat; but in its stead should have their bodies cooled with whey, greens, and thin meat. Without this precaution, the mange most probably would be the immediate consequence of hot weather; perhaps madness— Direful malady!

As a country life has been recommended in all ages (not less for the contentment of the mind than the health of the body), it is no wonder that hunting should be considered by so many as a necessary part of it, since nothing conduces more to both. A great genius has told us, that it is

> Better to hunt in fields for health unbought,
> Than fee the doctor for a nauseous draught.

With regard to its peaceful state, according to a modern poet,

> No fierce unruly senate threatens here,
> No axe or scaffold to the view appear,
> No envy, disappointment, and despair.

And, for the contentment which is supposed to accompany a country life, we have not only the best authority of our own time to support it, but even that of the best poets of the Augustan age. Virgil surely felt what he wrote, when he said, "*O fortunatos nimium, sua si bona, nôrint, agricolas!*" and Horace's famous ode, "*Beatus ille qui procul negotiis,*" seems not less to come from the heart of a man who is generally allowed to have had a perfect knowledge of mankind; and this, even at the time when he was the favourite of the greatest emperor, and in the midst of all the magnificence of the greatest city, in the world.

The elegant Pliny also, in his *Epistle to Minutius Fundanus,* which is admirably translated by the Earl of Orrery, whilst he arraigns the life that he leads at Rome, speaks with a kind of rapture of a country life: "Welcome," says he, "thou life of integrity and virtue! Welcome, sweet and innocent amusement! Thou art almost preferable to business and employment of every kind!" And it was *here,* we are told, that the great Bacon experienced his truest felicity. With regard to the *otium cum dignitate,* so much recommended, no one, I believe, understands the true meaning of it better, or practises it more successfully, than you do.

A rural life, I think, is better suited to this kingdom than to any other; because the country in England affords pleasures and amusements unknown in other countries; and because its rival, our English town (or ton) life, perhaps is a less pleasant one than may be found elsewhere. If this, upon a nice investigation of the matter, should appear to be strictly true, the conclusion that would necessarily result from it might prove more than I mean it should; therefore we will drop the subject. Should you, however, differ from me in opinion of your town-life, and disapprove what I have said concerning it, you may excuse me, if you please, as you would a lawyer who does the best he can for the party for whom he is retained. I think you will also excuse any expressions that I may have used, which may not be current *here*; if you find, as I verily believe you may, that I have not made use of a French word, but when I could not have expressed my meaning so well by an English one. It is only an unnecessary and affected application of a foreign language, that is deserving of censure.

To those who may think the danger which attends upon hunting a great objection to the pursuit of it, I must beg leave to observe, that the accidents which are occasioned by it are very few. I will venture to say, that more bad accidents happen to shooters in one year, than to those who follow hounds in seven. You will remind me, perhaps, of the death of T——k, and the fall of D——t; but do accidents never happen on the road? The most famous huntsman and boldest rider of his time, after having hunted a pack of hounds for several years, unhurt, lost his life at last by a fall from his horse, as he was returning home. A surgeon of my acquaintance has assured me, that, in thirty years' practice in a sporting country, he had not once an opportunity of setting a bone for a sportsman, though ten packs of hounds were kept in the neighbourhood. This gentleman, surely, must have been much out of luck, or hunting cannot be so dangerous as it is thought: besides, they are all timid animals that we pursue; nor is there any danger in attacking them: they are not like the furious beast of the *Gevaudan*, which, as a French author informs us, an army of twenty thousand French chasseurs went out in vain to kill.

If my time in writing to you has not been so well employed as it might have been, *you* at least will not find that fault with it: nor shall I repent of having employed it in this manner, unless it were more certain than it is, that I should have employed it *better*. It is true, these Letters are longer than I first intended they should be: they would have been *shorter*, could I have bestowed *more time* upon them. Some technical words have crept in imperceptibly, and with them, some expressions better suited to the field than to the closet: nor is it necessary, perhaps, that a sportsman, when he is writing to a sportsman, should make excuses for them. In some of my Letters you have found great variety of matter: the variety of questions contained in *yours*, made it sometimes unavoidable. I know that there must be some tautology. It is scarcely possible to remember all that has been said in former Letters; let that difficulty, if you please, excuse the fault. I fear there may be some contradictions for the same reason; and there may be many exceptions. I trust them all to your candour; nor can they be in better hands. I hope you will not find that I have at different times given different opinions; but, should that be the case, without doubt you will follow the opinion which coincides most with your own. If on any points I have differed from great authorities, I am sorry for it. I have never hunted with those who are looked up to as the great masters of this science; and, when I differ from them, it is without design. Other methods, doubtless, there are, to make the keeping of hounds much more expensive; which, as I do not practise myself, I shall not recommend to you:—treated after the manner here described, they will kill foxes, and show you sport. I have answered all your questions as concisely as I was able; and it has been my constant endeavour to say no more than I thought

the subject required. The time may come, when more
experienced sportsmen, and abler pens, may do it greater
justice: till then, accept the observations that I have made:
take them, read them, try them. There was a time when I
should readily have received the information which they
give, imperfect as it may be; for experience is ever a slow
teacher, and I have had no other. With regard to books,
Somerville is the only author whom I have found of any
use on this subject. You will admire the poet, and esteem
the man; yet I am not certain that you will be always
satisfied with the lessons of the huntsman. Proud of the
authority, I have quoted from him as often as it would suit
your purpose; and for your sake have I braved the evident
disadvantage that attended it. I wish this elegant poet
had answered all your questions: you then would have
received but one letter from me, to refer you to him. That
no other writer should have followed his steps, may, I
think, be thus accounted for:—Those gentlemen who make
a profession of writing live chiefly in town, consequently
cannot be supposed to know much of hunting; and those
who do know any thing of it, are either servants who cannot
write, or country gentlemen who will not give themselves the trouble. However, I have met with some curious
remarks, which I cannot help communicating to you.
One author tells us, that "coursing is more agreeable than
hunting, *because it is sooner over;*" "that a terrier *is a mongrel
greyhound;*" and, "*that dogs have often coughs from eating fish-
bones.*"

Another (a French author) advises us to give a horse,
after hunting, "a soup made of bread and wine, and an
onion." I fear an English groom would eat the onion and
drink the wine.

The same author has also a very peculiar method of
catching rabbits, which you will please to take in his own
words: he calls it, *Chasse du lapin à l'écrevisse.* "*Cette chasse
convient aux personnes qui ne veulent employer ni furets ni armes à
feu; on tend des poches à une extrémité d'un terrier, et à l'aûtre on
glisse une écrevisse; cet animal arrive peu-a-peu au fond de la*

retrait du lapine, le pique, s'y attache avec tant de force, que le quadrupède est obligé de fuir, emportant avec lui son ennemi, et vient se faire prendre dans le filet qu'on lui a tendu à l'ouverture du terrier. Cette chasse demande beaucoup de patience: les opérations de l'ecrevisse sont lentes, mais aussi elles sont quelquefois plus sures que celles du furet."

This gentleman's singular method of hunting rabbits *with a lobster*, reminds me of a method that Harlequin[1] has of killing hares (not less ingenious) with *Spanish snuff.* Brighella tells him, that the hares eat up all his master's green wheat, and that he knows not how to kill them. "Nothing more easy," replies Harlequin—"I will engage to kill them *all* with twopennyworth of snuff. They come in the night, you say, to feed on the green wheat: strew a little snuff over the field before they come: it will set them all a-sneezing: nobody will be by to say *God bless you !* and, of course, they will all die."

I believe that, during our present correspondence, I have twice quoted the Encyclopédie with some degree of ridicule: I must, notwithstanding, beg leave to say, in justice to myself, that I have great esteem for that valuable work.

On opening a very large book, called the *Gentleman's Recreation,* I met with the following remarkable passage: "Many have written of this subject, as well the ancients as moderns, yet but few of our countrymen to any purpose; and had one all the authors on this subject (as indeed on any other), there would be more trouble to pass by than to retain; most books being fuller of words than matter, and of that which is, for the most part, very erroneous." All who have written on the subject of hunting, seem to agree in this at least—to speak indifferently of one another.

You have observed in one of your letters, that I do not always follow my own rules; and, as a proof of it, you have remarked that many of my hounds are oddly named. I cannot deny the charge. I leave a great deal to my

---

[1] The Harlequin of the Italian theatre, whose *tongue* is at liberty, as well as his *heels.*

huntsman; but if you aim at perfection, leave as little as you can help to yours. It is easier, I believe, in every instance, to know what is right, than it is to follow it; but if the rules I have given are good, what does it signify to you whether I follow them or not? A country fellow used to call every directing post that he saw, a *doctor*. He was asked, Why he called them so? "Why, master," said he, "I never see them but they put me in mind of the parson of our parish, who constantly points out a road to us which he does not follow himself."

If I can add to the amusement of such as follow this diversion, I shall not think my time has been ill employed; and, if the rules which are here given may any way tend to preserve that friendly animal, the hound, from one unnecessary lash, I shall not think they have been written in vain.[1] It never was my expectation to be able to send you a complete treatise: *Thoughts upon Hunting, in a series of familiar Letters*, were all that I proposed to myself the pleasure of sending. The trouble I have taken in writing them entitles me to some indulgence; nor need I, therefore, whilst I endeavour to render them of use, stand in any fear of criticism. Yet if any man, as idle as I have already declared myself to be, should take the trouble to criticise these Letters, tell him this:—An acquaintance of mine, who had bestowed much time in improving his place, whenever he heard it found fault with, asked "Where the critic lived? Whether he had any place of his own? Whether he had attempted any improvements? and concluded with promising *a peep at it*." The gentleman here alluded to had

---

[1] Strangely unfortunate should I think myself, if, while I profess to be a friend to dogs, I should prove their bitterest enemy; and if those rules, which were intended to lessen, should increase their sufferings; convinced as I am by experience, that a regular system of education is the surest means to render correction unnecessary. Hard is that heart (if any such there be), which can ill-use a creature so affectionate and so good; who has renounced his native liberty to associate with man, to whose service his whole life is dedicated; who, sensible of every kindness, is grateful for the smallest favour; whilst the worst usage cannot estrange his affection, in which he is, beyond all example, constant, faithful, and disinterested; who guards him by night and amuses him by day, and is, perhaps, the only companion that will not forsake him in adversity.

less humility than your humble servant: take, therefore, my sentiments in the following lines:—

Si quid novisti rectius istis,
Candidus imperti; si non, his utere mecum.—HOR.

Farewell.

The inclosed curious manuscript was called by its author a *hunting song*; it is worth your notice:—once more farewell.

Hark! hark to the notes of the melodious French horn
How sweetly she calls you out in the morn
She tells you Jemme is mounted on Tartar his steed
And invites you all to the cover with speed
Of all pleasures or pastimes ever heard or seen
There's none in the world like to merry hunting.

Hark! cover hark! the hounds are all in
The fox they have found and to his kennel they fling
He's forced now thorow the woods for to fly
Tho' nothing can save him between the earth and the sky
    Of all pleasures

Hark! tally hark! out of cover they all break
And tell you the fox they ever will seek
They surely will run him until that he did
Unless some kind earth save him in his way
    Of all pleasures

The fox now panting sees he must die
The hounds with their ingoys resound to the sky
There's Stately and Empress the earth scarce touch with the feet
There's Chasir and Trimmer all together as fleet
    Of all pleasures

Triumph and Driver now push to head the whole pack
Whipster being stole his place for to take
I think such rascally treatment as these
Should be reproach'd by all those who seek for to please
    Of all pleasures

Bold Reynard now finding his speed will not do
Betakes to the woods the hounds may not him pursue
But the hounds as at first to the cover they fly
And swear old Reynard in the field of honour shall die
    Of all pleasures

There's Trimbush and Chirrup and others as good
Ralley Cleanly and Comfort drives on thorow the wood
Emperor and Conqueror will never him forsake
But drives on full speed thorow every breake
    Of all pleasures

Old Reynard finding the cover can't save him
Lurkes on for the earth that us'd to preserve him
But Smiler he sees him and soon overtake
And poor Reynard his exit in the field of honour doth make
    Of all pleasures

The hounds how eager to enjoy their reward
The huntsman as eager checks them with a word
He beheads old Reynard and takes off his brush
And to the hounds gives his karcass a toss
    Of all pleasures

The hounds now well pleased wallow on the ground
The huntsman as well pleased to see his company around
He buckles Reynard's head to his saddle with a strap
And with his ribbon tyes the brush to his cap
    Of all pleasures

Our sport being ended and our horses full jaded
We return home well pleased with our sport quite amazed
Saying was there ever such hounds as these
Or ever such hunting on . . . . weares
Of all pleasures or pastimes ever heard or seen
There's none in the world like to merry hunting

INDEX